THE
PAST
WE
STEP
INTO

THE
PAST
WE
STEP
INTO

RICHARD SCHARINE

atmosphere press

"Being American is more than a pride we inherit.
It's **The Past We Step Into** and how we repair it."

—Amanda Gorman—

To: Marilyn Hunt Scharine (1940-2002)
"The Author of My Identity"

CONTENTS

SATURDAY NIGHT IN FRONT OF THE IGA

This is a true story, although I don't remember who told it to me. I was probably there at the time, but I was either asleep or at the library.

My mother's people emigrated from Ireland during the Great Potato Famine. Her name was Margaret, after her mother, and they were the only two Margarets in the family.

My great-grandmother was coming out of church one Sunday, and a young man came riding down the street on a bicycle and stopped in front of her. He had come from the nearest village six miles away. It was the first bicycle she had ever seen. He offered her a ride, and making use of the base of the sign that noted the presence of the church, she tucked up her skirt and climbed on the handlebars, scandalizing the rest of the emerging congregation.

Why she would do such a thing I have no idea. I only know that when I was a little boy my mother always combined that story with a description of her family coming to America, and my young mind pictured my great-grandmother tucking up her skirt and climbing on to the prow of the ship in order to be the first to see the promised land, a sort of floating Statue of Liberty.

I mention this only to explain how in my family transportation and romance go hand in hand. Studying the genealogy of the family in Ireland, one sees the same names repeated generation after generation—until the appearance of the bicycle, when the pattern begins to break down. "Margaret" was the name of my great-grandfather's favorite aunt, and was a symbol of the new possibilities introduced into the village. Why was his granddaughter the last named Margaret born into the family? We were in America by then, and the options were endless.

Why shouldn't we all have new names?

When my father's father came to America from what was (and is now again) Poland, he went to school one winter. He already knew how to write his name, but when he did so, his teacher was confused. "How do you pronounce that?" she asked. "Shah-rine," he answered phonetically. "Well, that's not the way you spell it in America," she snapped, and wrote out the spelling you will find at the end of this piece. My grandfather went home and told his parents, "This is the way we spell our name in America," and that is the way it has been ever since.

New world, new name.

Transportation was a part of my grandfather's romantic story too. One day he walked out of Milwaukee and headed west to Watertown, where he'd been told he might find work. However, the driver of the wagon on which he hitched a ride misunderstood his accent and dropped him off in Whitewater instead. As he sat on a grassy knoll of what is now Starin Park, a Norwegian girl walked by. "Now that's the girl I am going to marry," he said to himself. And he did.

I wonder if she knew what she was getting into. My grandfather was a successful man, but a hard one. He never became a citizen, but he did eventually own 11 farms and run for office in Rock County. Once when I was standing on the Charles Street Bridge in Prague, I got to talking with a woman from Oklahoma who had gone to college in Beloit, Wisconsin. When I mentioned my name, she asked: "Do you have any connection to Scharine Road?"

It was named after my grandfather, and when he was a county commissioner, he had it paved as far as his house, stopping short of his neighbor who had challenged him on a land deal. You didn't want to cross him.

I was in Europe because I was teaching as a Senior Fulbright Lecturer at Poland's University of Gdansk, the city where my great-grandfather had died in the Prussian army. I didn't know that when I got there, and neither did anyone else I knew in the family. He existed only as a photo of an unnamed man in uniform, having carelessly died two months before my grandfather was born, without marrying his mother. My great-grandmother named the baby after his father, married his younger brother, and had six more children by him in two different countries.

My wife unearthed these facts while we were living in Gdansk, using her considerable research skills and even more considerable personal charm. When "Little Grandma," as we called her, came to America, there was a split in the family when some of its members refused to contribute to her passage. The genealogical truths died with that generation.

Armed with the name of a town (*Slonecznik*, a Polish word which means "sunflower"), a drawing of a house, and a 90-year-old letter, we went in search of Grandfather's origins. On a street lined with pine trees, we came across a façade unchanged in a century, knocked on a door, and read a letter to a Polish family who had lived in New Jersey.

The letter said, "We hope to soon have the railroad in *Sonnenborn* (a German word which means "sunflower") for which we have given the land at the bottom of the property, down next to the cemetery." The Polish family gasped in astonishment, and led us through the house down to the end of the property where railroad tracks passed by the cemetery.

Sometimes dumb luck is your best friend.

Speaking of dumb luck, romance, and transportation, I never would have been born if the gas tank of the Model-A Ford had been bigger. My mother had been dating my Uncle Herman, and he took her for a Sunday drive in the country in his 1927 Model A. My uncle didn't "accidentally" run out of gas behind some wooded knoll (which must already have been a cliché even then), but he did realize he was running low. In those days every farm had its own underground fuel tank, and Herman headed for home. Rather than risking getting gasoline on his Sunday best, he called for his brother to come out of the house and do the duty.

My mother never dated my Uncle Herman again.

When I *was* born, my father was out in the barn buying a 1937 4-door Chevrolet. He got a good deal. New, it cost $590. Used, with one owner and low mileage, it was much less, and the best evidence of its quality was that I was headed into the seventh grade before we saw its replacement. Even without a car dealer on the premises, my father would probably have been in the barn rather than at the bedside tenderly holding my mother's hand. The farm wouldn't run itself, and my father always saw childcare as women's work. A man who I once saw with his arm up to his elbow in a cow's vagina, rearranging the position of a calf so that it could be born alive, and who, after I had been out drinking one night until two in the afternoon, took me down in the pigpen to help him castrate boars (figuring that if my stomach could handle the one, it could handle the other), was uncomfortable minding children. Once my mother left my infant self with him when she went to help a sick neighbor. When she returned, she found me delicately balancing on a diaper of Baby Huey proportions. "I have never changed a baby in my life, and I never will," was his explanation.

Actually, I might never have been born at all. At different times in my life after I was grown, I was given different reasons for that. An aunt told me that my mother was believed to have a medical condition that would have caused all her children after the first to be still-born. After my sister's birth in 1931 they decided not to take the risk, but eventually they slipped up. I was a non-kicking baby, and for a while they were sure that the doctors were right. When I was born, however, and they weighed the nine pounds of me on the kitchen meat scale, they could see that I was just saving my strength. I always did like my sleep.

The second reason was economics. The farm never had two good years back-to-back, but we survived because we never had two bad years either. The bad years were the even ones, and the good years the odd. My father said that the difference between 1934 and 1936 was that he made fifty dollars in 1934 and in 1936 he didn't make anything. He talked about loading the milk cans in a horse-drawn sleigh in the winter of 1934 and driving it through the woods to Country Trunk A, because members of the National Farm Organization were waiting at the end of our road to pour out the milk in hopes the shortage would drive up prices. "Nineteen and Thirty-Seven was a good year," he would say to me. "If we knew what 1938 was going to be like, your future might have been just a bit different."

If you associate spring with flowers, new buds on the trees, and the return of the songbirds, my experience "might have been just a bit different" too. When I think of spring, I think of picking up rocks in the "Back Forty," the field behind the woods. In the spring of 1941, my father tried to move a 200-pound boulder all by himself and suffered a double hernia. When the War came six months later, he was 4-F from the get-go, and we never had to worry about what we were going to do without him. Farm prices went sky high, and while I was wearing underwear made out of feed sacks the day the Japanese bombed Pearl Harbor, by V-J Day we were middle-class.

It happens like that sometimes.

My father also wore a truss all those years. The word alone conjures up an image of him naked to the waist, washing himself for dinner as we called lunch then (the evening meal was supper) in one of the laundry tubs sitting on planks held up by cement blocks next to the garage: The truss peeks over the top of the bib overalls hanging down his back to the ground. His body is almost milk white. The idea of a tan would have been laughable to a farmer, who needed as much as possible to protect his body from the late July heat. His face is burned almost to a rust color as far up as the middle of his forehead, which was as far down as he wore his hat. He had two hats, a good one that he wore to town and to church, and a battered one in which he worked. When the good hat began to show its age, it became the work hat, and the other was thrown away.

It's been a long time since I've seen a man with a sunburned face and a white high forehead, but I believe that I would automatically trust him.

It is the summer of 1947 and the laundry tubs line the garage wall because we are feeding almost every man and boy within miles. It is time to harvest the oats, and I am excited because I get to wash myself with the men. Scharine road is not named yet. Nor is Hake road where we live, or the road that crosses Scharine road in front of Plainview School, the single room where all eight grades of kids will receive much of their formal education. But all the men and boys of the farms on those three roads are here today, and I am working with them, at my first harvest in my ninth summer, driving the John Deere "B" tractor pulling the grain wagon to the oat bins.

It is also the last time. As the township becomes more prosperous, farmers begin buying their own harvesting machinery. That way we don't have to worry about putting up crops that are still green, or having them destroyed in the field by a sudden summer storm.

But something was lost.

Nineteen forty-seven was also when I made my radio debut on WCLO in Janesville, as part of a program in which rural schools were periodically brought in to do 15-minute broadcasts. In our playlet a boy is small and undeveloped because he doesn't eat in a healthy way. I can still remember my only line: "I'm Vitamin A, you need me each day." My teacher said I was too "sing-song," but you act with what you're given.

That was also the year when my father and the hired man dug out the basement and we got running water in the house. For the first time I didn't have to take a bath sitting on the kitchen counter with my feet in the sink.

A momentous year.

Why is it that I remember what should have been bad times so happily? A prairie fire that all the neighbors joined together to fight—plows making furrows in the path of the flames, water barrels being loaded on wagons to wet down the fields. A tornado that ripped up the fence line but left the crop unharmed. A dust storm that came all the way from Kansas and stopped at the County Line three miles away.

I don't think I ever went to a family funeral that wasn't a happy occasion—everyone together again, all the promises remembered, all the animosities forgotten, all the shortcomings forgiven.

There is a color photo of my mother and me, taken when I was a baby. She is standing outside the house next to the cistern, holding me high in the air. She is just happy that I am healthy. Her favorite story is about carrying me into a grocery store, and being asked by the clerk: "And is that your little brother?" She is 32. Many years later, after I have left the farm for the army, they test the cistern and find it full of bacteria. I figured that was why I was so healthy. Any germ that entered my body found itself outnumbered and was immediately devoured.

And I knew that there were others worse off than me because I saw some of them: tinkers who would mend your pots and pans for a free meal and be allowed to sleep in the hay loft; gypsies in their wagons who were never encouraged to stop; black men who worked in the slaughterhouse in Cudahy and would come out to the farm because my father would let them hunt. They would buy and butcher a Poland China barrow in the grove west of the hen house.

And there was always fresh milk, eggs, a lot of pork, less beef, vegetables, apples, cherries, grapes, pears (canned in the winter), and fresh bread—coarse crusted, made by my mother on Saturday, and soft white, delivered by the Jaeger Bread Man three days a week.

And there was what I learned from my father.

It wasn't what he said so much, as what he did. The quiet concentration on his face as he carried the five gallon buckets of water down the hill from the stock tank to the hog troughs. The blood running down his face and arms, as he reattached the corn planter to the runaway horses that pulled him through a barbed wire fence. Milking the cows with his hands swollen with erysipelas, a disease that he caught from the pigs.

It was the simplest of lessons really, and the most profound. The cows have to be milked twice a day. Seven times out of ten is not a passing grade. You cannot promise them more quality time tomorrow. You cannot work twice as hard in the morning so that you can take the evening off. Milking the cows twice a day is your responsibility to the cows and to the task.

A colleague of mine was fond of quoting a Zen proverb: "When there is no solution, there is no problem." My father never studied Zen, but he lived that proverb. He lived all his life in the township where he was born, and the longest time he ever spent away from it was the four months he spent in University Hospital, dying of leukemia.

I drove 500 miles down from northern Minnesota to visit him, and it was in that hospital that he asked me if he was going to die. I have regretted for forty-five years not giving him an honest answer to that question. I would like to have heard what he had to say on the subject, even as I hope that one day my own children will be similarly curious.

It happens like that sometimes too.

I always blamed the cigarettes. He smoked two packs a day, at 15 cents a pack. Chesterfields, in my memory, but I'm sure he took what he could get—especially during the War. We went to town only once a week, unless work was being held up by a tractor needing a part. In those days even doctors came to your house, although I only remember that happening once—when my cousin and my best friend both came down with Polio right after I had been playing with them. Of course, I only had a cold.

For lesser purchases we could go to Richmond Center, where at the bottom of a hill a few houses nestled themselves around the junction of Country Trunk A and Highway 89. There was a feed mill run by my great-uncles and a general store owned by a second cousin. At the top of the hill there was a Methodist church, and at the bottom a Lutheran one next to the Town Hall.

It was at the Town Hall where I saw my first theatre.

The "Toby Players" were a product of the WPA Federal Theatre in Iowa, and they toured all over the Middle West. The Works Progress Administration, part of FDR's "New Deal," was run by Harry Hopkins, whose stroke of genius was to understand that artists are workers too, and that the country could benefit from the products they produced. "Free, Adult, and Uncensored," the Federal Theatre was only one program in the Federal Arts Project, but at its peak it had units in 35 of the contiguous 48 states. That peak wasn't long. Communist-hunting, budget-slashing congressmen killed it nationally in 1939, but some states supported their theatres until their final hour of death at the hands of television.

"Toby" was the brainchild of an actor/director/playwright named Fred Wilson. You can't find the plays he wrote in any anthology, but you'd recognize them if you saw them. The setting might be a western bunkhouse, a society drawing room, or a gangster's hideout, but the plot was pretty much the same. A good guy and the girl who was meant for him are kept apart by people who think they are better/smarter/tougher/richer. The guy has on his side a yokel sidekick and the sidekick's dim-witted but good-hearted girlfriend. Guess who wins out.

In addition to writing and directing the plays, Wilson played the yokel. One day he was accosted by a young boy who had seen three of his plays and wondered why, since the characters always looked alike, sounded alike, and essentially did the same things, they all had different names. Why not call them all "Toby?" From that time on all the yokel sidekicks in Wilson's plays were called "Toby" and their dim-witted girlfriends were "Suzy."

In college I discovered the same idea in a theatre history book. It was called *commedia dell'arte*.

The play was a western, and some of the actors onstage doubled as musicians. After it was over, there was a dance, complete with waltzes, polkas, and even the occasional schottische. My parents didn't dance and neither did I, so I went up onstage behind the band to see where the actors came from. There was a door on either end of the wall, and above the middle of the stage was a little balcony where Toby and Suzy crept to eavesdrop on the bad guys and foil their plans.

Thirty years later when I was touring Wales and England as an actor, moving from Cardiff to Bristol, to Birmingham, to York, and points North, I realized that every theatre we played in had the same set-up: doors at either end of the rear stage wall and a balcony above it.

If I could play in Richmond Center, I could play anywhere

in the English-speaking world. Now if only I could dance!

Nevertheless, I always associate Saturday night with Whitewater. Eventually I would go to high school there, the twists and turns of the back country roads making it a 52 mile bus ride. During the War, it seemed almost that long, synthetic rubber tires and unpaved roads making anything over 35 miles an hour unwise. A little further in the opposite direction was a bigger city, the county seat, where in the house of my great aunt and uncle, I encountered my first indoor toilet, embarrassing my mother because I didn't know to flush it. Where I came from, these things just went down and were forgotten.

If you were under 12 years old, you could go to the Strand movie theatre for 12 cents. The bill changed three times a week. Friday and Saturday there were westerns, Wednesday and Thursday had B movies (gangster films, Abbott and Costello, The Three Stooges), and Sunday through Tuesday you could see (if you lived in town) the big Technicolor features. I don't remember ever going by myself. For me, the big treat was the weekly purchase of a comic book.

Check that! Buying a comic book was the *last* thing I did. There were two general stores and a drugstore that had racks of comics. If I didn't read at least thirty before surrendering my dime, it was only because the store clerks were particularly impatient that night. I always went home with a western or an innocuous Disney comic—Roy Rogers or Donald Duck—that my parents wouldn't object to, knowing that when I visited my cousins, I could get *True Crime*, *Crime Does Not Pay*, and maybe even *Ranch Romances*. (It would be years before I discovered *Nyoka, the Jungle Girl*.)

The Chevy was always parked in front of the IGA grocery store, just off Main Street. After their shopping, my parents, who rarely saw a neighbor during the week, would sit there, watching anyone who passed in front of the windshield. I didn't pay much attention, twisting sideways in an attempt to get enough of the street lamp light to read my comic book for the fourth time, or at best trying to read the ration stamps on the window backwards.

34653170

8C

EGAELIM

The one thing I wasn't allowed to do in the car was listen to the radio, which occupied my attention every other night of the week—*Superman* (with Bud Collyer, who could drop his voice an octave just by stepping into a phone booth), *Tom Mix* (who apparently had done everything he was credited with on the radio, even though the *real* Tom was dead by that time), *Captain Midnight!* (who for a quarter and an Ovaltine label would send you messages on a secret decoder—one of which sits on the desk next to my laptop), and *The Lone Ranger* (whose nephew Dan Reid was the father of Britt Reid, *The Green Hornet*).

The Lone Ranger played Monday, Wednesday, and Friday, alternating with *Sergeant Preston of the Yukon* on Tuesday and Thursday. An army buddy and I developed our own version, "Sergeant Prestone of the Anti-Freeze Squad," whose job it was to keep villains from putting out the smudge pots which kept the Florida citrus fruits from freezing. Prestone made his arrests "in the name of the Orange Bowl Queen," and was assisted by "Pluton Thing," a 183 lb. frog who as a tadpole had been exposed to the radioactivity of an A-bomb test. It was "Thing" who inevitably tackled the terrified bad guys, but who, at the end of each episode, suddenly began to emit a series of gasps and collapsed, hovered over by Sergeant Prestone, who had the last line: "Good heavens, he's... he's croaked."

Coming back to the barracks from a particularly late night at the NCO club, my friend and I were given to acting out the occasional episode, emulating Thing by leaping on all fours from bunk to bunk. One night the mail clerk woke up screaming, sprinted out of the barracks in his underwear, and locked himself in the mail room.

Thank god we were between wars!

On other nights of the week my parents loved the radio too. On Monday there was *The Lux Radio Hour*, where in sixty minutes, minus the introduction, commercials, and an epilogue with the stars, we heard in our Technicolor minds the movies we didn't see play at the Strand from Sunday through Tuesday. Then there was *First Nighter*, whose host took us to "The Little Theatre just off Times Square" for a new story every week, or for an old favorite like "Little Town of Bethlehem" (which played every Christmas season from 1937 to 1953. And for comedy, there were Jack Benny, Bob Hope, Phil Harris, and later, Bob Eliot and Ray Goulding.

There was a family legend that depicted my mother, having finished the dishes and her other housework, picking up the baby and going out to the barn where my father was milking the cows, in order to listen to the only radio on the farm. Thus, I can make the claim of being one of the few living Americans to have been present for the broadcast which over a million Americans believed was the beginning of the end of humanity as we knew it—Orson Welles and the Mercury Theatre's *War of the Worlds*. I slept through it.

Network radio drama came to an end in October 1954. That Christmas my father bought a television set.

I always fell asleep during the last ritual of Saturday night as well—the gathering of the cigarettes. My father smoked 40 cigarettes a day, two packs. During the War it was impossible to buy cigarettes in cartons. You could only buy them two packs at a time. They could only be bought in bars. And the bar would only sell them to you if you bought a drink at the same time. We lived in a dry township, which meant a weekly trip to Whitewater Street—where there were seven bars in a single block—for my father, with my sister in tow. My mother stayed resolutely in the car, as my father went from swinging door to swinging door, ordering a beer for himself and a cherry coke for my sister, pocketing his cigarettes and moving on. The sound of the car starting would awaken me to my sister beside me, complaining of a stomachache, my father at the steering wheel, his faced flushed, and my mother, as far from him as she could get, her body stiff, tight lines around her mouth.

My father was not a drinker, and after the war things changed. My sister graduated from high school and went off to a nearby town with a hospital where she became a nurse's aide, a job she held with some variation for the rest of her life. My father convinced me that comic books were a one-time pleasure, but a 25 cent western paperback could last most of the week. (He liked to read them too.) Eventually, I walked up Main Street past the fountain surrounded by colored lights to the City Library, where I found books that would last a lifetime, even if I couldn't always figure them out. I have a picture of myself at 13, riding a tractor cultivating corn in a field, with F. Scott Fitzgerald's *Tender is the Night* in my hip pocket. It would be a quarter century before I read it again and understood what was happening.

Incest! Who would have guessed?

When my sister graduated from high school, I heard my father say to her: "If you want to go to college, I'll pay for it." Until then my mother had been the educated one in the family. She had graduated from high school and was working as a secretary in a stationery store in Whitewater when my Uncle Herman dropped by one day. Getting that far in school hadn't been easy. After grade school her older sister, May, had stayed home a year, and my mother finished a year early. Every Sunday night for four school years, their father hitched up a horse to the buggy and drove his two oldest daughters to a Milton boarding house, where they lived during the week and went to high school during the day. On Friday nights my grandfather appeared at the door of the boarding house with the horse and buggy, and they went home for the weekend.

I have a program noting their appearance in the Milton Senior Class play. I always thought my mother was a natural actress, had she the opportunities given to me.

When my father was in the sixth grade and it came time to prepare the land for spring planting, he left school and never returned.

Yet, there was always something to read in the house. There was a *Collier's* magazine every week from as long as I can remember to its very last issue on January 4, 1957. *Collier's* invented the short-short story, which fit on a single page, and Ray Bradbury was its master. It serialized longer stories over as many as ten issues. John Wyndham's *Day of the Triffids* became such a part of our family's mythology that we still refer to weeds impossible to clear out of our garden as "Triffids." And that doesn't even count stories from Earle Stanley Gardner, Roald Dahl, J.D. Salinger, and Kurt Vonnegut that were in the issues of that era.

And what do I remember from the book club to which my father belonged?

James Ramsey Ullman's *The White Tower*, which made me look at the land and the woods around me and wonder if there was a magic and a mystery there that I was missing. Ernest Hemingway's *A Farewell to Arms* and James Jones' *From Here to Eternity*, both of which I read over and over before I went into the Army, thinking somehow that they would prepare a farm boy who had never been away from home—not realizing that the ability to read and understand was the preparation in itself.

My sister didn't want to go to college, but I was listening, and I did (although I had no clue what I was to study). My mother thought I should be a minister, like our church minister, who was living at the boarding house and going to Milton College when she and her sister were in high school.

My father thought it would be more practical for me to be a large animal veterinarian.

After 55 years of mostly being a college teacher, I've come to the conclusion that they both may have been right.

Since those days, I've never returned to Whitewater except for the shortest of visits. Still, sometimes in my dreams I see someone walking down through the darkness of Main Street toward the more brightly lit shopping area of a Saturday night. Not a boy, an older man with a white beard. His pace is not fast, but he knows where he is going. He walks past Starin Park, and out of the darkness to his left a wagon takes shape. A young man is sitting on it, and he is looking at a girl walking past him on the sidewalk. Ahead of the old man is a fountain, still surrounded by colored lights, but behind it a child daycare center reforms itself into an Andrew Carnegie Library. Still further down the street, the lights from a Good Will store reveal at closer glance a drugstore door, through which a shiny rack of comic books can be seen. And above what in the daytime is a yoga studio is a marquee for the Strand Theatre. The film is *Exodus*.

The old man turns a corner and walks up the street to a spot where a '37 Chevy stands in front of a grocery store. He opens the rear door and slides in behind a middle-aged couple who sit watching the people who pass in front of the windshield. The light from the street lamp passes through the open door and a patch of it falls across the front seat. They are holding hands.

Love! Who would have guessed?

--February 24, 2018

THIRTEEN SPRINGS

Janesville Gazette (April 18, 1953)

Miss Alma Hansen, 85, a longtime resident of Richmond Township, died Monday morning in the Welcome Home nursing facility of Whitewater, where she had been a patient.

She was born February 29, 1868, on a farm not far from Skien, Norway, the second daughter of Charles and Anna Knutsdaughter Hansen. In 1874 she immigrated to America with her parents, who homesteaded a farm in the Norwegian community south of Whitewater Lake. For many years she acted as housekeeper to her uncle, Hans Anderson, who operated the farm, and moved to Welcome Home after the expansion of the lake last year. Three sisters and a brother preceded her in death, and she is survived by a number of nieces and nephews.

Services will be held at 2 p.m. Wednesday in the Schneidermann Funeral Home, the Rev. Ole Knudson officiating. Burial will be in the Heart of the Hills Lutheran Cemetery. Friends may call at the funeral home Tuesday evening.

*****

The kids were already growing restless by the time I found the driveway and turned in. Technically, it was a park entrance, but the Morning Glory vines that covered the fence gave the opening the appearance of a cow path, and negotiating the twisting, hilly two-lane blacktop, I'd missed it twice. It was a July mid-afternoon in Wisconsin, and the temperature was fighting a valiant but losing battle with the humidity. I could only hope there was enough direct sunlight to discourage the mosquitoes. Lynne was taking her mother to a doctor's appointment in Ft. Atkinson, and I had thought to combine my baby-sitting chore with a compensatory visit to my mother on the farm. We were halfway down Highway 89 when I realized how little we would have to go out of our way to stop at Thirteen Springs.

What I remembered was a long double-rutted road to the clearing in front of the house. What I found almost immediately inside the gate was a parking area built up with landfill at some time in the past, now covered with long grass kept at a negotiable level by a visit two or three times a summer from an alfalfa hay mower. At the far edge of the lot, next to the path leading down the hill, sat a lonesome picnic table, its stain pealing like last month's sunburn. The sweet smell of decay was almost tactile.

Annie walked to the picnic table and sat down, barely lifting her eyes from the pages of *Little House on the Prairie* in the process. It was perhaps her third time through the series, fourth if you counted her mother's having read it to her, and earlier in the year she had talked the family into making a pilgrimage to the Laura Ingalls Wilder home in Missouri. Despite our Volkswagen micro-bus having much of the speed and certainly the wind resistance of a Conestoga wagon, we'd all enjoyed it, and I resisted forcing upon her the fact that she was ignoring the site of similar stories from her own family. Meanwhile, Karl had settled his "rattle-rattle dump truck" down on what I could clearly see was an anthill, and seemed no more inclined to leave his own fantasy world than was his big sister.

I walked down the path, looking in vain for a familiar landmark, and much sooner than expected, came to the edge of the lake. More accurately, I came to an indeterminate patch of swampy wetlands, where humps of grass and mud contended for position with pools of stagnant water. Further out the lake registered a post-card blue, and on its far edge a brave little marina reflected the town's hope for a tourist-based prosperity. This side was favored only by water snakes, a thought which turned me back up to the children in the parking lot. As I headed up the hill, the different perspective revealed a darker patch of foliage to my left and just below the ridge. I risked the tall grass, and as I approached the space, it revealed itself as a depression in the earth overgrown with bridal vines. Only within five feet of the space could it be recognized as the foundation of a house. I walked around the edge, trying to dredge up in my mind any details of the structure. Beneath the vines, twisted beams were still visible at points where the loads of gravel intended to fill the pit had sunk into the earth. At one corner, in a dip in the gravel protected by a rotting two by six, a distinctively shaped object caught my eye. It was a corncob pipe.

*****

My Great-Aunt Alma smoked a corncob pipe, the only woman in my family to smoke at all in my presence (although I had my suspicion about some of my aunts). All the men smoked, but only Grandpa Temple and my Uncle Bert favored pipes, straight-stemmed Briars. Grandpa alternated his pipe with La Palina cigars, memorable because of the maiden with the deep cleavage who stared seductively at me from the cigar box top. For a time he even raised tobacco; only the coarse outer leaves (all tobaccos products are blends) would grow in Wisconsin's climate. They had to be transplanted and picked by hand. My father remembered this work as rough and disagreeable, leaving his hands raw and sometimes bleeding. Perhaps for this reason he preferred cigarettes, as did all the other men in the family.

My father smoked Chesterfields, which cost 15 cents a package. Filtered cigarettes were for women until Marlboro's brilliant advertising campaign of the late 50s. (A throaty-voiced Julie London purring "Filter, Flavor, Flip-Top Box" directly into a television camera yanked many an unwary boy into smoking and puberty at about the same rate.) My father never drank, except for a single glass of Manischewitz, a sweet Jewish wine my Lutheran grandfather served at all family occasions. Possibly this was because, unlike his brothers who had all married German women, my mother was a fierce Scotch-Irish teetotaler. When he did drink, it was to support his smoking habit during the cigarette rationing of World War II. In those days, my father smoked two packages of cigarettes a day, and with gasoline rationing and synthesized rubber tires, the family went to town only once a week on Saturday nights to shop. On that night, my father had to manage to find a way of buying 14 packages of cigarettes to last him through the week. Cigarettes were only sold in saloons. That in itself wasn't a problem, in that Whitewater Street (whose false-fronted buildings would have done Dodge City proud) was an uninterrupted line of taverns. However, no drinking establishment would sell any one customer more than two packages of cigarettes a day, and only then if alcohol was purchased at the same time. Therefore, our Saturday night shopping trips always ended the same way. After parking the car just off Whitewater Street (my mother believed that Eternal Damnation was reserved for the owners of any car parked in front of a Whitewater Street tavern with unattended children playing or sleeping in it), my father, accompanied by my sister, would go to seven consecutive bars, ordering in each a beer for himself and a cherry coke for Marti.

After the War ended, I never saw my father take a drink again, but, of course, it was the smoking that killed him. Like all the men in his family, it first cost him his teeth. My Uncle Bert got his false teeth only when he could no longer hold his pipe in his yellowed stumps. I associate smoking with being awakened at five on winter mornings by cough after hacking cough from my father before he went out to the barn to milk the cows, and with smoke being puffed in my face as my father tied my tie before Church on Sunday morning. When I left home for the Army at 18, I quickly learned to tie my own tie, but I never learned to smoke.

Aunt Alma's corncob pipe was different. She smoked it because she had a crush on General Douglas MacArthur, whose dramatic visage with its sunglasses and pipe clinched in a jutting jaw was one of the most familiar icons of the era—literally in the case of my Aunt Alma. This wasn't just an attempt to delude a small boy. She kept a picture of MacArthur clipped from a Sunday supplement on the wall of her living room, with a kerosene lamp always burning underneath like a votive flame—an eerie night-time sight in a house with no electricity.

"In the Philippines, Rikart!" MacArthur says, "'I Shall Return'! And he did! I think I would trust him with my life!"

I was with Aunt Alma on that one. My only complaint about MacArthur's Inchon landing on September 25, 1950, was that I was sure it would make the Korean War the shortest in American history, even shorter than the Spanish American War. Even when the intervention of the Chinese exploded that misapprehension and Truman sacked MacArthur the following April for contradicting American policy, she and I remained true believers. On April 19, my teacher at Plainview School took me and the other four eighth-graders to the nearest neighbor with a television set, and we watched MacArthur speak to a joint session of Congress, which interrupted him with applause thirty times:

"Old Soldiers never die; they just fade away." Aunt Alma and I thought MacArthur should be president. Six years later in Basic Training, I bought a history of the U.S. Army just to read about him. The book was cheaply made and fell apart faster than the General's post-Korean War reputation. By the time of the 1952 election Aunt Alma was no longer at Thirteen Springs, the General's star had faded, and my concern about the Korean War was a distant second to my desperation to survive high school.

Aunt Alma drank too, but in a far more subtle way than she smoked. Every grocery list my mother picked up from Thirteen Springs on Saturday included a request for "Hadacol." Almost everyone had heard of Hadacol. It was the most advertised pain reliever on radio. How Aunt Alma, who didn't have a radio, became a believer I don't know, but my guess would be an advertisement in the *Chicago Herald-American,* of which she was a daily and devoted reader. "Hadacol" was the invention of a Louisiana State Senator named Dudley LeBlanc. Essentially, it was a Vitamin-B elixir. It also contained 12 % alcohol. When my father, who could read labels as well as anybody, asked my abstinence-believing mother about the contents, she just shook her head wearily.

"If I had to live out there without electricity or indoor plumbing, and with only cats for company, I wouldn't be filtering my alcohol through patent medicine."

From the time of his double hernia, my father had a

bottle of Old Crow Bourbon on the top shelf of the cabinet in the basement, which he described as "snake bite medicine." I sipped it a couple of times myself, and suspect at least one of the hired men of helping himself. I never saw my father drink it, but then I never saw him bit by a snake either, although he once explained why:

"If you should be walking through the woods and step on a snake, that snake is apt to be pretty riled up! However, if you sit down and offer him a drink of that Old Crow-man to the snake, so to speak-that snake will get really mellow, and after a couple of drinks not only will he never bite you again, he'll tell all his friends and relatives, and you can walk through the woods without ever worrying about snakes again. I did that years ago, which is why I can leave that bottle at home in the basement."

There were plenty of snakes around Whitewater Lake and the hills above it, but I never heard Aunt Alma express concern about them, so maybe she shared the Hadacol as well. Certainly, the snakes would have gotten along with Bob Hope, George Bums and Gracie Allen, Dorothy Lamour, and James Cagney, all of whom touted the pain reliever at one time or another. On his radio show, Groucho Marx once asked Senator LeBlanc what Hadacol was good for. The Senator's answer was prompt and candid.

"Last year it was good for five and a half million for me."

I never tasted Hadacol, but Aunt Alma did make oatmeal cookies especially for me. I knew they were oatmeal because she always put them in a Quaker Oats box; they were round and just small enough to fit in the cylinder shape, and there were just enough of them to completely fill the box. We would come very close to decimating an entire baking on those afternoons I stayed with her when my mother was visiting in the neighborhood, although she always made me save some for my sister Marti.

There really were "Thirteen Springs," just as there really were fourteen cats. I don't recall the names of any of the cats, but I do remember that each of the springs had a name and a story attached to it. I was told these stories as we walked the lowlands below the house, but I have forgotten most of them and the springs and the *griot* who gave them their identities have both been gone for more than a half-century now. The closest spring was just down the path from the house, where the lake now begins, and probably the reason why the house was built where it was. Aunt Alma called it "Uncle Hans' Spring," after the man for whom she had kept house so many years. He died before I was born, and I should have been curious as to why she had no stories of him. But then, no one in my family did. My parents described him as a quiet man, without the language necessary to express himself fluently in English, who gradually lost the habit of expressing himself to his niece in Norwegian. Uncle Hans had built the long wooden box, now green with living organisms, into which the spring poured from the hillside, and which in earlier times must have also served as a stock tank. An oaken stave bucket with iron straps holding it together hung from a stake next to the tank, as did a metal cup. I always made certain to drink from it, as nightly I drank a cup of warm milk from one of the thirty-one and a half gallon cans standing in the cold water of the milk house. I never saw either cup changed. Years after I left home, the well on our farm was closed because of bacteria, but I was never sick from it and, in fact, have enjoyed remarkably good health all my life.

I remember the names of three of the other springs. "Two Beavers Spring" was so-called because of the animals' attempt to divert it with a dam. They would labor all day long, and late in the afternoon, Aunt Alma would come down with a long pole to dismantle their handiwork. Finally, she decided that with no cattle in the area anymore, likely to break a leg in an unfamiliar hole, she might as well let the beavers do their worst and came to enjoy watching their construction even more than she used to enjoy tearing it apart. The beavers had left by the time I was around, but the dam was still there.

"Tinkers' Spring" was named for an unfortunate mender of pots and pans who tried to find his way around the south side of Whitewater Lake one Saturday night when Alma was still a young woman. Out searching for birds' eggs after Church the next afternoon, she came upon him, lying on his back and staring up at her from under perhaps ten inches of water. He was a forlorn man whom nobody knew well. There was no evidence of foul play, suicide would have taken uncommon reserves of will power, so drink, and a lost sense of direction was probably the answer. The image bothered me for days, and I took to going to bed when it was still light and getting up after dawn to avoid seeing the dead man in the dark.

Then, of course, there was "Raccoons' Spring."

One summer evening, my Aunt Alma encountered a pair of raccoons with a young family near one of the western springs. They seemed remarkably unafraid of her, and on other occasions, she found that if she sat quietly, she could watch them diligently washing their food in the spring water. She took to leaving them food near the spring—vegetables going wooden and fruit just a little bruised. As time passed, she found that she could put down the offerings right at her feet and they would come to pick them up. Eventually, she was able to walk down to the spring, show the animals the food, and turn around and walk back to the clearing with them following.

We had often heard Aunt Alma sing to herself as she snapped beans or peeled potatoes on the porch of her house, and when the time came that such things had to be done, my mother found among her effects the words to two songs written in a beautiful cursive and stored in an envelope dated April 1, 1888: "*I Wandered Today by the Seashore,*" and "*Little Maggie May.*" For some time we wondered if she might have written them herself, but a while ago, I discovered the titles in a book of sentimental American songs from the 1860s. (Nevertheless, I kept both words and envelope, and they sit on the desk in front of me, looking as they must have when a 20-year-old girl who was never to marry tried to commit them to memory a century and a quarter ago.) Still, it was something of a surprise one Saturday night when Aunt Alma claimed to be able to charm raccoons into eating from her hands by singing to them.

It could hardly have been a more theatrical setting, and initially I could hardly have been a less appreciative audience. It was my last summer of western comic books, and I was eager to get home with my latest copy of *Johnny Mack Brown.* Like Randolph Scott movies, and unlike Gene Autry or Roy Rogers, Johnny was not averse to showing as much interest in the rancher's daughter, with her long legs flashing out from under her split riding skirt, as he was in catching the rustlers after her father's steers. Fortunately, my parents prevailed, and as a full moon gave dramatic dimension to mountains of high cumulus clouds above, the pageant began.

Aunt Alma perched on a stool in the clearing, and we sat on the porch behind her. The moon was so bright that when the passing clouds briefly came between it and us, I had the impression of a pivoting searchlight from a Warner Brothers prison break movie. She sang in a high, cracked voice, but with surprising range, words that I didn't recognize—Norwegian perhaps—and within a couple of minutes, the grass around the clearing began to answer her, waving and chirping like an encore-hungry crowd at a rock concert. Out into the open they tumbled, seven of them, two adults and five kits of that April's litter. They circled my aunt, and she lowered her voice and sang to each one personally, raising her hand with its pieces of bread, carrots, turnips, and plums so far off the ground that the masked intruders each had to stand on their hind legs to get a promised treat. It was a circus act of choreographic precision. I rose to join the circle, but my mother touched my arm and motioned me to sit. This was Aunt Alma's show, and we were there to witness, not participate. One by one, the tidbits of food disappeared, Aunt Alma ceased to sing and began to whisper, and one by one, the raccoons dropped back to all fours. Chattering happily and looking back frequently, they scrambled back into the underbrush, and we were left with the quiet of the moon, the clouds, and the clearing.

I once told some of my friends about Aunt Alma charming the raccoons, and one suggested that she might be a witch. As much as I might have wished to believe that, it seemed unlikely since she took me to Heart of the Hills Church one Sunday when I was a little boy.

Heart of the Hills was an old, Norwegian Church built on a slope overlooking Whitewater Lake. It was not far from Thirteen Springs as modem transportation measures these things, but Aunt Alma who had no transportation other than her feet, did not attend often. My mother drove us there and picked us up afterward. No doubt, she justified the venture as cultural education. Having rescued my father from one Lutheran Church, she would not have risked losing her only son to another. (For ten years after I left Wisconsin forever, she kept me on the rolls of the Scotch Prairie Presbyterian Church.) Whether Heart of the Hills still stands, I don't know. Aunt Alma said it was the oldest church in the synod. Even in those days, services were only held there in the summer. A few elderly Norwegian farmers might have attended had there been a year-round preacher (even though services were now only in English), but most of the people in the pews were from cottages on the Lake, augmented by a few curiosity-seekers like myself. Heart of the Hills had not been modernized. I found it uncomfortable sitting in the straight-back benches, envied the boy who worked the pump on the organ, and wondered how long it had been since the kerosene lamps that lined the walls had been lit. The hymns were mostly unfamiliar, and even when I knew the words—Old *Hundredth,* for example—the melody was different. I remember nothing of the sermon, only that the minister made much of me for coming to Church with my aunt.

The service was relatively short, and while we waited for my mother, Aunt Alma took me through the cemetery. I was old enough to read the names on the tombstones, and she seemed to know most of them. Aunt Alma had come to America on a steamship, but twenty years earlier, Anna Oslock had come on a "three-masted" sailing ship. Mr. Halvorsen, the blacksmith, had regularly driven to and from the fifty miles to Milwaukee on the plank toll road over the mud. Mr. Swenson (a Swedish outsider) had walked over the hills to court her more than sixty years ago when she was in her teens.

"One day he just decided that there were too many hills and he married somebody else."

I asked her if she remembered Norway, which she had left when she was six. "Oh ya! We lived in Wibeto, maybe five or six families. We all lived together, and each family had a farm in the land around the village. We were three-and-a-half miles from Skien, but a Norwegian mile was seven American miles. I don't know how that works."

"What did the land look like?"

"Wibeto? Like here, only bigger. I can understand why Papa and Uncle Hans wanted to settle here. The Holden Church was on a hill above a lake, like this one is. Wibeto is on a hill with a road leading up to it, just like Thirteen Springs. There we had fjords, mountains, and paths. Here we have lakes, hills, and paved roads. Of course, I was just a little girl, but everything seemed bigger there. The water, the hills, even the people—ya, especially the people! Like they try to cut everybody down to size here, wanna make everybody chust like everybody else."

*****

Somebody was having big ideas during the summer of the singing raccoons. The County Commission was looking at the future of Whitewater Lake, and they didn't see agriculture; they saw tourism. Their model was nearby Lake Geneva, with its beaches, its marina, its cruise ship, and the mansions of Chicago millionaires that ringed the lake. The problem was that Whitewater Lake was too small. There were no sailboats, and no place to launch them. The cottages had no amenities and brought little income into the community. The only place to swim was the Milk Company condensary pond. There was no money to be made in that!

I was in high school when the decision to dam the streams that fed into the lake was made. The 52-mile bus ride and the necessity to adapt from a one-room country schoolhouse didn't leave a lot of time for ecological speculation. If I was aware of any controversy; it was over the push to change the nickname of the school's athletic teams to "Lakers," after the Minneapolis teams that of that period which dominated the National Basketball Association. If I thought about Thirteen Springs at all, it was that the expansion of the lake would bring me opportunities for swimming and boating on Aunt Alma's land. I didn't realize that as the lake grew larger, the springs would dry up.

It was my father who first noticed the smell. It was autumn, following the second summer after the damming. We had taken to coming by twice a week instead of once. In the post-war prosperity, extra trips had been downgraded from an impossibility to an inconvenience. Aunt Alma was 83 years old, and the last of the springs— Uncle Hans' Spring—was running slower and slower. My mother was worried that the water was no longer safe.

Aunt Alma was sitting on the porch as we drove in. She nodded at my father as he walked up to the house but didn't speak. Since he was a boy my father had been acutely aware of any potential change in the weather. He could tell you what field the cows were pasturing in by the taste of the milk. Something in the air was not right. He paused only a moment at the steps, and then went into the house. A few minutes later he came out of the door, and walking past Aunt Alma, approached the car on my mother's side.

"The cats are dead. I counted six of them. There may be more in the cellar, probably in the walls too."

I couldn't see my mother's face, only her hand tighten on the window post. "What happened?"

"Distemper, if I had to make a guess. It's hard to tell. Lots of living things from the wetlands have come further up the hill because of the high water. Could even have been the raccoons."

There was a pause. My father's face was impassive. My mother's voice was controlled: "She can't stay here."

*****

Janesville Gazette (March 1, 1952) Octogenarian Celebrates "21st Birthday"

Miss Alma Hansen, formerly of Whitewater Lake, was given a party by friends and relatives on Friday afternoon, February 29, in honor of her 84th birthday in the Welcome

Home nursing facility of Whitewater, where she currently resides. The occasion for this Leap Year Lady was her "official 21st birthday."

"I am a grownup now, I guess," Miss Hansen joked. The "Birthday Girl" received many nice gifts. Traveling Bingo was played, and guests participated in a sing along. Refreshments, including a birthday cake, were served at the close of the afternoon.

When it came her turn to sing, Aunt Alma tried to beg off, but my mother urged her, and she finally gave in.

"But now we are growing in years, Maud.
Our locks are all silvered and gray;
But the vows that we made on the shore, Maud,
Are fresh in our memories today.
There still is a charm in those bright shells
Set free from the deep ocean's roar,
And those were the happiest of days, Maud,
As we gathered the shells from the shore."

My mother finished gathering together whatever we would have to take with us and touched my arm.

"You go sit with Aunt Alma for a little while. I'll get the car from the parking lot and bring it around to the front door so we can load these things."

I looked around. Aunt Alma was sitting in the common room with three other Welcome Home women. The WTMJ *Five O'Clock News* was on. She rose and began walking around the room.

"What are those men in the box doing in my house?"
"It's a television set, Aunt Alma."
"I think it's time I went home, Rikart."
"You are home, Aunt Alma."

"It's time I should feed the cats, Rikart."
"I know, Aunt Alma."

RUMSPRINGA

The subject was homosexual metaphors in the plays of Tennessee Williams. Lynne served tea to Monika and me.

Our apartment was at the south end of the Physics and Mathematics Building, which was itself south of the Languages and Literature Building where I had an office and taught my classes. These two architectural post-war relics were the only part of the University of Gdansk then located in *Przymorze*. The rest could be found in numerous areas throughout the city, created between the two World Wars when Gdansk technically wasn't part of Poland, but rather was Danzig, an International City under the League of Nations. Look at the shoddy functionalism of these educational sites built in the 1950s and you will see Communism. In the same city look at the *Stare Miatso*, which the retreating Nazis shelled into rubble, at the 800-year-old Hanseatic League buildings so lovingly recreated in those same years, and you will see Poland. An underlying truth will always best an imposed system.

Monika glances around the room. "Do you like it here?"

The Poles are a beautiful people, and Monika is both a typical and exceptional representative of the race—translucent skin, piercing blue eyes, and a shiny, black page-boy bob framing high, Asiatic cheekbones—a moment of perfection when the Teutonic encounters the East. As most men would, I had been dividing my time between her and the plate of cookies Lynne had placed on the table between us. (I had missed lunch because of an English Institute faculty meeting.) I look around, confused.

Lynne laughs. The combination dining room/living room we are in is at the end of a hall flanked on the west by a small kitchen and a bathroom just big to enough to hold a tub, and on the east by a bedroom and a tiny office. In the Spring, the sunrise assaults our theatre-conditioned bedroom eyes at 3 a.m., and in the winter the University heating plant shut down from 8 p.m. Friday until 8 a.m. Monday (until Lynne made friends with the *concierge* who repairs cars on weekends in the power plant just beyond the west wall). A few months after my employment, we were given a washing machine whose Tasmanian Devil-replicated spin cycle provides me with my Sioux name, "Dances with Washing Machine." There is a black and white television set with two channels, one with picture and one with sound, and a telephone which can occasionally connect to America, but never the English Institute office in the next building. The rest of the furniture Lynne describes as "Zakopane Wal-Mart," in that it was inspired by the meticulously crafted folk art of the mountains south of Krakow, but in the journey north every communist bureaucrat and every nascent capitalist from the southern mountains to the northern sea has hacked away at its originality until it can no longer shame the building around it.

"We're very comfortable," Lynne says.

And we are. I have taken to holding thesis discussions with my students in the apartment. It is only a five-minute walk from the Languages and Literature Building, and in addition to what she can bring to the subject, Lynne has a positive gift for putting people at ease—especially me. Eight moves in nearly three decades of marriage have led me to define home as where she is.

The Polish university system is an unforgiving one. There is no such thing as a baccalaureate. A liberal arts education is a five-year process, culminating in a master's degree. By design less than half of the students survive the first year. Despite a national shortage of three million college educated people, that first year is dominated by archaic required courses (for example, in English an oral mastery of Middle English, judged by professors whose native tongue isn't English). The system does not inspire give and take.

This is not a problem today. Monika is Lynne's favorite student as well, a former waitress in a Greenwich Village coffee shop, a frequent visitor to our apartment, and our bridge to a culture we frequently misunderstand. Her thesis derives from her friendship with Broadway set designer Robin Wagner, who supplies her with Tennessee Williams letters about *The Red Devil Battery Sign*, an out-of-town failure late in Williams' career, and Robin's own analysis of an upcoming gay-themed epic, *Angels in America*.

I'm doubtful about the subject. "Isn't the way Williams dealt with his homosexuality *passé*? There are a lot of openly gay writers in America now, and because of AIDS, they're dealing with life and death, not just social exile."

Monika frowns. "We're not in America. There are some things we still have to talk about in code here."

I know what she means. A Warsaw production of *Hamlet* a few years ago didn't alter the text, but featured as the Prince a famous folk singer costumed as a hippy, and a Claudius dressed in the uniform of General Jaruzelski, the Secretary of the Communist Party. Still, I feel stubborn. "Why? The Wall is down. Lech Walesa is an elected president. Shouldn't Polish writers be saying straight out what they couldn't say before?

"Do you think a whole culture changes when a form of government changes? In the *Sejm*, the parliament, the Communist Party required that a certain percentage of the representatives be women. Under Capitalism there are half as many women in the *Sejm* as before. The Party used to tell us how to vote. Now the Church does. As for writers, under Communism there were 364 professional theatres speaking to the people—*in code!* How many do you think the Marketplace will allow to "speak straight out"?

"Then the students have to take action—the same way that they did in the '88 strike against the government in this very building! Can they do that? You were in class the last two days when we were supposed to be discussing interracial marriage in *Wedding Band* and AIDS in *As Is*. No one would talk about it—and when they did, it was obvious that they saw the people in them as alien, examples of perversion."

"They opposed Communism because they *knew* Communism, the way it works in real life. You want them to fight for minorities they've never seen? Poland is 95% ethnic Pole, 96% Catholic. If you want them to understand minorities, first you have to explain what a minority is. That's what metaphors are for."

I try a different tack. "You see these problems so clearly. Why didn't you stay in New York where you didn't have to deal with them?"

Across the table the blue eyes flash. "This is my home. Wouldn't you rather be where you belong?"

I hesitate before responding, absentmindedly reaching for a cookie.

"You might want to take it easy on those," Lynne advises. "There's a dinner at the Rector's after the honorary doctorate ceremony."

*****

I'm too late to find a place in the Languages and Literature auditorium, which has probably been packed since noon. The recipient of the honorary doctorate is the novelist Gunter Grass, a native son of Gdansk/Danzig, his fame already established by the so-called "Danzig Trilogy" of *The Tin Drum*, *Cat and Mouse*, and *Dog Years*, and with a Nobel Prize for Literature rumored to come. I stand in a sea of students, watching the Great Man's acceptance speech on a soundless television monitor. The crowd is far from silent, however. Conversations float by in the leaf-rustling music of the Polish language, and popular tunes in English leak from the headsets of a dozen nearby watchers. On the screen the image of a dignified Grass perfectly lip-synchs a stanza from the Eric Idle *Always Look on the Bright Side of Life* playing in my ear: "Life's a bowl of shit/ when you think of it"—nicely summarizing his novelistic philosophy.

As I leave the Languages and Literature building, I see Andrzej Grzegorczyk, the University Vice-Rector and head of the American division of the English Institute, walking toward me, a well-dressed, older American man in tow.

"Rickart, I want you to meet Ernest Williams, who's here from the States to help us with our local telephone problems. He's going to be meeting with some of the Municipal Council members at the Rector's dinner tonight. Can you and Lynne escort him over? I have another stop to make first. Mr. Williams, this is Dr. Rickart Temple, one of our native speaking faculty."

Andrzej hurries off, as we exchange greetings and start on the walk across the field to the Administration Building where the dinner will be held.

"Have you been in Gdansk long, Mr. Williams?"

"Only two days. Still suffering from jet lag, I'm afraid. I retired from AT&T last year, and a friend of mine in government asked me if I might be interested in coming over here and offering a little advice.

"Where are you from?"

"Upstate New York. A little town you've probably never heard of. Malone?

I give a snort of laughter, and he turns toward me with

curiosity. I know I am smiling, if not entirely with amusement.

"I've not only heard of Malone, thirty years ago I was in jail there."

*****

The Norwegian-American cruise ship, *Mitt Hjemland*, sailed down the St. Lawrence Seaway and docked in Montreal on a crisp Monday morning, September 12, 1960. Originally launched as a Norwegian liner at Rissa in 1937, the *Mitt Hjemland* was on its way to New York at the time of Pearl Harbor. With Norway occupied, the United States appropriated it and took it to the Norfolk Naval Base, where it was refitted as a minesweeper, *Sanctuary*, and re-launched in 1942. Within a year, it had been captured by the Germans (some said there were Quislings among the officers), and wasn't returned to its original country, name, and purpose until 1947.

These days the passengers of the *Mitt Hjemland* are largely college students, and except for an early brush with the fringe winds of Hurricane Donna, the nine-day trip from Rotterdam has been largely uneventful: days of sunbathing on the observation desk, nights spent drinking in one of the several bars below, dancing to cover bands attempting to channel Perez Prado, Paul Anka, Bobby Darrin, or (given the right combination of break time liquor and backstage pot) Chuck Berry. In smaller rooms, their lights covered with improvised paper lanterns, would-be Beat poets read aloud from Ginsburg, Kerouac, Ferlinghetti, and Henry Miller. The first summer of The Pill is winding down, and still further below in two or three person cabins whose doorknobs are wrapped with a warning towel, a few recently introduced couples are testing its effectiveness.

Rik has become one of the serious drinkers. In a relatively brief time after loading his three-speed Raleigh Sports Bicycle on board the *Mitt Hjemland*, he'd established a fairly fixed routine: late afternoon reading on the port side of the upper deck now that September winds had robbed the swimming pool of its appeal (a snapshot tracking him down years later shows a sun-tanned boy in need of a haircut earnestly attempting to navigate Albert Camus' *Les Justes* in the original French); dinner at seven; four hours of lubrication in one of the bars; a continental midnight supper of enormous proportions; followed by sweaty grappling with some young woman who matched him in hormonal urges and indifference to background and future. This relationship almost invariably ends with the first call to breakfast (in French for some reason: "*La premiere portion de la petit-dejeuner aura lieu en dix minutes*"), and a retreat to the bunk in his own cabin. He awakes at 4 p.m. to an expansive tea, and the cycle begins again.

The routine changes the first time the girl joins him at breakfast. Actually, it must have begun the night before because Rik could remember that they had talked, and he even knew her name: Mary Jane Parkland.

"Shoes or dope?" he asked, and was immediately ashamed.

She took it without rancor. "When you grow up with a white bread name, you learn to roll with the jokes. Call me M.J. What's Rick short for?"

"It's Rickart. When you grow up with a vaguely ethnic name, you learn to shorten it to avoid explanations."

She was from Orlando and a theatre student at the University of Florida. It was *Les Justes* that had tipped her off that Rik had interests above the waist, and inspired her to take the bar stool next to him. (Perhaps it was just as well he hadn't been reading *Lolita* that day.) Shipboard girls tended to travel in pairs until one of them focused on a guy with the right combination of sexual energy and willingness to accept no at the critical point. Their character analyses weren't always correct, requiring consequent improvisation. Rik had traveled with a group of girls simultaneously making their first acquaintance with ouzo and Eastern European men in a Yugoslavia Socialist Youth camp, and twice in the same night found himself being introduced as a jealous fiancé. M.J. was on her own because her cabin mate, Janet, had been seasick the entire voyage. Rik had sobered immediately when she sat down, aware of both her curvy form and curly black hair, and behind her the weightlifter, from whom she'd turned away to talk to him.

The second night they sought one another out, silently joining hands, leaving the bar and climbing to the deck above, following the curve of the ship until the rhythm of the sea replaced the mambo beat of the band below. The sky was cloudy and starless. M.J. shivered. Impulsively, he lifted his arm and wrapped it around her shoulders.

"Fall is coming," she said. "Strasbourg is near the mountains, and I was cool all summer. What will it be like there in the winter?"

"You're going back?"

"Not this year. But maybe when I'm a senior. This summer was just for the language, the *Institut International d'Etudes Francaises*. I'd like to study political science there, maybe prepare for the Diplomatic Service."

"What about the theatre?"

"I'm not sure I want to stay in the theatre. I like being on the stage, but people think you're the person you play. And the better you are at it, the more they think that. And in order to be really good, you have to believe it too. There was a guy—"

"What guy?"

"He started following me around last year. He'd be in the hallway outside my classes. He'd call me late at night. Even when he didn't say anything, I knew it was him. He saw me onstage in Tennessee Williams' *27 Wagons of Cotton*, playing Flora. I think he thought I was her, a woman who wanted to be dominated, to be hurt. Then—when he realized I was afraid of him—that was proof to him that I wanted what Flora wanted."

"You should have called a cop."

"He didn't *do* anything! It was just what he thought!"

"You can't let anybody scare you out of being what you want to be."

"He didn't, but he made me think. Listen. What makes me good on stage? My voice is average, I'd never make it in a chorus line, and the theatre is full of pretty girls, (she said modestly). I'm good because I *re*-act. I'm good at listening, at picking up cues from other actors. They trust me on stage. Why can't I use those talents another way?"

"I don't get you."

"Being able to sense the atmosphere in a room, being able to hear what people are actually saying, being open to them, creating a condition of trust. Being prepared, but being in the moment, being able to improvise without losing the sense of the whole. The best kind of theatre! Diplomacy! What if everything I've done to this point was just to get me ready to do something I never anticipated?"

*****

Despite a calm sea, Rik slept restlessly. The cabin made him feel claustrophobic. Tomorrow was the last day before the *Mitt Hjemland* docked in Montreal. In his luggage was a train ticket, purchased (and only redeemable) in Milwaukee. What then? His father once told him, "You can be a farmer with a college degree." But what had he learned in college? He had no pre-professional skills, no teaching certificate (even if teaching had ever appealed to him), had never demonstrated any potential as a leader or for advancing in the wake of one. Even his obsession with acting had come relatively late at a school unconnected to the theatrical profession. He could go back to the Army, but that would be pointless unless it were a springboard to something more compatible. In three months in Europe, he'd spent nearly every cent he'd saved.

He had all the qualities of a loner, except the ability to survive as one.

*****

In the late afternoon, Rik roamed the upper decks, hoping to casually come across M.J., but she was nowhere to be seen. Perhaps she was packing, an activity that Rik (with nothing that couldn't be fitted on a bicycle) could complete in minutes. He struggled to remember the face of her continually seasick cabin mate, Janet, who, M.J. said, was determined to take part in tonight's last celebration, but neither girl appeared.

In his first hour at the bar, Rik downed five shots of Rye, exhausting the dollar budget he'd allotted for mood alteration. As the bartender returned to him in anticipation, a familiar voice whispered in his ear.

"How come ya drink so much, pardner?

He turned to face a smiling Mary Jane, standing before him in a belted raincoat. "I drink to forget, Ma'am."

"What are ya trying to forget, pardner?"

"I don't rightly recall, Ma'am."

He slid off the bar stool, kissing her hungrily. And because they wanted to do it again, they lurched toward the door in an awkward, entwined three-legged lope. Last night's clouds were tonight's storm, and after some energetic kissing in the stairwell, they scrambled laughing down two flights of rain-washed steps to M.J.'s cabin. It's a difficult task to insert a key and open a lock in the midst of a closed-eyes clinch, but she managed it, and they sprawled across the high doorsill into the room. M.J. disentangled herself and scuttled into the cabin's toilet. Rik hesitated, but she was back in a moment with an obviously pre-prepared tray, complete with an uncorked bottle of wine, two glasses, and a dish of treats commandeered from the afternoon's tea. She sat the tray in the middle of the floor, placed a candle in its center, and lit it as she motioned for him to close the door.

She poured the wine and they touched glasses. "What are you going to do?"

"You know what I'm going to do," he said as he arched his body over the tray in an attempt to kiss her without setting himself on fire.

She responded to his kiss, then pulled away. "I mean now that we're back. I decided today. I'm changing my major; next year it's back to Strasbourg and *l'Institut d'Etudes Politique*, and on to Brandeis for a doctorate in International Studies. That's what we're celebrating! I called my parents today. It took me all afternoon to get through. What are *you* going to do?"

"Well, until it's corn picking time, I'll probably just help out in the barn."

Even in the candlelight he could see her face flush. "That's silly! You don't even like the farm. Even worse, it would be a waste of what you *can* do."

"M.J., do you know what a "Gentleman's C" is? It's a grade higher than I averaged at a college nobody ever heard of, and I'm not a gentleman. I have a major in history and a minor in physical education. I am known for a couple of acting awards at a school which doesn't have a theatre department, and for editing an underground magazine that never would have been read if it hadn't been banned in the student union. I'd say I've pretty much pissed away my possibilities."

She didn't flinch. "I don't believe that, and I don't think you do either. Or maybe you think it's romantic to throw away your life."

Rik stood up and opened the door. The flame of the candle flickered out, leaving Mary Jane in the shadows. "I'm sorry if I spoiled your celebration."

She stood, and in the dim light from the passageway, he could see her white hands move to the belt of the raincoat. "The celebration isn't over yet." The coat fell away from her bare shoulders and she beckoned as he closed the door behind him. A moment later he was leaning over her as she lay back upon the lower bunk.

From beneath M.J. a high-pitched scream shattered the tension of the night. Janet hadn't made it to the party upstairs after all.

*****

Rik stood on the top deck of the *Mitt Hjemland,* leaning on the railing and looking down at the milling crowd below. He'd done enough of the "hurry up and wait" routine in his infantry days not to be eager to join the Customs lines that preceded embarkation. Why rush? Even though his train wouldn't leave for hours, there still wouldn't be time enough to see anything of Montreal. The sky was cloudless and the sun was warm on his face, even as the wind off the water cooled his back. At one point he saw below him the dark, curly head of Mary Jane Parkland. She strode from side to side, looking in either direction and down at the dock, but never up. Was she looking for him, or for Janet? A fleeting smile crossed his face as he wondered whether M.J.'s cabin mate, her feet firmly on dry land, would remember last night's rude awakening as funny or frightening, ironic or rude. He would probably not see either of them again. Would he have a place in their mythology? Why not call out? Why not go down? At the very least there would be a tender goodbye, a warm memory for a frosty morning scooping manure out of the pigpen.

M.J. suddenly plunged into the crowd and disappeared down the gang plank. For the fortieth time in the past 36 hours Rik contemplated his future. Like M.J., he reacted rather than acted, but while she'd done it onstage, he'd done it in life. He had no realistic assessment of his possibilities. He went to college to play football because he wanted to think of himself as an athlete. When that didn't work out, he volunteered for the draft—service but not a commitment. He became an actor when a director approached him on a campus sidewalk. He prospered (he was aware) because he was a physical presence among pencil-necks. He became an editor (and a controversial figure) because of creative friends whose work was turned down by administration-sponsored outlets. He chose his major because he had the largest number of credits in that discipline when he decided to graduate. It could easily have been one of three others.

Unrealistic dreams and impulsive actions. How was insanity defined? Doing the same thing over and over again and expecting different results? Well, why change a lifetime of habit? He couldn't avoid going home, but he just might be able to delay it.

*****

It was four o'clock in the afternoon before he found the right road heading south out of Montreal—Highway 138, two paved lanes, smooth enough to make good time, narrow enough to be avoided by international trucks and impatient tourists. He'd spent nearly every day this summer on his three-speed Raleigh, a bicycle (like him) built for endurance rather than speed, pedaling from Southampton to Dubrovnik, and almost every night in his homemade sleeping bag in youth hostels, train stations, and garbage pits. How far was it to Wisconsin? Less than a thousand miles as the crow flies! Not that much of a challenge for legs that had conquered the Italian Alps and coasted down into Venice in seven hours.

Of course, that was summer and there was a drought in Italy. Drivers in their mini-Fiats expected to see bicycles on the road. There *were* other bicycles on the road. By the time Rik passed through Kensington and arrived at the United States border, it was raining. He had $3.75 in American money to declare.

At the border, Canadian Highway 138 becomes U.S. Highway 30. Sixty miles south of Montreal it neatly intersects Malone, New York. On the outskirts Rik passed a row of battered tourist cabins ("$1.50 a night, $3.00 heated") and chose a still open A&P instead. A day-old loaf of wheat bread and a jar of jam, and 85 cents was gone. The bicycle turned right on Main Street/U.S. Highway 11 and headed west. To his left he could see a city park with a picnic table and a roof sheltering it from the rain. Bedtime.

About the time the bone ache from the hard boards superseded the chill of his soaked clothes, he became aware of the flashlight shining in his face.

A figure wearing a stiff cap and covered by a poncho stood beside him, silhouetted by a street lamp. "It's time for you to go home, Buddy. The park closes at 9 p.m. after Labor Day."

"I don't live here. I'm just passing through."

"Where do you live?"

Rik pulled his feet out of the sleeping bag and began to pull on his shoes. "Wisconsin," he said.

The cop sighed. "Well, you're not going to get there tonight. I'm going to drive back up Main Street and take a left turn on Elm. I want you to follow me and don't get lost. Cause if you do, you're gonna spend more time with me than either of us wants."

The municipal building was three stories of turn-of-the-century red brick topped by a steeple, but the cell block off the rear parking lot was much more modern. Rik hoisted the Raleigh up the steps behind the cop, who, slapping the rain off his hat, nodded to another officer drinking coffee behind a desk.

"Hey, we got space for this kid until morning?"

The coffee drinker looked up from his crossword puzzle

just long enough to state the obvious. "It's Monday night, Frank. We got nothin' *but* empty cells."

Frank led the way down the hall, pausing at a rear cell. "I'm gonna put you back here, kid, so the light from the desk won't keep you awake. I'm gonna leave the door open so you can use the can, but I don't want you leavin' until I've had a chance to talk to you in the morning. Now I'm not gonna ask your name, 'cause if I did I'd have to make out a report. But I do want you to be here in the morning. Okay?"

Rik hung his clothes to dry on the cell's wash stand and climbed onto the bunk, which folded down from the wall on chains. It had a leather sleeping pad, shiny, hard, and uncomfortable. He drifted off in seconds.

*****

The cell block john had a shower, and after he dressed, Rik followed Frank down the street to a café where the waitress and several of the patrons greeted the cop by name. Rik was on his second cup of coffee and second helping of toast that followed the sausage and eggs when Frank produced a New York State roadmap.

"Don't you have any family that can help you?"

"They will if I can get to them."

Frank sighed and unfolded the map. "When I was a kid, I rode the rails out to Ogden, Utah, to work on my cousin's sugar beet farm. But the freights don't run through here anymore. Some police stations will let you stay the night, some won't. The best bet is to start out on Highway 11 and circle the Great Lakes, but I still think you're crazy."

*****

Rik had estimated he could make a hundred miles a day, but Tuesday had been as hot as Monday was wet, and he was exhausted as the Raleigh rolled into Gouverneur just 85 miles west of Malone on Highway 11. His mouth was as dry as the tad end of the wheat bread, which could no longer be folded into pads small enough to wipe jam out of the inside of the jar. Ahead of him in the downtown area was a narrow strip of triangular land identified by a roadside sign as "Gouverneur Municipal Park." Rik searched for a water fountain, but saw instead at the end of the park something that looked like a—

Giant roll of Lifesavers?

"That's right," said the man on the park bench with an affirming grin. He kicked at the ducks he'd been feeding and waved Rik to a place beside him. "It's been one of the town's biggest employers for nearly fifty years. Beechnut Gum too, for close to forty. I like to sit here sometimes and watch the faces of tourists when they see the statue for the first time. They can't believe their eyes!"

He was a genial looking man in his late thirties. Ruddy complexion, tight curly hair starting to recede from his forehead, khaki pants topped off with a Hawaiian shirt not quite concealing an incipient paunch: The look of a high school sprinter who had parlayed his local fame into a career as a used car salesman.

The man held out his hand. "My name is Patrick McRae. What can the town of Gouverneur do for you?

Rik looked around at the gathering shadows. "Well, the first thing would be to direct me to the police station."

"Really! Our artistic taste in statuary may not be very good, but I don't think it's illegal."

Rik explained his situation.

Patrick McRae grinned. "I just might be able to do you one better than that. Follow me."

A half block beyond the park, McRae in the lead, Rik pushing his Raleigh, the pair turned onto Morris Avenue, a tree-lined street of stately homes, some of which had been converted into offices and businesses. The third from the highway on the right had a stoop and a wide porch. The front door sign read "Gouverneur Salvation Army."

McRae bounded up the steps. "Leave your bike on the front porch. Nobody will bother it." Inside, a bespectacled woman of indeterminate years was working at a roll-top desk, and McRae spoke to her with an air of familiar command. "Sally, this young man is Rik Temple. I want you to put him up in one of the upstairs rooms for tonight, and give him a breakfast voucher for Carter's." He turned and shook Rik's hand, and held it for a second. "Sally will take care of you, and maybe I'll see you later."

A smiling Sally came out from behind the desk. "You'd better bring your bicycle inside. I know what Mr. McRae said, but sometimes he just expects too much of people."

*****

Downstairs Sally is watching *Bourbon Street Beat* on television. The furniture in the room upstairs overwhelms the space. Rik sits in a stuffed armchair, a three-legged dresser to his right, reading the copy of *Lolita* he'd bought on the Left Bank of the *Seine*. Humbert Humbert—obsessive, a manipulator, a pedophile. Why did he feel sympathy for him? He looked at the Victorian bed, with its iron frame incongruously woven into floral designs with soft curves. When did he last sleep in a real bed? Even one with a too soft mattress, an overly cool sheet and a stiflingly heavy quilt. The trapped air is stagnant on the inside of the sealed window. The book slips out of his hand and hits the floor.

*****

Rik hurries out of Carter's Restaurant. The weather has turned chilly again and he's overslept. On the other side of Beechnut Street, leaning up against a new Corvette, is a man in a denim jacket and sunglasses. The day is cloudy.

"Rik, did you sleep well?"

Rik waits for a car to pass, then pushes the Raleigh across the street. He takes in the "vette." Maybe the used car salesman's guess underrated McRae. Maybe he had a dealership. "Very well, thank you. And thanks for the breakfast."

"Look, I have to meet with a client a couple of hours down Highway 11. Why don't I give you a ride? I get some company and you get a good start on the day. We should be able to strap the bicycle on the back."

*****

For a man who wanted company, Patrick McRae is quiet, his eyes on the road ahead. On the car radio a D.J. does sports chat between playing records. An 18-year-old outfielder, Danny Murphy, is the youngest Chicago Cub in history to hit a home run when he connects with two on against Bob Purkey of Cincinnati. Obviously a great future ahead of him, but the Reds win anyway, 8-6. An Elvis Presley ballad comes on—recorded, released, a hit, and faded from the charts while Rik was in Europe.

"It's now or never,
Come hold me tight.
Kiss me my darling,
Be mine tonight.
Tomorrow will be too late,
It's now or never.
My love won't wait."

Patrick takes a right turn onto a secondary road. "I have to drop something off on the way. It won't take long." After a time, he switches off the radio. "So, where'd you go in Europe?"

Rik launches into the full tour: to Southampton on the *Mitt Hjemland*, London, the English Channel to Cherbourg,

Paris (the *Lido*, the Louvre), Lucerne, Montreux (Lake Geneva), Rome (pre-Olympics), the Italian Alps, Venice (his birthday), a livestock boat to Croatia (the Socialist Youth Camp), Oberammergau (the Passion Play), Lyons, back to Paris, back to London, Edinburgh, Rotterdam, the ship again—a long story.

"Alone all that time?"

"No, for quite a while I hooked on as a bike mechanic with a group of girls—16 of them."

"That must have kept you excited."

"I never had an experience like it."

"New experiences are good. Yeah, I bet they kept you excited all the time. You able to keep all of them happy?"

"Well, I did what I could."

"Yeah, I bet you were in a state of non-stop excitement. I bet I could I reach over there and find out just how excited you were."

Rik gave the driver a fleeting glance. McRae was looking straight ahead, his hands on the wheel, and his face inscrutable beneath the sunglasses.

"Yeah, I bet I could just reach over there and see how excited you can get."

Rik's racing mind weighed his options. He was younger than McRae, taller. Surely he could defend himself if it came to that. And if it came to that, then what? A respected resident of the community befriends a drifter, offers him a much-needed ride, and is attacked for his trouble? He wouldn't have to worry about being able to spend nights in jail for a long time. Then there was another possibility he couldn't keep out of his mind. Suppose he did what McRae wanted? Could he turn that into a cross-country bus ticket? There was nothing he wanted at that moment more than to be home.

Then it was over.

Patrick McRae switches back on the radio. Bobby Darrin is singing.

"Somewhere beyond the sea,
Somewhere, waiting for me,
My lover stands on golden sands
And watches the ships that go sailing."

"Look, I've gotta take a turn at the next crossroad, and it'll only take you out of your way. Why don't I let you out there? Just follow the road to the next town and you'll be back on Highway 11 in no time."

*****

The day is dark and cold, but it isn't raining and the wind is behind him. Rik makes good time. What must it be like to be Patrick McRae in Gouverneur, New York—a town of what? Seven thousand? A town where the only jobs are in the candy factory or the marble quarry? To be a prominent citizen (the car, the influence at the Salvation Army)? How many people knew? Sally seemed to be genuinely admiring. Rik strained to remember the presence of a wedding ring. Were there business trips to New York City? How often did a pliable stranger come through? How did they recognize one another? He'd been wrong about Rik. Had he inadvertently used a code word which inspired McRae to take the risk?

A town loomed up in the distance. Rik dug in at the pedals. The afternoon was waning, and this time he wanted to check out the town thoroughly before he talked to anyone. As he rounded the bend, a huge pit became visible on his left. Rik cursed. It was the Gouverneur marble quarry. McRae had driven him in a circle.

*****

It was late Thursday afternoon when Rik reached Pulaski, seventy-five miles from Gouverneur. He hadn't eaten since Wednesday morning. On an impulse he turned right at the

Pulaski turnoff, heading for Selkirk Beach on Lake Ontario's shore. On the ship someone had told him it was a hangout for college students. Even this late in the season he might be able to cadge a meal or a ride—or both. As it happened, he was in luck.

The party on the beach could have been going on for days, pausing only to restock combustibles and participants. Rik moved easily from fire to fire, exchanging greetings with people who thought they knew him—devouring an offered shish-ka-bob, sucking on an unguarded Ballantine, being kissed by a drunken girl who mistook him for her boyfriend. Just another shabbily dressed student with longish hair and a stubbly beard. In the early morning hours, with the party still raging around him, he curled up in the sand as close as he could to one of the fires without being burned, and went to sleep.

He woke struggling to breathe, a morning breeze from the fogged-in lake blowing the smoke of the guttering fire into his face. He sat up, momentarily unaware of where he was, conscious only of the gritty taste in his mouth, part meat gristle, part sand. His smarting eyes eventually focused on a young man opposite him who was using a still glowing faggot end to light a joint.

"Good morning."

Rik muttered something incomprehensible.

"My name is Nick Russell. I don't think I know you.

"I don't know you either."

"Fair enough. But my family owns the beach house directly behind you, and presumably everyone at last night's party was someone I invited, or came with someone I invited." There was a pause. The young man smiled at his own thoughtlessness and offered to pass Rik the joint.

Rik shook his head and stood up. "I was just riding by," he said, trying to remember where he'd stashed the Raleigh. "I guess it's time to ride on."

"No hurry. By the way, your bicycle is in the boat house. There's a shower there that you might want to use. I'll get you some soap and a towel. Where're you headed?"

"Anywhere west. The Middle West, eventually. Anyone headed in that direction?"

"Just one."

"Who?"

"Me, but not until tomorrow afternoon. I'm a graduate student in English at Cornell in Ithaca."

"How far is that?"

"A three or four hour drive. Maybe 200 miles. Want a lift?"

"I guess not. Thanks for asking."

"No problem. The offer stays open. There's some fruit on the table next to the beach house. You might want to use that too."

*****

Just short of the intersection with Highway 11, Rik saw a faded sign which hadn't been there yesterday. It was on the nearest of two oaks whose branches formed a celebratory arch over the entrance to a private lane.

"DAY LABOR NEEDED. INQUIRE AT THE HOUSE"

"You know that the sign means there's nothin' permanent. I only got a day's work to be done."

"Perfect. I only got a day to spend on it."

The woman in front of him was nearly sixty—wire-rimmed glasses, graying hair gathered in a bun, a tall, strong body, slightly stooped with labor or maybe the beginnings of osteoporosis. She wore a faded print dress, a cloth belt at the waist, cotton stockings and sensible shoes. Her expression was not unfriendly, just matter-of-fact.

"You a student here?"

"I'm a student, but not here. Just passing through."

"Lots of students go back and forth between the Lake and

the Highway. Usually high school, if they're on bikes. I put out that sign whenever I need help. Usually high school kids. People in cars don't even see the sign."

She led him down a driveway circling the two-story farmhouse. Grass growing between the wheel ruts suggested the path wasn't used much. Behind the path was a deserted barn, a still in-use chicken house, and a carriage house-like structure. Still further was a late-season garden, and back of the barn stood a small apple orchard.

"After Papa passed on, I sold the stock and most of the land. Didn't really need it, what with social security and the Air Force pension. But I had to keep busy, so I kept the garden for myself, and the orchard. I still got my weekly egg customers, and a lot of them buy apples in the fall, and sometimes stuff I've canned. I raise more than I can eat, and storing more than a winter's worth in the fruit cellar is pointless."

Rik looked at the fruit above him—red, sometimes flecked with green, but still appearing ripe. "I didn't know they raised apples in New York."

She snorted. "We grow more apples in New York than any other state except Washington, as many as they do in all of Canada. These are McIntosh, but within a hundred miles of here you could find Delicious, Golden Delicious, Tydeman Early, Arkansas Black, Earliblaze, Winesap, Courtland, even Winter Banana—"Zone 4" apples, which means that the trees will survive a winter that gets down to 25 or 30 below zero."

"The trees aren't very tall. Are they young?"

"They're spur trees—won't get any bigger. That's why we planted McIntosh. We raise apples, not wood. Otherwise, we would have put in Courtland. If I was starting again, I'd put in some of the newer strains—something that would catch people's interest, be the apple of their eye, so to speak: Holly, Mutsu, Empire, Jonagold. Papa wasn't interested in the orchard, but I always wanted apples, and, by god, I got 'em."

In the barn there was a ladder, a bucket with a hook that could be hung from a limb or a ladder rung, and dozens of wooden baskets. Rik determined that if he could finish the picking by Friday noon, he could catch the ride to Ithaca with Nick Russell, arrive as soon as he could have done on his Raleigh, and have a little money in his pocket. His bicycle-conditioned legs stood him well on the ladder, but by the time the long shadows sliced through the orchard, his back and shoulders ached with fatigue.

The woman suddenly appeared below him. "It's getting dark. You'd better stop now and come back in the morning."

"I've got a sleeping bag. If you don't mind, I'll just sack out in the barn."

She paused for a moment. "That won't be necessary."

The meal was of the huge proportions he remembered growing up on the farm: meatloaf, homemade bread, potatoes, peas and corn from the garden, pickled watermelon rind, coffee, and cantaloupe for dessert. When he could push himself away from the table, she switched on the yard light and led him across the clearing to the carriage house.

"Papa built this about twenty years ago. He was always good with his hands, building things, repairing machinery, and so forth. It was going to be a *Grossvater* house, like the Amish have, for him and me after Davy got married and took over the farm. I thought about moving out here after Papa died, but what was the point?"

The bottom half of the building was a garage, and Rik could make out the indistinct shape of a '49 Ford as they climbed the stairs to the second floor. The flick of a light switch revealed a neatly organized, surprisingly clean, living space. At one end there was a kitchen with an old refrigerator, a gas stove, built-in cupboards, a Formica-topped table, and metal-framed chairs. In the middle was a sofa, a small table with a plastic radio, and an elderly, comfortable looking recliner. At the far end was a sleeping area: a double bed parallel to the wall, a rag rug beside it, a floor lamp and a chair at its head, and a bookcase at its foot. Directly above the bed, suspended in an intricate pattern was a mobile consisting of a half dozen, lovingly crafted model airplanes. They circled in the evening breeze as the woman opened a window and turned on the floor lamp.

"It looks better this way," she said apologetically, as she crossed to the head of the stairs and switched off the overhead light.

Rik touched one of the model planes, sending it into a steep glide to the starboard side. A military medal he didn't recognize swung around to the front.

"Davy lived up here the whole time when he was a teenager. Gave him a sense of independence, I guess. His friends envied him, loved to visit him here. No girls though! Me and Papa wouldn't allow that kind of stuff. He was crazy about airplanes! Usedta stop the horses in the field to watch whenever one went over. He wanted to be a pilot in the War so bad, but we wouldn't sign for him until after he graduated from high school. That was June 17, 1945. The war in Europe had been over a month. It broke his heart when he couldn't get into flight school. He was just out of high school and didn't have any training. The Bomb was dropped, the Japs surrendered, and they were cutting back in the Armed Services. He stayed in the Air Force though—as a mechanic, and spent his spare time studying and taking flying lessons. It took him *five* years, but he got accepted, went through the training and got his commission. We were so proud!"

Rik wandered over to the bookcase. Magazines, books— *How to Fly in Ten Easy Lessons*, *The Future of Aviation*, *Hitler's Luftwaffe*, and many others.

She walked to the bed. A gust of wind blew through the window. The formation of flying birds shivered. "That's a Messerschmitt ME-109. This is a Heinkel HE-11. Here's a Focke-Wolfe FW-190. The big bomber is a Dornier DO 17, and the fighter's a Junker JU-87. Davy told me their names so many times that I can't never forget 'em."

"What happened?"

"It was his first day in Korea. He took off in his P-51 from the base at Pusan and somehow got separated from his formation. They never saw him again."

"That must have been hard."

"It was for Papa. He didn't say much, just kept working—even after he stopped hoping that Davy would come back. He just got littler and littler each season. Five years ago he was up on the ladder picking apples, and he just looked up, sighed, and pitched over backwards. Doc Willard says he was probably dead before he hit the ground."

"What about you?"

"I don't know. I've had ten years to think about it. To be there, to fly combat, is something Davy'd been wantin' to do his whole life. He did that. Nobody can take that away from him. It's like me and my apples. How many people get to do the one thing in their life they wanted to do? Have you?"

*****

The VW microbus roared down the highway, a Raleigh three-speed bicycle tied to its roof. Sitting next to Nick Russell, Rik thumbed through a Cornell University catalogue.

"Literature 646: Twentieth-Century Russian Novels"
Instructor: Vladimir Nabokov
(Reading knowledge of Russian required)
"Would you mind if I kept this?"

Nick Russell smiled sweetly through the haze of a reefer. "Not at all," he said. "You can have it for your share of the gas money to Ithaca."

Rik sighed and opened the envelope the woman had given him. There were four dollars in it. At that moment he realized that he had forgotten to ask her name.

*****

It rained all day. Rik stayed in the Public Library until the peak of the dinner hour, then steered the Raleigh down the street leading to the Highway. He was looking for a particular type of restaurant, one with a buffet where the help stayed behind the counter, crowded enough to assure that personal attention would be kept to a minimum.

"Will that be all, Sir?"

Rik raised his eyes to meet those of the operator of the cash register. He had tried not to be noticeable, not to make eye contact with anyone in the serving line, but this question could not be avoided. In front of him stood a very fair girl of what he first guessed as about fifteen years. Like the other waitresses, she wore a faded cherry-colored uniform, with a white cap over her pulled-back, center-parted, blonde hair.

However, her cap was distinctly different, with what looked like horizontal slats on the sides and worn lower on the head so that the hair was tucked into it, making her pale blue eyes seem all the larger. Rik was reminded of the picture of the Maid on an Old Dutch Cleanser can. He glanced at the tag on the breast pocket of her uniform: "Rachel."

She looked at the tray in front of him, with its cup and single tea-bag. "That will be ten cents, Sir. The hot water is there to your right."

"Can I have more hot water if I want to make a second cup?"

"Of course."

*****

When he slipped out of the side door an hour or so later, she was waiting for him under the edge of the roof that led to the parking lot.

"I saw what you did."

"And what was that?"

"After you finished your tea, you came back to the hot water three times. Each time you picked up a package of crackers from the condiments rack. You took the top off the ketchup bottle and added it to the hot water until it was empty. You made tomato soup and seasoned it with salt and pepper. You thought no one saw you, but I did."

"Don't you have to get back to work?"

"No, my shift is from noon to eight."

"Are you going to turn me in?"

She stood before him, a small and determined figure. "No, I'm going to feed you."

*****

Rik secured the Raleigh under the dripping porch roof and followed Rachel up the wooden steps to the second floor apartment. The first floor was an appliance store that fronted on a street adjacent to that of the restaurant. The living space was accessible only from the alley. The furniture was an accumulation of hand-me-downs—the gas stove and the refrigerator probably from the store below, the tables, chairs, a sofa, etc., totally mismatched but given a modicum of unity by tasteful arrangement and an abundance of decorative doilies and rugs clearly made by the same hands that fashioned the curtains.

She opened a window a crack, then climbed a chair and pulled down a gas lamp from the ceiling above the table. She lit it, stepped down and smiled at him. "There's electricity of course, but I feel more at home this way. Please, make yourself comfortable while I change," she said, and then disappeared into a curtained area.

Rik placed his wet backpack and his bedroll on the mat in front of the door, and looked around. The space had a comfortable, lived in feeling, small, but suitable to the stature of its occupant. Yet there was something odd about it, and Rik suddenly realized that there was no television set or radio, not even a family photograph on the wall.

Then she was back, still with the same cap, but having traded her waitress uniform for a long-sleeved, single piece, almost floor length plum-colored dress. A white apron was tied at her waist with a decorative bow in the back, its strings hanging in scallops almost to the hinge of her knees. She smiled again. "You can take off your clothes if you like. I have to go to the Laundromat around the corner anyway."

There was a knock at the door. Rik started. He was alone with a girl who was probably underage—in her room. In another moment he might have been undressed. Was this planned? Rachel seemed unconcerned. She crossed to the door. Standing on the other side of the threshold was a broad-shouldered young man, younger than Rik and almost as blonde as Rachel. He was clean-shaven, and on his head he wore a flat-brimmed black felt hat. His black cloth coat was open, revealing a tie-less white shirt and black suspenders holding up a pair of barrel legged black trousers.

Rachel turned to Rik. "Would you excuse us, please?" She stepped out onto the landing and closed the door.

Rik rose and looked around the room for another exit. There were none. Even the two windows in view were in the same wall as the door. Behind the curtain to the left of the door, he found a bed covered by a spectacular quilt. Above the bed was a high window, and to its left was a large cardboard cupboard. On the right was a door to an alcove which stood out from the wall. Inside was a miniscule bathroom—commode, sink and mirror, and shower—a space incapable of accommodating two people at once. On his way out he noticed something on the bed and brought it out into the light of the room. It was a tiny cloth figure, delicately shaped to give it a human form and dressed in a manner very much like Rachel, complete with cap. But the face was featureless.

He was still studying the miniature when the original herself re-entered the room alone, apparently not in the least disturbed by his invasion of her private space.

"I see you've met Miss Peanut, my *lumba bubba*."

"Lumba bubba?"

"My rag doll. When Mama first made her for me, before she had clothes, I didn't know what she was. I thought she looked like a peanut, three nuts in a shell." She took the doll from him and arranged its clothes to reveal the shape. "See?"

"Why doesn't it have a face?"

Rachel looked serious. "'Thou shalt not make unto thyself a graven image, nor any likeness of anything that is in the heaven above, or that is in the earth beneath, or that is in the water under the earth.' I can see Miss Peanut in my heart, I don't need a picture."

"Who was at the door?"

Rachel is all smiles again. "That was just Aaron. He wanted me to go to a party with his Buddy Bunch. Wasn't he cute? He usually wears English clothes—he works for a landscaper in town—but he put on his *Ordnung* garments to ask me to go with him."

Rik was trying to process all this information. "What happens at the party?"

"The usual things." She opened the refrigerator and began arranging covered dishes on the counter next to the stove. "It'll be in a barn. Loud Rock n' Roll music, dancing, lots of drinking, food in the milk house. Fooling around in the hay loft." She glanced at him shyly, then turned on the gas and lit it. "There'll be at least a hundred people there, some—like me—from Pennsylvania or Indiana, maybe even further away. It'll last all night, probably most of tomorrow. No one has to work. It'll be Sunday."

"You're allowed to do that?"

Rachel looked at him with surprise. "Of course, it's our

rumspringa! I keep forgetting you're English."

Of the multitude of Northern European countries that had belched his family up on the shores of America, England was not one, but Rik didn't bother to correct her. "*Rumspringa?*" he asked.

"Our 'running around' time." Rachel tried to be patient. "Until we're sixteen our family decides. After we're baptized the Church decides. That's good, but the Church wants us to know the world before we give ourselves to the Church. So when we're sixteen we have our *rumspringa*. We're on our own until we decide to be baptized, or maybe forever. Either way we decide. That way we know we're not making a mistake. A girl like me from out of state is a prize at a Buddy party. Maybe I won't go back to Lancaster. Maybe Aaron and I will get baptized together. Maybe we'll get married."

"What did Aaron think of my being here?"

It was like explaining something to a child. "It doesn't matter. It's *my rumspringa too*," she said. "Now, do you want to put the dishes on the table or would you rather take off your clothes first?"

*****

A commotion at the door awakened Rik. He lay on the couch, staring at an unfamiliar ceiling. A cheerful Rachel rustled past, carrying a basket full of laundry.

"Wake up, sleepyhead. It's our Day of Rest and we have a lot of work to do." She laughed at what was apparently a familiar joke.

He sat up on the edge of the couch, looking around for the trousers he'd kept behind. He'd showered the night before, taking several serious bumps in the lightless, tiny bathroom space because he was too shy to leave the door open. This modesty came to an end after one particularly painful knock was followed by Rachel collapsing in giggles in the bedroom.

"What's first on the agenda?"

"After breakfast," she said firmly, "I'm giving you a shave and a haircut. Two bits!"

Fortunately, the "two bits" wasn't required, because Rik couldn't have paid it, but that in no way diminished the girl's skill with a scissors and a razor. She'd obviously done this before. And as she circled him with an observant eye and flying hands, he pieced together the story of her life.

Rachel's family was Old Order Amish in rural Lancaster County, Pennsylvania, and she was the oldest of eight children, including a sister two years younger, four evenly spaced brothers, and after a hiatus of five years, a surprise pair of twin girls. Her mother had never fully recovered from that delivery and died a year later. And with her mother passed (Rachel thought) her *rumspringa* opportunity.

The ally she had not reckoned on was her father, who was determined that she receive her test. The twins were no longer infants, and, more important, her sister had completed the eighth grades the Pennsylvania State Board of Education required for the Amish, and could supervise the household under the guidance of a covey of nearby aunts.

"You don't know how much fun it is to be in a school where you can help teach your sister and three of your brothers."

Rik laughed, remembering Prairie View School and being allowed as a first grader to climb up into the desk of Marti, his eighth-grade sister. There were never more than twenty to thirty students there during his grade school years, a fair percentage of whom were related to him. The next generation had lost that experience of continuity due to school consolidation, something that would never happen to Rachel's family.

"The hardest part was to say goodbye to the littlest girls. I'd been their *mutti*, the only one they remembered. They called me 'Rashee,' and wouldn't stop crying."

The family had chosen Big Flats, New York, for a number of reasons. It was far enough away that that she wouldn't be tempted to come home, and they wouldn't be tempted to ask her. There was an Amish community close by in case she was homesick, and another neighborhood girl had been well-liked as a waitress in the restaurant where Rachel worked. It was hard at first, but eventually she began to feel at home. There was more than one "Buddy Bunch" of late teenagers in situations much like hers, and more than one boy like Aaron who was smitten enough to transport her anywhere she wanted to go. She watched television at the home of an "English" friend (as all non-Amish were called) and went to the movies for the first time. (*A Summer Place* was her favorite. She'd borrowed the Percy Faith record from the Library, and the appliance store below had lent her a record player. She'd play it and her other favorites for Rik if he wanted.)

She stepped back in delight. "It's finished," she said, and ran to the bedroom for a mirror. In its reflection he could see a sun-tanned young man who could have easily passed for an Amish youth—his previously shaggy hair now in a modified bowl cut and his upper lip, cheeks, and chin shaved, but with the stubble preserved on the underside of his jaw line. "I just wanted to see what you'd look like as a marriageable young man."

"Thanks, but if you'll hand me the razor I think I'll finish the job.

She wrinkled her nose, then leaned forward and lightly kissed his. Rik reached out quickly and pulled her onto his lap, kissing her once, twice. The third time she relaxed and took an active part in the process.

Rachel put her arms around his neck, leaned back and looked him in the face gravely. "I hope you realize I've still got the razor in my right hand," she began, and broke off into squeals of laughter as he tickled her.

"If you nick me, you'll get blood on your prayer cap."

An instant later they crashed to the floor, and just as quickly she ceased to struggle. He straightened up, his knees astride her waist.

"I think you'd better let me up now," she said quietly.

*****

They walked hand in hand along the path next to Gardner Creek Pond. The afternoon had been warm, but the evenings would be chill from now on.

"Why did you wait for me outside the restaurant?"

"I don't know. I saw something in you. Maybe it's silly, but it was like looking at myself in a mirror."

"I've never looked so good," he said, drawing her to him and kissing her.

She broke away and walked ahead, seeking out a park bench where he joined her. "That's not it," she said, taking his hands and looking up at him. "I saw a boy who didn't know where he belonged and was trying to find out. I used to be someone like that."

"But not any longer." He was angry and didn't know why.

"No. I'm seventeen, Rik. I'm grown-up. I'll stay here until next spring, and I'll go to movies and listen to records. I'll go to Buddy parties with Aaron or somebody else, and I'll dance to Rock n' Roll and have fun. And when May comes and my sister turns sixteen, I'll go home so she can have her *rumspringa*. I'll cook and I'll clean, and I'll make dresses for the babies and I'll sing to them at night. My aunts will teach me *Gelassenheit*, the way to be myself by being part of the whole. I will disappear as an individual, and when I do so, I will fulfill my destiny. And when my sister comes home, my brother will leave on his *rumspringa*. My other brothers will be teenagers, working with my father in the fields. The little girls will be in school, and I will be baptized and I will marry a man who will work on his father's farm and move into his father's house when his father and mother build a *Grossvater* house in the back yard. And I will fill that house with children and love, and things will be as they have always been."

"What if I stayed here?"

She put a finger on his lips. "You don't belong here. You don't know where it is you belong, but you already know it's not here. Have you seen the quilt on my bed?"

He nodded.

"My mother made that for me before she died. She thought that it was important that I have it. The pattern is called 'Rabbits Paw', and every first daughter in my family has been given one for as long as anybody can remember. There is a red border on a blue quilt, and inside it are twenty rabbit paws, and nineteen of them are perfect. Just one of them has a toenail that points in the wrong direction. I asked my mother about it. She smiled, and said she had never noticed it before. But I know better! Only God can create perfection. The rest of us must practice *Gelassenheit* and accept what we are given."

"What can I do to get you to come with me?"

"Nothing! But I can help you on your way, and you can help me while you're here."

"How?"

"I'll buy your bus ticket."

"I can't take that from you."

"It wouldn't be charity. I'd have your bicycle. Every time I ride it, I'll think of you."

"It's a boy's bicycle."

"It doesn't matter. We have to tuck up our skirts anyway to keep them from catching in the chain. This will make it easier."

"How can I help you while I'm here?"

"You can sleep with me tonight. The only man other than my husband with whom I'll ever share a bed. That's the way we court in the Old Order. Bundling on a Sunday evening after an afternoon together! We'll roll up my quilt and put it between us. It won't be perfect, but"—a tremulous smile passed quickly over her face—"Oh well!"

*****

In the night Rik got up to use the bathroom. When he returned there was a full moon visible through the window above the bed. A Harvest Moon. Autumn would be here soon. A time to reap what had been sown. The light shone on the unformed face of the *lumba bubba* lying on the floor. He picked it up and tucked it under Rachel's arm. Miss Peanut. He would always see Miss Peanut in his heart, he wouldn't need a picture. Gently he lay down upon the bed, wrapped his arm around the sleeping girl, and buried his face in the mane of fine-spun golden hair.

*****

As the bus pulled onto Canal Street, Rik looked up at the clock on the Courthouse wall. It was four in the afternoon, exactly one week since he'd left Montreal.

*****

Seventeen hours later, the mighty Greyhound completed its last lap, crossing the bridge under which the old brewery had once connected to Tripp Lake, loping up Main Street, and wearily turning right on Second to come to rest in the parking lot opposite "Ketterhausen Buick." Rik climbed stiffly down the steps, checked the lashing of the bedroll, stuck an arm in a strap of the backpack, and swung them both up onto his shoulders. He stood, a stranger in the only town he'd ever spent a full day in as a boy, and walked back up to Main Street. The marquis on the Strand Theatre trumpeted the current attraction: *"EXODUS!* Starring Paul Newman and Eva Marie Saint."

Exodus.

Rik eased off the backpack and sat down on the bench in front of the bowling alley. A paperback with a broken spine slipped out of the bedroll onto the pavement in front of him. He opened it randomly.

"My Lolita remarked: 'you know what's so dreadful about dying is that you are completely on your own.'"

Rik leaned back on the bench. This time of year the morning sun had yet to clear the Livingwell Haberdashery store across the street.

What if Nabokov had it backward? What if being completely on your own was a *form* of dying? Still, Davy had died alone, but only in that moment did he fulfill his greatest dream. Patrick McRae was alone, trapped in a seemingly bucolic system as inflexible in reality as the Salvation Army's flower-shaped iron bed. Rachel is returning to a world where her every gesture is pre-ordained, but doing so will give *her* complete freedom—because she chose it. What was it Mary Jane had said? "What if everything I've done to this point was just to get me ready to do something I never anticipated?"

So many questions!

"Rik?"

The sun had cleared Livingwell's store at his eye level, and he blinked at the silhouetted figure in front of him, until the image resolved itself into the smiling face and blonde ponytail of Lynne Chase.

"I haven't seen you all summer. Where have you been?"

He stood, a broad grin stretching over his face, but carefully choosing his words. He knew—without formulating the thought—that in front of him stood the one person in his world he needed to understand him.

"I've been on *Rumspringa*," he said.

DRESS REHEARSAL

The harsh December wind struck him full in the face as he stepped out into the compound, stopping to grind out a Marlboro under his boot heel. Behind him one voice among many rose in shrill disapproval.

"Jesus Christ! Will you close that fucking door! It's fucking Siberia out there."

Todd Larson slammed the door behind him, happy to vent his anger. His long strides ate up the Post Road toward the NCO club, his face reddened more by rage and humiliation than the coming storm. Smartass bastard! Who the fuck did he think he was? Everybody had to teach a class. Everybody! It didn't have anything to do with your real training. Your ability to take orders or to give them. To read a map or deploy a squad. Ideological background? Useless crap! You need to know the enemy's terrain, their tactics, not their fucking philosophy. Somebody needed an ass-kicking.

Again and again, Todd went over the events of the preceding hour, the last Saturday morning OCS class of the year. Next week most of the barracks would be on Christmas leave, and after the first of the year they would start on Field Tactics—real soldiering, not intellectual shit! He'd volunteered to teach this class because he didn't want to be distracted when real training started. All of the trainees had to teach one class. He didn't see the value of it, but he didn't question it. Command set up the regimen and you followed it. Simple as that! Chinese Communism—that was the subject, and he taught it right. They gave him a manual and he taught it. He didn't leave anything out and he didn't put anything in. He did it just the way the manual said to!

And then that smartass Temple started raising his hand. You don't do that! You don't ask questions! You just write down what the teacher said, or at least pretend to. There's no test, for Christ's sake. What kind of question could there be? It's all from the god-damned manual! Who gives a good goddamn about the Long March? Some World War II pact between Mao and Chiang Kai-shek? They're all Communists, for God's sake! Tito, Ho Chi Minh—all of 'em! And if we don't stop 'em there, we'll have to fight 'em here. That's what we're being trained for.

"In the jungle, the quiet jungle
The Lion sleeps tonight.
In the jungle, the quiet jungle
The Lion sleeps tonight."

Inside the NCO club the stringent silence of the compound was deflated by a jukebox blasting the Tokens and the sounds of men preparing for a duty-free weekend by pumping alcoholic warmth into bodies as numbed by routine as the weather. The smell of drying fatigues and an overachieving heating system mingled with urinal fumes leaking from a door in the right wall. Beside it an arrow imprinted with the familiar Olympia Beer slogan pointed the way to the latrine: *"It's the Water!"*

Todd's eyes swept the room from the crowded bar to the tables near the rear exit. Through the window behind he could see snow falling on the parking lot, already obscuring the metal clotheslines in front of the row of barracks. Between the windows a poster-depicted red-cheeked Santa offering a Coca-Cola to an equally rosy-cheeked sweater girl, who prettily accepted it: *"Merry Christmas, 1961!"* At the table in front of the poster a young man his own age leaned back in a chair, reading a bulky paperback as the rising steam from his mug of coffee bent in response to a back wall draft.

Rik Temple, Todd thought, his shaved neck reddening all the way to his buzz cut.

The chair jamming into the table sent the coffee splattering. The young man on the opposite side carefully inserted a napkin into the paperback, closed it, and reached out to steady the cup, whose contents still lapped the side. He looked up at Todd calmly. "Maybe I should have had a saucer?"

Todd's hands gripped the back of the chair in front of him. A soldier at the nearest table rose casually and headed to the bar for a grilled cheese sandwich that would take several minutes to make. "Cut the crap, Temple. What the hell did you think you were doing in there?"

"Doing?" The other man leaned back, feigning an infuriating innocence.

"Asking asshole questions. Making me look bad. I don't need help from you!"

A faint smile played across Rik Temple's face. "No," he agreed. "No, you certainly don't."

Todd added the insult to the sum total without comment. His eyes fell on the book on the table. *The Poetry of Ralph Waldo Emerson.* Figures—a fruit poet! "I've been watching you since training began. Listening to your snide little remarks. You can't take an order without having your say. You think you're smarter than everybody else. You're not here to tell us what *you* think; you're here to be *told* what to think!"

Rik Temple looked maddeningly thoughtful. "Well, that's a theory with some validity, Larson. Learn how to give orders by learning how to take orders? But what if the orders don't make sense? Did ya ever read Barnard Baruch: 'Everybody has a right to his own opinion, but nobody has a right to his own facts'?"

Todd leaned over the table. "I *had* the facts. The Army gave 'em to me, and I gave 'em to you. All Commies are alike, and anybody who can't see that might just as well be a Commie himself."

"So you want to be like all the other officers? Never think for yourself?"

"Maybe if you feel that way about officers, maybe you shouldn't be one."

Rik Temple slowly rose from the table. "Maybe you're right." He looked at Todd and then at the other men in the club who had formed a discreet horseshoe around them. "But I've got the feeling you're not going to be satisfied with just being right. You want something else."

*****

The roar in his ears dissolved into the recognizable blood cry of the men around them. The muddied slush of the parking lot took shape before his eyes. How long had they been out there? The ground had been pure white when the fight started.

Rik bounced to his feet with more energy than he felt. He'd fallen for that one. Have to remember to keep his left up. Pop! Pop! His head snapped back twice. Got to hand it to him. The guy was quick! Rik took a left to the body, but rolled with the right to the head. Thank god for all those sit-ups. Larson wouldn't be able to take him out working on the abdomen, and he had faith in his rock-hard head. The eyes and the nose were something else. It was hard enough to see with snow falling in the twilight, and he had to be able to breathe if he was going to last.

He elbowed aside a second roundhouse right and wrapped both arms around the other man. Let Larson push him around for a while—maybe he would get frustrated and careless. Wrong! A rain of blows fell on his head and shoulders. He hadn't been able to trap Larson's arms. He shoved the other man backward with a two-handed push and snapped out his own left hand. It fell short. Larson had the reach on him. He'd have to work inside somehow. For the time being there was no ice on the pavement, and the combat boots, whatever they did to your foot speed, provided good traction. But that wouldn't last, and the longer the fight, the more important long arms would be.

How long had it been since he was this tired? He had a muscle memory of the summer he'd worked as a deliveryman for the appliance store—moving a refrigerator up a set of wooden steps to a second-floor rear apartment. The belt had popped loose and he'd suddenly found himself trying to balance the weight of the 45-degree angled fridge on the dolly so it wouldn't be smashed—or smash him!

The micro-moment's reverie was interrupted by Larson's bull-rush. Rik covered his face and upper body with his elbows, forearms, and hands, but his ears rang from a hail of punches as he desperately tried to force a clinch. Inside his grip Larson threw him from left to right like a rag doll, his feet leaving the ground!

There was no referee to break them apart. As long as he held on, the other man couldn't hit him, and as Rik's ears regained their focus he heard another sound—half gasp, half grunt. A sudden realization flashed into his battered senses— Larson was a fighter who didn't know how to breathe! He could attack and he could punch, but he couldn't pace himself, didn't know to get oxygen into his blood. Rik's memory flew back to the refrigerator, which hadn't fallen on either him or the steps. All he'd had to do was not panic, keep low enough so that the fridge stayed on the dolly, high enough so it didn't tip over on him, and keep moving forward. It would be the same here. The longer the fight lasted, the less stamina Larson would have. It was Saturday evening. Rik had all night and all of tomorrow.

He broke free from the clinch first, flicking out a sharp left hand into the other man's chest, missing the thoracic diaphragm but getting his attention. Larson attacked again, throwing punches with both hands. This time Rik stayed low, taking most of the blows on his shoulders and above his ears, and ending the other man's assault with two left hooks to the ribs with all his weight behind them. Larson twisted to his right and Rik landed two right hooks on the other side. For the first time his opponent stepped backward, flicking out his own left, which Rik parried easily.

Another rush, and yet another—with Rik content to take six, seven, or eight blows on his shoulders and lowered head in return for landing three or four hooks to the ribs. A third charge was broken off when he feinted at Larson's body. Rik dropped his hands, taunting the other man for his caution. Larson was on the attack instantly, landing a wild right hand high on Rik's head. Too close! A little lower and it might have ended the fight. But Rik laughed, warding off the charge with a straight left. Larson was throwing avoidable haymakers now, rather than the stiff left leads that had been so effective earlier, and he could hear the panting breaths two arm-lengths away.

It was now Rik who was moving forward. Larson parried the left to his head, opening himself up to another right to the ribs. He tried to clinch, but Rik slipped through and landed a crushing elbow to the kidneys. No referee, right? Something between a gasp and a scream escaped Larson's clinched teeth, and he responded with another flurry of blows. Good boy, Rik thought, no quit in you—but the punches had lost their sting. Rik stepped through them, unimpeded, and landed another right on Larson's chest. Missed the thoracic diaphragm again, but the ribs wouldn't stand up much longer. The howl from the men around them was now for Larson's blood, not his. He lowered his head and moved in.

A shrill metallic whistle sliced through the night air. *MP!!*

Suddenly, men were running in all directions, the fight forgotten! What had happened to Larson? Which direction were the MPs coming from? Rik scrambled over the low cement barrier surrounding the parking lot, slipped and fell in a ditch on the other side, and was on his feet in an instant, racing toward the row of barracks. If he could get to their other side without being caught, he could duck into any one of them. Unless there was a bloody body in the parking lot, the MPs would be unlikely to undertake a building-by-building search.

He ran like a deer through a space made even darker by his just having left the lighted parking lot, toward snow being driven at an almost horizontal angle.

Or was it the metal clothesline?

*****

Second Lieutenant Boston "Beans" McMartin, Executive Officer of Company A, Officers Candidate School, Second Battle Group, 128th Infantry Regiment, shivered inside his service overcoat. If this man's army ever invades Antarctica, he thought to himself, I will fucking desert! Ordinarily, as Officer of the Day on a weekend he would use any excuse to escape of the tedium of HQ. (Christ, he even went to chapel!) But last night's snow had given way to a knife-like chill he'd never known growing up in Georgia. If the Army had shown him this place before he joined the ROTC in Athens, he'd still be working in his father's office, no matter the family tradition.

What the hell was he doing in the infantry anyway? He'd signed up to be an army doctor—your second choice had to be a combat MOS; it never occurred to him he'd have to follow through on it. The McMartin family had subscribed to the same pattern for a hundred and fifty years. The oldest son got the plantation, the second son became a doctor, and the rest went to the military. His father had doubled the ante by having the Army pay for his medical education, and when his Uncle Arthur ran the family estate into the ground, Beans had just assumed he'd follow his father's footsteps. Who knew he'd come in at the one time in military history when there was a glut in physicians? In six months, they told him, there would be a medical school opening in this part of the country. Meanwhile, no infantry company wanted him because he wasn't expected to stay, so he wound up as the XO of an OCS company because his years of handling the insurance forms in his father's office made him good at paperwork. Christ! He should have been a lawyer!

Meanwhile, here he was—in the cold—walking the length of Ridgeway Road to check on one half of the participants in a Saturday night fight behind the NCO club. It happened all the time. If the other guy wasn't in the hospital, it could have been ignored. Even then, if the two weren't part of the same OCS class, Beans would have been tempted to let it go. Larson wouldn't say what happened, said he just fell. On both sides? Not likely! It was a buddy of his who fingered the other soldier.

He must have walked at least a mile. He should have requisitioned a jeep. Why in God's name didn't they bunk the whole OCS class in the same barracks instead of keeping them with their original unit? Lack of space, he supposed. Beans walked along Ridgeway, checking off numbers of otherwise identical buildings. Even in the cold he could smell dry rot. Built in 1940 in the frantic run-up to WW-2, they were intended to last ten years. How long was it now—21, 22 years? Same old Army! A billion dollars for an ICBM they never used, but the troops lived in dumps. 1117?—finally!

"TEN-HUTT!" A PFC, pulling up his pants as he came out of the latrine, was the first to notice him. Except for a four-handed euchre game on a footlocker near the door, the first floor was almost empty.

"As you were," McMartin drawled. "Now, if you would be so kind as to direct me to Specialist Temple? One of the card players pointed wordlessly to a figure standing by a bunk at the end of the room.

McMartin strode down the aisle formed by the rectangular posts holding up the second floor, each one with a tin can for cigarette butts nailed to it. He stopped and looked back at the motionless witnesses observing his progress. "Gentlemen," he said. "It has come to my attention that the PX is holding a pre-Christmas sale this afternoon. As many of you will be going home on leave soon, this would be a good opportunity for you to pick up some small token of appreciation for one or more of your loved ones." In a moment, caps slapped hastily on heads, arms pulled into unbuttoned field jackets, the other men piled through the barracks door into the white glow of the compound.

Rik Temple stood at parade rest in front of his footlocker. Beans McMartin crossed down in front of him and turned to face a visage with a cut that slanted up the bridge of the nose and resumed through the left eyebrow like a rejection line between a pair of eyes surrounded by a yellowish-purple bruising. "Jesus," said McMartin. "And I thought the other guy looked bad."

"I ran into a metal clothesline," the soldier answered stoically.

"Yeah? And Larson fell down. Twice!" The Lieutenant turned toward the cadre room by the front barracks. "SERGEANT!" Seconds later, a bleary-eyed, middle-aged man, with a sagging gut appeared at the cadre room door. He'd had his own rough Saturday night at the NCO club, and it looked like his weekend wasn't over.

McMartin looked him over briefly before speaking in a consciously courteous, southern-accented voice. "Do you happen to have a first aid kit, and if so, would you be so kind as to fetch it for me?"

The sergeant threw an expressionless glance at Rik Temple and disappeared into his room, returning with a grimy leather package which he gave to McMartin. Beans looked at him for a moment, and the sergeant turned on his heel and exited wordlessly into the cadre room.

McMartin looked at the light above their heads and gestured toward the area between the two beds. "Pull that footlocker around here and sit down so that I can have a look at you."

"That's not necessary."

"I can make it an order if you like."

The soldier shrugged, dragged the trunk over to the space and sat down on the edge of the bed. McMartin perched on the footlocker opposite him and examined the contents of the first aid kit—scissors, cloth tape, adhesive bandages, aspirin, antibiotic ointment, antiseptic wipes, and three packages of condoms. Right, Beans thought—good to know what injuries to worry about most.

Ripping open the top of an antiseptic wipe packet, Beans went to work. "You might consider having a stitch taken in that eyebrow."

"I'd rather not, Lieutenant. I'm not too fond of sick call, filling out official forms, etc."

"Unofficially—and I mean that. What happened?"

Rik Temple winced as antiseptic ointment found its way into a cut. "Let's just say I had a disagreement with someone over whether I should be an officer."

"Larson?" Beans chuckled, washing a bruise. "I don't think he'll raise that point for a while. He's in the dispensary with three cracked ribs, and in a couple of days he'll be on Christmas leave. When he gets back, I'll have him transferred to Charlie Company and you guys will have to go out of your way to bother one another. Problem solved."

A mirthless grin creased the soldier's face. "Don't do that.

He was right. I'm dropping out of OCS."

McMartin's hands stopped in mid-air, an adhesive bandage poised for application. "I just told you. You don't have to do that. You'll have a couple of shiners, but you took him fair and square and you hurt him. He won't mess with you again."

Temple looked pensive. "When does this class get its commission, Lieutenant?"

Beans shrugged. "Next October, as a guess. Nine and a half months?"

"And I'll have a commitment of two years active duty after that?"

"At least."

"October 1964? I don't know if I'll want to be an army officer three years from now. Are you sure that you will?"

Beans thought about his medical schooling. "The Army is changing. Not every posting is like this one. At least not so cold," he laughed.

"I didn't enlist." Rik Temple pressed his point. "This was a call-up—a pure and simple political response to the building of a wall in Berlin. We weren't sent to Europe. They don't expect us to fight. Kennedy made his point. If Khrushchev doesn't raise the stakes, I could be out of here next September. Maybe even sooner."

Beans McMartin repacked the first aid kit and thought hard. "What will you do when you get out? Do you have a career plan? A job? A girl?"

"No," the soldier admitted. "Maybe study languages? History? Travel?"

"Okay." The Lieutenant stood up. "I'm not giving you any advice here. But I am going to lay out some possibilities. First, there's nothing you just talked about that can't be done in the Army—and done faster than it can be done in civilian life. You finish up here and apply for the Languages School at the Aberdeen Proving Grounds in Maryland, and I'll recommend you. More important, the CO too. He likes ambition. Every American Embassy in the world has a military attaché, and every attaché has a staff of young officers who can advance fast if they know enough of the language and customs of where they are to be of use as an observer." He was pacing in the aisle now.

"Second, that raising of the stakes you were talking about just might happen pretty soon."

Rik, who was moving the footlocker back in front of the bed, stopped still.

McMartin grinned. "That caught your attention, didn't it? Have you ever asked yourself why all those Intelligence briefings we've been giving are about Asia rather than Europe? And you'll notice after the first of the year that our training exercises will be focused less on mechanized movements and more on guerilla warfare. Though God knows how we're going to carry them out in all this snow."

"There's snow in Germany, and even more the farther east you go in Europe."

"That's the beauty of it," said McMartin, pleased with himself. "We won't be in Europe. We'll be in Southeast Asia—Laos probably, if what JFK has been saying in the papers is true. Or maybe the home of the Domino Theory that Ike used to talk about—French Indochina."

"Vietnam?"

"Exactly! You see what I'm saying? You *know* that! Larson would never have heard of it unless it was in his manual.

"I don't know anything about Southeast Asia."

"But *you* can learn. And we're going to need guys like you who can learn history and languages and customs. You've heard our Intelligence lectures. They're shit! Written by guys who don't know, given by guys who don't care, to guys who have no idea that stupidity is as deadly as a bullet. You've got a future in the Army because the Army needs guys like you. What other future do you have?"

Rik Temple sat down on his footlocker and looked at the floor. "I don't know."

Beans McMartin looked down at him. "Just promise me one thing. Don't make up your mind about dropping out until you get back from leave. You make the right choice and I'll back you all the way. And remember something else about Southeast Asia."

"What's that?"

"It's hot there!"

*****

Dutch's Sukiyaki House! Not a place somebody who had been based at the Yokota Air Force Base would have chosen, but it passed for a Japanese restaurant in Milwaukee, and Lynne liked it. The movie had been her idea too. *Through a Glass Darkly*? Roy spent half the time waiting for Ingrid Bergman to make an entrance, and the other half waiting for the film to end. What the hell was the point? What's her name—Harriet Andersson?—was sexy, but that character was crazy! Did she really fuck her brother? Roy couldn't tell, and he'd bet no one else in the theatre could either. That was just like Lynne—wanting to see something that made no sense just because it was playing in an Art film house. They should have gone to *Guns of Navarone*, like he wanted.

Ah, hell! He couldn't stay mad at Lynne. Watching her walk away from the table, toward the Little Girls' Room? Long blond hair in a French roll, set off by a green Tyrolean cape, through which you could imagine the firm derriere, and below which legs reached all the way down to the ground? She was sleek! Like the B-47s he used to fly—swept wings, inboard turbojet engines! He laughed at the—what was it Lynne called it?

The metaphor? She had style. Roy liked the way other men looked at her in public, liked them knowing that she was his.

She had a few of the B-47 faults too. Sluggish to get off the ground? Hard to control in landings? He'd fix that when they got married. Roy knew how to handle women.

They'd be married already if she wasn't so stubborn. Lynne didn't know her own mind! Roy was fifteen years older than she was; god knows he'd seen more of the world then she had. So determined to get that diploma! Why? Once she had kids and was helping him with the business, what use would a BA be? They would be a team. Shit, she'd already helped him with the required English papers—although he didn't know what the hell English had to do with a business degree. Not being a college graduate hadn't stopped him from making Captain in the Air Force! He'd still be there if he'd wanted to re-train for the B-52, if he hadn't wanted to settle down and take over the Old Man's business. He had ideas for expansion. If Lynne wanted a challenge, she could run the home office while he was setting up in other towns.

And now Lynne was walking back toward him. Those blue eyes had turned a lot of heads, but women respected a man who was in control. While she was gone, he'd had the waitress clear away the Tempura appetizer, and had ordered Negimaki with Teriyaki sauce, the Fresh Seaweed salad, and another sake. After all, Roy had lived in Japan. He had taste. He knew Japanese food even better than he knew the feminine mind.

Lynne had almost reached the table when she stopped short, a startled look on her face. Roy turned and followed her gaze to a young man in Army blues, seated on the floor at one of the low tables by the far wall.

"Rik?"

Then she was in front of him; the soldier scrambling to his feet, a forgotten paperback dangling from his hand. Roy strained to see around Lynne. The guy looked vaguely familiar—and slightly confused, in that half eager, half hesitant way Lynne had a habit of inspiring in young men. It was a situation Roy often enjoyed. Tonight he wasn't so sure.

It was almost Christmas, for god's sake, not a time for sharing with strangers!

A moment later she had taken the young man by the hand and brought him to their table. "Roy, this is Rik Temple, whom I'm sure you've met before. Rik, this is my fiancé, Roy Evans."

Mollified by the way he had been introduced, Roy did the only thing he could do under the circumstances. He invited the young man to join them, anticipating the response good manners required: "Thank you, I don't want to intrude. I was about to leave. It was great to see you both again." But by that time Lynne's hand was pressing down on Rik's arm, a gesture trumping any pretense of manners, and the three were all seated at the table.

Roy sized up the interloper and was unimpressed: an E-4 who wore his uniform off the base, a face that looked worked over, so without buddies or a girl that he dined alone reading a book! Nobody to worry about.

Lynne was looking to him for confirmation, her soothing hand now moved to his arm. "Rik and I were in several plays together in college. You remember!"

Roy pulled a momentary blank, then recalled. "That English Department poetry reading you dragged me to. You were both in that, right?"

A sheepish smile crossed the young man's face. He held up the paperback. *The Poetry of Ralph Waldo Emerson.* Lynne laughed and clapped her hands in glee. "Please tell me you remember the piece we did together!"

Rik Temple dropped his head momentarily, then carefully recited.

> *They put their finger on their lip,--*
> *The powers above;*
> *The seas their islands clip,*
> *The moons in Ocean dip,--*
> *They love but name not love.*

Lynne's face softened and she answered in a voice so low that Roy strained to hear it.

Gifts of one who loved me,--
Twas high time they came;
When he ceased to love me,
Time they stopped for shame.

"Wow, not exactly the stuff you associate with Brook Farm," Roy hazarded. "So, what are you doing here tonight, Dick? Army sponsoring poetry readings?"

Lynne frowned, but the other man ignored the mistake, unintended or not. "I caught a late afternoon military transport from McChord into Billy Mitchell Field. You have to be in uniform to get on free, even if they store you with the luggage. One of the crew gave me a ride downtown. The Trailways Terminal is only two blocks from here and I had a couple of hours before the Tripp Lake bus left, so I came over here to see if Dutch would let me hang out for a while."

Roy was impressed. "You know Dutch?"

"A cousin of mine knew him when he was a heavyweight prize fighter twenty years ago. He was stationed in Tokyo after the War and fell in love with Japanese cooking. This place opened in '53. My cousin says he's a much better restaurateur than he was a fighter."

Lynne's interruption was spirited. "There is no way you're going to sit on that cold bus for an hour-plus. You'll ride home with us."

Roy's failure to second the offer went unnoticed in Rik's response. "No! Thank you! I already have my ticket; the bus leaves in twenty minutes and your order hasn't even arrived yet." He smiled apologetically. "I'll be home long before you are."

Rik rose to his feet, and after shaking Roy's hand and nodding appreciatively at Lynne, returned to the table at the far wall, behind which his great coat, cap, and duffel bag were stashed. Roy noted with satisfaction that it wouldn't be necessary for him to pass by their table when he exited. Lynne took a sip of her sake, as the waitress arrived with the Negimaki and Seaweed Salad. The Muzak system slipped unobtrusively from "The First Noel" into the Carmen McRae vocal of Paul Desmond's "Take Five."

Though I'm going out of my way
Just so I can pass by each day
Not a single word do we say
It's a pantomime and not a play

Still, I know our eyes often meet
I feel tingles down to my feet
When you smile, that's much too discreet
Sends me on my way

To put down a plate the waitress moved something on the table. In a flash Lynne was on her feet, the forgotten Emerson in her hand.

She caught him at the door, and for a moment the poetry volume was a palpable link between them. "I've always wanted to ask you something." He waited expectantly.

"We did so many plays together, so many plays in which we were married—*Diary of Anne Frank, The Adding Machine, Cat on a Hot Tin Roof*—but never one where we were happy. Why do you think that was?"

Rik thought for a moment. "Well, you know what they say about the theatre. 'Lousy dress rehearsal, great performance.'"

*****

Sort of a purplish-pink—magenta really! And a medium blue green—like the teal ducks on the pond in the woods. Now there were traces of yellow, violet and indigo flowing through the stagnant pools, blurring their edges.

Werner Temple looked down into the gutter of the cow barn. People would think he was crazy if they knew it, but he'd always found the mixed colors of bovine urine and fecal waste beautiful. Sometimes in the winter on the grounds of the cow yard outside they froze in patterns that put the stained-glass windows of the Presbyterian Church to shame. The windows were made by men, but everything on the farm—even manure—was made by God. He could sense it in the air. The longer the cows were outside, the more the air chilled, and the chillier the air the more it suppressed the other smells in the barn—the hay, the ground feed, the whitewash. He could smell it though, and something inside of him recorded the changes from moment to moment, a something that never grew tired of those changes. He registered them as easily as he could tell what field the cows were pasturing in by the taste of their milk. Some might call farming a hard life, but it had its compensations.

Scrape! On the east side of the driveway Werner's son had begun scooping waste from the other gutter into the manure spreader between them. After fifteen feet of gutters had been cleared, one of them would whistle to the horses to move up a wagon's length. Three whistles and the job would be done for the day. Werner sighed and adjusted the truss he had worn ever since the double hernia he got when he was clearing rocks in the Back Forty twenty years ago. If Rik finished too far ahead of him, he'd tease him for being an old man and he couldn't have that.

Rik didn't have the same feeling for the farm that he did. He wasn't lazy; he'd always pulled his weight, but he didn't sense what the farm needed. It wasn't a *calling* to him. Well, Werner didn't learn everything overnight either. He hadn't finished the sixth grade, but there was more than one kind of education. The fact is that even when Rik was home working on the farm, he wasn't *there*! There was a book in his hip pocket that he couldn't wait to get back to, a radio program that he'd rather escape to than appreciate the world around him. His wife's mother called him a woolgatherer, which Werner knew hurt Peggy. Still, there was some truth in it. Rik was more at home someplace else; it's just that he didn't know where that place was.

His mother had wanted him to be a minister. Werner hadn't pooh-poohed it, but figured the situation was something like the time he'd asked Rik why he hadn't been promoted in the Army. He was smart, sturdy, and reliable enough. His son had smiled at him. "Dad, they look in my eyes and they can tell I don't believe." Maybe OCS had made him a believer. He never talked about it. Rik was the only one of his kids to take him up on his offer of a college education, but nothing he studied there had led to a profession. He'd played football for a while—and then he didn't. The literary magazine he edited had been shut down by the college. Werner read the issue. Religion—nothing to get *that* upset about. He was a good actor on the Old Main stage, reminding Werner of how well he'd done back at Prairie View grade school—the upside of wool gathering, he suspected. (Peggy didn't exactly approve, which surprised Werner. She was a natural performer herself.)

Yes, the truth was Rik would never get anywhere until he committed himself to something. Yet the wrong something would be worse than woolgathering. Werner and the farm were a perfect match. Whatever it was, that's all he wanted for his son.

He looked up to see his son standing at the end of the gutter, smiling at him.

"What's next?" he asked.

*****

Hit the road Jack and don't you come back no more, no more, no more, no more.

Hit the road Jack and don't you come back no more. (What you say?)

Hit the road Jack and don't you come back no more, no more, no more, no more.
Hit the road Jack and don't you come back no more.

Oh! Woman, oh woman, don't treat me so mean,
You're the meanest old woman that I've ever seen.
I guess if you said so
I'd have to pack my things and go. (That's right.)

Hit the road Jack and don't you come back no more, no more, no more, no more.
Hit the road Jack and don't you come back no more.

New Year's Eve! Gillian threw herself into the dance with renewed energy. Her flip haircut whipped around her head in coordination with her pumping arms, and a shimmer of light rolled across the throbbing curves of the little black dress like a surf's up at midnight. She couldn't remember if she'd begun this dance with a partner or not. It didn't matter! People were all around her now—couples, lone men, their clapping hands trying to keep up with the rhythm in her head. She could feel the glow on her skin! She might have come to the party alone, but she wasn't alone now. Not as long as she was dancing! And when it was time for her to leave, she could have her pick of escorts; or she could steal away like Cinderella, leaving a slipper behind. She'd be remembered. They wouldn't be able to get the dancing out their heads—even if she was dancing alone!

As I walk along I wonder a-what went wrong
With our love, a love that was so strong.
And as I still walk on, I think of the things we've done
Together, a-while our hearts were young.

I'm a-walkin' in the rain.
Tears are fallin' and I feel the pain,
Wishin' you were here by me.
To end this misery.
And I wonder,
I wa-wa-wa-wonder
Why,
Ah-why-why-why-why-why you ran away.
And I wonder where you will stay,
My little runaway, run-run-run-run-runaway!

They'd danced together, of course. It was as natural as
their skating routine. People applauded then too, but it was
different when they were on ice. A figure skating audience
wasn't a participant. It was disciplined, admiring but
judgmental. Tchaikovsky wasn't Del Shannon. Their skating
movements were long, graceful, carefully balanced, not
frenetic. They had their audience's esteem, not their passion.
Anyone watching them skate as one must have assumed, as
Gillian did, they never could be separated, that their
compatibility on ice was a reflection of their love.

Love—she couldn't even think the word now. No one had
ever loved her; not for a million years! But she hadn't known
it until yesterday—not until she'd found Robbie in the locker
room with Carl, their choreographer. One thing was sure. The
men who watched her when she danced were different from
the audiences who watched her and Robbie when they skated.
They had no interest in elegance, and Gillian would never
mistake symmetry for passion again.

Tonight you're mine completely.
You give your love so sweetly.
Tonight the light of love is in your eyes.
But will you love me tomorrow?

Is this a lasting treasure,
Or just a moment's pleasure?
Can I believe the magic of your sighs?
Will you still love me tomorrow?

I'd like to know that your love
Is love I can be sure of.
So tell me now, and I won't ask again.
Will you still love me tomorrow?

She knew him by sight, of course. They'd been in a French class together, and everyone remembered the editorial in the campus paper about the literary magazine. How he'd resigned as editor when the administration wouldn't publish what he'd approved? Some people had wanted him to be kicked out of college. He hadn't even written the article! Why was it so important to him? Gillian had seen him onstage in that Tennessee Williams' play that they made the movie of with Elizabeth Taylor and Paul Newman. She'd wondered if he was like the character—didn't even suspect (like a fool!) that *Robbie* was like the character.

But he couldn't be! He was nothing like Robbie. Robbie was ethereal, always almost on the verge of escaping gravity, a perfect figure skater's body. This man, with his post-like legs, could walk a hundred miles, but he could never make Tchaikovsky come alive. Gillian had seen him across the room—the deep chest and strong upper body, a Band-Aid on an eyebrow—and decided he was the one. He couldn't skate, but he could do other things, things that Gillian needed badly!

At last,
My love has come along,
My lonely days are over,
And life is like a song.

At last,
The skies above are blue.
My heart was wrapped in clover
The night I looked at you.

You smile,
And then the spell was cast.
And here we are in heaven,
For you are mine at last!

Before their dance was over, the decision had been made. Gillian crossed the room, looking for her roommate to say they wouldn't be going home together, struggling to remember where she'd put her coat. When she returned, Rik was deep in conversation with a blonde girl. Steps away, Gillian heard her last words: "If that's the case, I want a ride home too, and I want to be the last one to be let off!"

$$*\,*\,*\,*\,*$$

It was a 1951 Mercury Monarch, with bathtub curves on a body built so low to the ground that the first impression was that of an alien surface vehicle in an old Flash Gordon serial. Werner Temple's way of celebrating the paving of the road past the farmhouse, its sleek symmetry would never have survived the Wisconsin March and April ruts of the first half of the 20th century. "Four thousand pounds of decadence at 65 cents a pound," the dealer called it. A V-8 engine with 112-horse power and a MPH for every BHP.

Lynne Chase loved this car! She called it *Hermes*, after the

Greek guide to the Underworld, the god of speed and patron of thieves. She couldn't confirm the 112 MPH, but she had seen the speedometer at 92 while riding with Rik on one of these dark country roads. Yet, more than speed, she associated *Hermes* with being still, parked in the driveway of the family house while she told Rik of her hopes and plans—what it was like to grow up in Tripp Lake's "Bloody First Ward, between a corn field and a graveyard," her fights with her mother, and the stories about her father, the union man who was killed when the "sonsabitches" (the bosses) assigned him to a job with unsafe conditions. She told him about the neighbor who had introduced her to the theatre by taking her to Milwaukee to see Julie Harris as Joan of Arc in Jean Anouilh's *The Lark* at the Pabst Theater, about the scholarship she gave up to the University of Wisconsin in order to take a bicycle trip through Europe, about climbing the Alps, about smoking *Gauloises* in a Paris *bistro*. She told him everything!

He gave her lifts home when they were in a play together. She had a cold and the buses stopped running before rehearsal was over. It was months before she discovered he lived in the opposite direction.

"When is your leave over?"

"What time is it?" Rik looked at the clock on the dashboard. "Technically? Tomorrow, Monday, January 2nd. As long as I get there before midnight on Tuesday, I'll be okay. Nothing much will be going on this week, anyway."

Lynne wished she had a cigarette. Her New Year's resolution for the last three years had been to quit. "Are you going to stay in OCS?"

Rik leaned forward to adjust the heater, his face serious in the light of the dashboard. "I haven't made up my mind. It's an opportunity; I don't have very many of those. Some of the officers know I'm thinking of leaving. I can't put off telling them much longer. I can always come back to the farm, I suppose."

"I've never heard you say anything that would make me believe you cared anything about the farm."

Rik shrugged. "Maybe not. But I've never found a reason to permanently leave it either. What about you? What are you going to do?"

Lynne found herself answering a question she'd never formally asked herself. "I'm going to graduate school—where I always intended to go."

"Really!" Rik's eyes were firmly fixed on a road that was now curving through a wooded area. "What does Roy think about that?"

Lynne studied the shadowy profile far away at the other end of the seat. "About what you'd imagine. He's seen the world. He wants to settle down and build a life, a home. His father wants to retire, so somebody has to take over the business now. He wants to have kids while he's still young enough to enjoy them. He's sure a family is a woman's greatest fulfillment and the sooner I have one, the happier I'll be. He wants to take care of me, so I'll never have anything to worry about. I've heard it all before. Do you remember Bennie?"

"The guy from my high school class?"

"I dated him while I was still in high school. The spring I graduated he asked me to marry him. I'd always assumed I would, eventually. But Bennie was adopted—late! He was also Catholic. His folks ran the floral agency, remember? And they weren't in good health—heart disease, diabetes. (Bennie was as thin as a rail.) He couldn't stand the idea of being without a family. I couldn't blame him—and he gave me an ultimatum. Marry him that June. That June I went to Europe, and that Fall I started college. Bennie was engaged to another girl by Labor Day. He wouldn't wait."

Rik carefully chose his words. "And Roy? Will he—wait?"

The voice of the woman on the passenger side was husky. "He might. He said he was willing to think about it—to negotiate. I told him it wasn't necessary. I'd already made my choice—and it involved someone else."

Rik turned—a stunned look on his face. He slowly raised his right arm, and Lynne shot across the seat, crashing into him even as the car wheels hit an icy patch on the highway that divided the counties of Walworth and Rock, and skidded sideways!

*****

On New Year's Day, 1962, Augie Deegan finished milking his cows shortly after 5 a.m. Not that there was anything unusual about that. Augie Deegan *always* finished milking his cows shortly after 5 a.m.—just as every noon he took a nap on the cot in the basement of his house.

"*Why?*" his wife would ask. "I can understand why in the summer when the sun is up at 5 a.m. you'd want to be milking, and why when the temperature and the humidity are both at eighty you'd want to take a mid-day siesta. But why in the middle of the winter when you don't have anything *else* to do all day long, do you have to get up—and get *me* up—at four o'clock in the morning?"

And Augie would explain for the hundredth time or so that things are just *easier* if you keep the same routine all year round. So, yes, he fell asleep every night in front of the television set just like in the old days he fell asleep with the newspaper on his lap. And, yes, he got up every morning at 4 o'clock and did the milking, and after he was done, he took a wagon load of corn over to the pigs on the Heenan place, and he would keep on doing it! Besides, those two jobs were the hardest things he had to do all day long, and it was like swallowing a live toad before breakfast. No matter what happened the rest of the day, it wasn't that big a deal!

But she wasn't listening. If she had the power to pay no more attention to him at 4 a.m. than she did the rest of the day, she'd be a lot less bothered—and so would he.

So, at 5:30 on New Year's morning Augie pulled the John Deere Model A with a steel wagon half-full of corn out on to the County Line highway. He'd have to be careful this morning. The cold snap had broken during the night and the contact between the frozen ground and the warmer air produced a fog so thick that sometimes he couldn't see more than ten feet in front of the Johnny Popper's exhaust pipe. Even worse, he thought to himself, any New Year's Eve drunk coming home at this hour was liable to be in a fog that would put nature to shame.

The fog cleared for a moment as Augie was easing into the curve a quarter mile south of the Heenan place, and a huge presence took shape left of the road. Damn, he thought. If I didn't know better, I'd say it was a Polar Bear! Augie pushed in the clutch and throttled back the Model A, but as quickly as it had cleared the fog settled in again.

Augie put the tractor in neutral, stepped on the brake lock, scrambled down, and started walking towards whatever it was. He was only ten yards away before he could be certain it wasn't anything alive, but rather a car almost up to its doors in the ditch, its organic curves blurred by snow.

On closer inspection he could see on the windows at least, it wasn't snow at all. They were completely steamed over— front, back, and sides. The engine was off, and yet it seemed to Augie there was an almost imperceptible movement of the chassis—as if it were alive! Very gingerly, he reached out and tapped twice on a side window. "Is anyone in there?"

The movement stopped. The car stood quiet for a moment. Then from deep in the recesses of the back seat came the growl of a female voice.

"Go Away!!!"

*****

January thaw! The smile on Beans McMartin's face could

have raised the temperature another two degrees. This was more like it! Nothing was certain in the world, but according to the long-range forecast, next week's field training would at least *start* at fifty degrees or above. This war might be worth winning after all. McMartin interlocked his hands and stretched them as high above his head as possible. Now to the Officers Mess for the house breakfast specialty of shit-on-a-shingle and Cookie's delectable sphincter-dissolving coffee!

As McMartin turned, squinting into the morning sun, he saw a familiar figure spiritedly walking across the compound toward him, wearing a smile almost the equal of his own. "Specialist Temple! If I may judge by your limber gait and your shit-assed grin, you've had an amenable leave and you are tickled pussy-pink to return to our little coterie of positively channeled psychopaths."

The shorter man snapped off a by-the-book salute. "Lieutenant McMartin! If I remember correctly, at our last meeting you offered to write me a recommendation letter. If that offer still holds, Sir, I would like to take you up on it."

Beans returned the salute nonchalantly. "Ah yes, the Aberdeen Proving Grounds matter. I will take time to do that on the first *cold* day of the upcoming field exercises. First, however, I will attend to the transferring of Corporal Larson to "C" Company."

"That won't be necessary." Rik Temple's smile broadened. "I'm leaving OCS and going back to supply. Is my telling you sufficient, or do I have to sign something?

A look of bewilderment came over the Officer's face. "I don't get it. What about the letter?"

The other man produced two sheets of typed paper from inside his field jacket. Pointing to one of them, he explained: "I need a letter of recommendation to this official at this graduate school—and this graduate school only. The other sheet is a rather fanciful exaggeration of my qualifications and accomplishments. And the letter better be good! It has a lot of bureaucratically recorded mediocrity to counteract."

"Yeah? And to what am I to attribute this Great Leap Forward?"

"Tell them that I've found my passion. Tell them that I've achieved focus. Tell them that they're lucky to get me. Tell them—" Rik Temple paused in thought. "Tell them—in the words of Ralph Waldo Emerson—that I've become my own man.

I will not live out of me.
I will not see with others' eyes.
My good is good, my evil ill;
I would be free.

GULF

It's a Saturday in late August 1964 in a lakeside mountain village in Austria, where the University holds its summer sessions away from the heat of Vienna. Our characters are young Americans, winding up their student days, and at the point of embarking on other avenues of life—marriage, careers, and (for some of them) a soul-wrenching adventure in Southeast Asia. There is a gulf between them and the truth of their futures, but its crossing cannot be put off for long.

What Billy's Bar had begun, the morning sun completed. Rik awoke, a small but persistent throb at his temples, and his eyes squinting into the rays pouring through the window. Mentally he calculated the time. As the Austrian summer advanced, the sun cleared the sill ever later, but it still couldn't be more than eight A.M. Last night's party had been a surprise. Lynne must have told some of the other actors about his birthday, and the word had spread to friends among the students and faculty.

Rik rolled over and his elbow cracked into the wooden frame of the bed. He cursed under his breath. Two months spent in a hastily assigned room in a men's dormitory and he still wasn't used to sleeping apart from Lynne, in a narrow bunk with one feather bed as a mattress and another as a blanket. He looked over at his wife in the bunk opposite him.

Her comforter was wedged against the wall behind her. Her slip had worked its way up almost to her hip and the sun was just lighting the blonde hair on the pillow. He sighed nosily, but the rhythm of her regular breathing continued undisturbed.

On the low table between them stood his gift from last night—a commemorative plate inscribed "University of Vienna *Sommerhochschule*, Strobl, Austria, 1964." The presentation was made during the meal in the dining hall last night, and the celebration continued at the bar in the *Seegasthof*, the town's largest hotel, with predictable results: lots of beer, dancing, and effusive thanks shouted over loud music. Thanks for holding the group together! Thanks for finding venues to play in! Thanks for the *Sommerhochschule* as a home base!

In fact, they must have known Rik bore little responsibility for their good fortune. When the professor who had organized their performance tour didn't show up, when their university support vanished, the mantle of leadership was arbitrarily passed to him as the only married male graduate student, and he didn't have the courage to turn it down. In self-defense, he'd adopted the same brusqueness he'd experienced in army boot camp and was amazed to receive the same fear and respect he'd shown his sergeants. People with problems or suggestions came to Lynne rather than face him, and a group discipline created itself. The performers didn't lack for talent, and the sponsors of the playing dates they did find (most of them students themselves) connected them to a network of assistance across Western Europe from the Netherlands to Austria—student travel cards, free hostels, names and addresses at other universities along the way where they might share digs, sing for their supper, etc.

At the lakeside mountain village of Strobl, the home of the University of Vienna summer school, they discovered that their absent professor was expected to teach two courses, but no one had anticipated a student entourage. Nevertheless, acting with perfect Viennese urbanity, an unruffled provost quickly produced a contract which Rik signed. The professor's salary was converted into tuition waivers and room and board for twelve actors who were now committed to perform a musical and dramatic performance each Saturday night for the term. In addition, they received dress rehearsal tickets for the theatre and music events of the nearby Salzburg Festival, plus three days off to play at the student drama festival at the University of Erlangen in Germany. And now it was almost over.

In the men's bathroom at the end of the hallway, Rik leaned his forehead on the cool plaster wall, contemplating the seemingly endless yellow stream splashing down on the urinal cake below him. No more calling the group together for an early morning meeting which inevitably began with the question: "Now what's the *worst* thing that could have happened today?" No more booking night trains when there was no money for both travel and shelter. No more renting a room for himself and Lynne, and sneaking ten other actors up the fire escape to the second floor. No more balancing a load of costumes on your shoulder as you ride through the streets of Utrecht on the back of a motorbike. No more walking a half block down an Amsterdam canal street before realizing that the mannequins in the store windows *aren't* mannequins, and they aren't selling *clothes*. No more artistic diplomacy and aesthetic trade-offs as you try to balance actors' egos and a show's needs. No more last second check of the lighting as you stand with your back to an already opening curtain. No more attending dress rehearsals of Goethe's *Faust*, Strauss' *Electra*, Reinhardt's *Jedermann*.

Tonight was their last performance. They would all meet at four o'clock to finalize the bill and run through entrances and exits. Next week would be final exams. (What should he be studying? Bach's Leipzig period? The German subjunctive?

Existentialism and Sartre's *The Condemned of Altoona*?) Then what? A junior college in Iowa, the teaching of eight sections of public speaking, a forensics program, a play to direct every now and then—so long as it didn't upset or offend anyone. He'd had only three job offers for a M.A. with no previous experience. Lynne wanted to be within a half-day's drive of her widowed mother, which eliminated the potentially more exciting Texas Gulf coast and Appalachian Virginia.

Rik sighed, waggled his spent member, tucked, zipped, and walked out into the hallway. From the shadows to his left came a low, teasing feminine voice.

"Hey sailor, want to do a girl a favor?"

He turned, a smile spreading slowly across his face: "Hey, aren't you supposed to be leaning against a lamp post some place?"

"No point when the fleet is out." Michelle stepped into the beam of the ceiling's single lamp, its light forming a halo behind her curly red hair and the shoulders bare under the haltered sun dress. Trust an actress to know where her spotlight is.

"Look, I was the last one up after the party last night. All the other girls went to *Schafberg*, and they used all the hot water. So I thought I'd come over here for a shower." She waved a plastic bag stuffed with toiletries in explanation. "Would you mind watching the door? I'll only be a few minutes, I promise."

Rik nodded and she disappeared into the bathroom. A moment later she was back. "I forgot my towel. Do you have an extra one?"

"You can use my terrycloth robe. It's hanging on the back of the door."

"Thanks, you're a *mensch*," and she was gone again.

Rik settled down on the floor, his back to the door frame. It was a familiar task, something he did every day when Lynne took her shower, but it didn't matter. Michelle would have found some guy to act as her watchdog. At the party last night, Rik had been asked to explain to a young German man who had followed Michelle from Erlangen to Salzburg to Strobl that her friendliness had no future. He guessed that she was aware of the power she exercised over men; the only question was its deliberateness. Everything about her was a promise, but only could remain so if it was never kept.

Michelle was Rik's dance partner in the first half of the show, which was always an American musical comedy montage in which everyone had to appear. His primary value was as an actor in the scenes or one-acts that were performed after intermission. Lynne had refused to dance with him.

"It's not just that he has two left feet," she explained. "He's not that consistent. I never know if he's going to show up with two left feet, two right feet, a right-left, or a left-right combination. I'd be in less danger with Sonny Liston."

Michelle, on the other hand, could make him appear almost competent—especially to a male audience paying no attention to him whatsoever. She led when they danced, while giving the impression that she was responding to him. Her every movement was in complete control, yet one was always aware of every limb, every muscle from which her fluidity derived. Her dancing was her own metaphor.

"See, that didn't take long." She stood in front of him, his wet terrycloth robe clinging to her body, her dancers' legs visible from the mid-thigh down, the sun dress over her arm. Rik was simultaneously aware of not having washed his hands in the bathroom, and of a reluctance to stand up in her presence.

"Look." Her voice dropped even lower. "I didn't say anything last night because it was so noisy in Billy's Bar. But I want to thank you for all you did for us. Some of the kids think you were too tough, but if you hadn't taken charge, we'd have all been back in the States long ago, and with a sour taste in our mouths. I just want to say that we couldn't have made it without you—you and Lynne."

Rik mumbled something that sounded like thanks. He had to stand up now.

"I have one more request to make." She stepped closer to him and her face momentarily disappeared into the shadow. "I want to do a solo song tonight."

Rik cleared his throat uncomfortably, momentarily glad that she was looking at his eyes, and not lower. "That's not my decision, Michelle. Tom's the music director. He determines whether a number's in or out."

"Tom's down with it, definitely! He's been working with me. He just needs you to confirm it. It's a farewell love song to Strobl. It's a promise that we'll be back, that this wasn't just a one summer thing! Listen!" She stepped back and raised her head, the light catching her green eyes as she launched into an old Frankie Laine ballad.

"No tears, no fears.
Remember, there's always tomorrow.
So what if we have to part,
We'll be together again.

Some day, some way.
We both have a lifetime before us.
For parting is not goodbye.
We'll be together again."

Rik glanced around, but the hallway remained empty. "I can't promise anything, Michelle. I'll talk to Tom at four o'clock when we work out the bill. If he says you're ready, the song's in."

The redhead kissed him on the cheek, hugging him an instant longer than impulsiveness demanded. "Thanks! I knew you'd come through. It'll be great! You'll see!" A moment later she had disappeared down the hallway.

*****

Across the room from him as he entered, the sun shone on Lynne's bare back. He knelt beside the bunk and gently stroked her neck. In one motion she turned her face down into one feather bed and reached back to pull the other atop her. "Go away and leave me alone," she groaned.

*****

He left the path and cut across the campus toward the village. The grounds were deserted, but in the recreation hall that butted up against the dining room, someone was picking out on the piano a popular tune that Rik couldn't quite place. The wet grass gave way under his feet to the brick-block main street. To his right as he walked into the town square was an unopened gelato stand, to his left the Catholic Church with its onion-shaped minaret of a tower, a cultural remnant of the Turkish invasion three centuries earlier. A gardener, hard at work on the tiny, beautifully cultivated flower gardens atop the graves, returned Rik's nod with a cheerful *"Gros Gutt."* Many of the stones next to the street contained short biographies and even pictures of the young men who lay beneath them—the nation's unripe fruit plucked by the frozen fingers of a winter on the Eastern Front more than twenty years ago.

On the far side of the square stood the *Kino*, which in the largely television-free town still did a lively business, especially among the international students on the weekend when the bill changed. Rik paused to watch as two men in coveralls pasted up the advertising posters of a cheap German Sax Rohmer knock-off. In one illustration, a muscular Teutonic, his shirt ripped to shreds, laid waste with his fists a horde of knife-wielding, black-clad Orientals, while in the second, a Dragon Lady type with a mane of jet-black hair stood in profile, her slightly-flexed left leg visible through the hip high slit in her red *Ao Dai* as she threw a seductively contemptuous glance over her shoulder at the young American man on the sidewalk. Finally, an amply endowed, mini-skirted young woman, her arms tied behind her, *en pointe* like a ballet dancer, kicked well above her head to shatter the window of the cellar in which she was imprisoned. Michelle's image flashed through Rik's mind. Heroism, adventure, and sex. Ah, the movies!

Down the street beyond the town square was a 300-acre park of unevenly spaced spruce, elm, and linden trees, at the center of which stood the *Seegasthof*. Through the trees he could see the lake which ran parallel to the campus and the town. Here it was barely a hundred meters from the street. The fresh air cleared his head, and Rik was suddenly aware of being ravenously hungry. The café outside *Wilhelm's Hofbrauhaus* (which the students called "Billy's Bar") would be open and he could get an omelet, some coffee, and perhaps a newspaper from the kiosk next to the hotel.

The International Edition of the New York Herald Tribune was prominently displayed on the kiosk, but with the reading of its headline Rik's appetite vanished.

Saturday, August 8, 1964
"CONGRESSIONAL RESOLUTION GRANTS LBJ RETALIATORY POWERS IN GULF OF TONKIN INCIDENT"

A ten Schilling coin and the newspaper was in his hands. Rik's eyes raced through the text, singling out the relevant facts—an attack the night of August 2 by North Vietnamese pursuit boats on the destroyer *Maddox* patrolling the Gulf of Tonkin in international waters—a second attack two nights later on the *Maddox* and the *Turner Joy*—bombings of North Vietnam ordered by LBJ—and, yesterday, a Resolution by both houses of Congress giving the President the right *"to take all necessary steps, including the use of armed force, to assist any member or protocol state of the Southeast Asia Collective Defense Treaty requesting assistance in defense of its freedom."*

War. A chill ran down Rik's back. War. Not advisors. Not strongly worded admonitions in the United Nations. War—Armageddon! The ultimate confrontation of Good and Evil! Face to Face with Godless, Atheist Communism at last!—except he wouldn't be there.

The summons to arms of a decade and a half flowed through Rik's memory. Fulton Lewis, Jr. exposing Communist Front Groups on Mutual radio each weeknight at six. Racing out in the field to tell his uncle about the beginning of the Korean War. General MacArthur's "Old Soldiers Never Die; They Just Fade Away." Dwight Eisenhower on the Domino Theory. *The Angel of Dien Bien Phu* at the Strand. Signing the Loyalty Oath at Fort Leonard Wood. The Bay of Pigs. Being reactivated as the Berlin Wall went up. All without ever firing a shot in Defense of the Free World.

And now what? Teaching public speaking to 18-year-olds in Keokuk?

At a table across the courtyard of the café, two familiar figures were engaged in a war of words of their own. The quieter of the two leaned back in his chair, a lanky man of about fifty with the wind-burned face of a lifetime skier visible above the collar of his Tyrolean jacket. The other—younger, darker, Jewish—leaned forward, elbows on the table, expressive hands accentuating the points of his argument. Professor Willy Kriesky of the University of Graz, a Strobl summer German teacher, waved Rik over to join them. Aaron Podheretz, a Columbia University history and journalism double major, nodded his acknowledgement without interrupting his accusations.

"Any American—any democracy—not taking a stand

against Communism in Southeast Asia is just as guilty as the Austrians who didn't resist the *Anschluss*. That's what the Truman Doctrine is all about! Containing Communism wherever it rears its ugly head. If Vienna had the same policy toward National Socialism in 1938, attendance at the Podheretz family reunions would be a little larger today."

"Excuse me, Aaron," the professor interrupted him. "What happened to your grandparents was, of course, deplorable. But Hanoi is not 1938 Berlin, and America is not 1938 Austria. My wife and I were married on Saturday, March 5th, 1938, and for our honeymoon went skiing in the Schladming region of Styria in the sovereign nation of Austria. When we returned home two weeks later, there was no Austria, just a German province called *Ostmark*. Are you seriously suggesting to me that this will be America's fate if Communism is victorious in French Indochina?"

"Not if we act now! Besides, Ho Chi Minh is just a pawn for Moscow, another domino on the Cominform game board. This war has nothing to do with Vietnamese nationalism! Claim that this war has nothing to do with American security, and next year you'll be making the same claim about Laos, then Taiwan, then the Philippines! Ninety percent of Austrian voters approved the *Anschluss*, and after the War, the Soviets occupied the country for *ten* years! Did you learn nothing from your own history?"

Kriesky grinned mirthlessly. "We learned the futility of trading one form of fascism for another. Do you think the first Brownshirts ever to knock on a Viennese door came from Hitler? You should have been there in 1934 when the "Christian" Socialists sent their tanks to open fire on the Social Democrat neighborhoods, disband the labor unions, and set up a state based on 'Catholic Social Principles'. Hitler was Austrian. Some people thought they were giving up an incompetent dictatorship for a successful one. If I were to walk around this courtyard and present your argument to five different natives, one would agree with me, two wouldn't know what I was talking about, and two would call me a *nestbeschmutzer*. You are familiar with the word? 'One who befouls his nest?'"

Podheretz was unimpressed. "The refusal to face the truth now is proof that you should have acted to support the truth then."

The professor tried again. "You are from Columbia, right? Perhaps you are more familiar with the American saying, 'Hindsight is 20-20.' In 1933 Hans Luther, Hitler's ambassador to the United States, was a guest speaker at Columbia University's Institute of Arts and Sciences. Afterward, three students asked for his justification of the firing of anti-Nazi professors from the universities and the confiscation of their houses. They were forcibly removed from the lecture hall. At the reception given Luther afterward by Nicholas Murray Butler, Columbia's president, Russell Potter, the Institute's Dean, called the protestors 'ill-mannered children'. Perhaps they were. Or perhaps I should categorize Columbia as permanently immoral for something that happened thirty years ago. The truth is not always obvious. By the time I figured it out, I was less concerned with ideology than with *not* being sent to the Eastern Front."

"You could have refused to go."

"Could I?" Kriesky was amused. "As it happened, I didn't have to. I was sent to Italy, and during my first skirmish with the Americans I was captured. I and the surviving members of my squad were shipped to a prison camp in Texas where we saw no life outside our stockade fence for two years. In the middle of the third year a longhorn steer walked across the desert and up to the fence where it stared at us, as we stared at it. It was lost. We were cheered. I spent my time teaching German to the guards, other soldiers, and some civilians whose presence was never explained to us. In return, they taught me the songs of Bing Crosby. 'White Christmas' was my favorite."

The Columbia student was stubborn. "How personally fortunate for you—but there is nothing in your narrative that refutes the necessity of my country taking action as yours did not."

"Well then I will provide one thing." Professor Kriesky was tiring of the dispute. "Germany occupied us and annexed us. If you are going to 'save' Vietnam, you will have to go there and occupy it."

The café was momentarily quiet. In the park beyond the courtyard, birds sang a late summer song in the trees. The leathery Austrian turned to the third person at the table. "Rikart, you have been unusually silent during this discussion. What's on your mind?"

Rik tossed the copy of the newspaper on the table

*****

She wheeled about as Rik entered the room, bumping the table and tipping over a half cup of cold coffee. A dark stain slowly spread down the side of the commemorative birthday plate. Without ever taking her eyes off him, Lynne grabbed a towel and began wiping the table. There was an unnatural pallor beneath her summer tan.

"Where have you been?" She had been crying.

"Down at the *Seegasthof*, having coffee and listening to Podheretz and Professor Kriesky argue politics as usual. What's wrong?"

She perched on the edge of her bed, her hands twisting the forgotten towel. Rik crossed the room and sat by her, his arm around her. She was trembling.

"Carol came by earlier. She got a telegram from her father. There's something big happening in French Indochina. He's being called to Washington from Manila."

"Carol's father is a senior officer in the Air Force. He's

always being called to Washington for some reason or another. Why is she so worried about him now?"

"Then the mail came." Lynne pointed to a bulky envelope lying on the bed opposite them.

Rik walked slowly around the table and sat on the bed. He picked up the envelope and examined it. It was smudged, battered, and obviously well-traveled. The address was Lynne and Rik's apartment in University Married Housing—crossed out and replaced with that of his parents' farm—crossed out and replaced with that of the *Sommerhochschule* in Strobl. The addressee was Sp5 Rickart Gottfried Temple, and the return address was "Headquarters, Department of the Army, Washington 25, D.C." The postmark was so badly smeared that it was impossible to read the mailing date.

The envelope was unopened.

"You're not going to go again." Rik looked up to face his wife's intense blue eyes. "They called you back once before. You're not going to go again."

"I may not have a choice in the matter."

"Yes, you do. I've thought it all out." She was kneeling, facing him from the other side of the low table. Unwillingly, he found himself on his knees opposite her. "We're on a different continent. We have no idea when the letter was sent, and it would be perfectly understandable if we never got it! We don't even have an address in Iowa yet. By the time the Army found us, I could be pregnant. They'd never take you then!"

Rik tried to sound reasonable. "You don't know that. And if the orders are already cut, I'll have to go anyway. If I don't go, it could mean a court-martial."

"Then *let* it be a court-martial! Let it be a dishonorable discharge! I don't care. I waited for you once." Lynne's voice suddenly became calm. "I won't do it again."

"It won't be so bad. No matter where I am, there'll be married housing nearby."

"In Vietnam?" The fear was mixed with anger now. "You're Infantry! Jungle patrols aren't nine to five jobs, and you won't come home in the evening. And you won't come home to me either. I didn't wait tables through two university degrees in two university towns so that I could wait tables outside an army post. And I'm not going to sit at home, waiting in terror for the doorbell to ring and two officers and a chaplain to appear outside. I was there, a little girl, when that happened to my Aunt June during the Korean War. I won't let it happen to me."

"Look, Lynne. Let it go for now. Later we'll know what our options are. We won't make any decisions till then."

She rose slowly to her feet, her eyes searching his face. "You want to go, don't you? You want to fly away out the window, like some camouflaged Peter Pan. To some Never-Never Land, where you never have to grow up, never have to worry about making good at a job, never have to worry about taking care of a family, never have to worry about house payments, car payments, never have to worry about coming home to a *wife*!"

Rik felt his face reddening. "Look, this is a national emergency. I could be needed."

"*Needed*," she hissed. "I've never heard you say that the Army did anything but give you time to think of something else to do. You said a reasonably obedient chimpanzee could do anything you were asked to do. *Needed*! You're "needed" to be a college teacher."

Rik was on his feet now, pacing the room, his temper rising. "Yeah, I'm needed as a teacher all right—needed in some Mississippi River town which hasn't seen a new idea since Mark Twain passed through a hundred years ago. I'm needed to teach bored teenagers how to make an introductory, an informative, and a persuasive speech about the necessity to change the school's nickname from bobcats to tigers—students who are only there because there's a layoff at the button factory, or worse, because they want to avoid being drafted into an army I'm running away from myself!"

"If you're not happy with their ideas, teach them new ones!" Lynne's voice was transmuting from anger into a reasoned pleading. "You'll have a forensics team. You don't have to stick to the same old subject matter. You can combine technique and content."

"What do you want from me?"

"I want what I've seen this summer. You've always run away, avoided taking charge, acted like you were too smart to accept responsibility. This summer you were put in a situation where you had to make decisions, show leadership—and you did fine! Not perfect, but pretty good at times when a wrong move could have really messed things up. That was new for you, and you showed you were up to it. Now something else new is about to happen, and you want to run away again. Well, I've got a hot tip for you; dealing with the unfamiliar is what life is all about. I want you *to grow up!*

Rik reached for the envelope on the table.

"Don't open it—not yet!" Lynne's voice was a warning, not a plea. "First, tell me that you're going to Iowa—that you're making a commitment to a life for the two of us together, not to something that will separate us again. Because if you leave me again, I promise I won't do anything to stop you."

He looked at his wife across the room, trying to gauge the strength of her resolve, trying to find the words that would undermine her argument, that would justify what he was about to do. Then he dropped his eyes and in a single motion tore open the envelope.

At the bottom of the envelope was a crumpled booklet, above it an official certificate, and at the top a folded page, which began with the following summary:

DD FORM 256A (1 MAY 50)

DATE: 28 JUNE 64
TO: TEMPLE, RICKART GOTTFRIED/ ER 27
        898 346/SP5/USAR

HQ & HQ CO/ 2D BG/ 128 INF/ 32D DIV
LAST ORDERED AD PER EX O 10957/ 10 AUG 61

FROM: SPAHR, D.D. / COL/ AGC/ 128 INF/ 32D DIV
SUBJECT: NOT REL/ INACT RES/ USAR

HON DIS/ AFUSA

He handed the papers to Lynne, who stared at the jargon in utter bafflement. "I don't understand. What do they mean?"

Rik took the documents from her hands and methodically shuffled through them. "The first page is a notification of my release from the Army's Inactive Reserve. This certificate is an Honorable Discharge from the Armed Forces of the United States of America 'awarded as a testimonial of Honest and Faithful Service,' and the pamphlet is an explanation of my rights and obligations as a veteran newly separated from the service." He tossed the documents on the table between them, and turned to the shelf above his bunk, retrieving a towel and a pair of trunks.

"Where are you going? Lynne's eyes remained fixated on the papers in front of her.

"I thought I'd go for a swim before the four o'clock rehearsal."

She broke from her reverie and crossed to the closet. "Then you'll want this," she said evenly, handing him the terrycloth robe. "Michelle brought it back this morning."

*****

His path to the lake took Rik past the other side of the recreation hall. As if trapped in time, the piano repeated the same plaintive melody of the morning. Only this time he could hear his music director, Tom Lawson, singing the lyric.

"Michelle, *ma belle*
These are words that go together well,
My Michelle

Michelle, *ma belle*
Sont les Mots qui vont tres bien ensemble
Tres bien ensemble"

So Tom was "down" with Michelle singing "We'll be together again." Rik hoped that he would be let down easy. He knew that he had been.

Rik walked down to the end of the dock and looked out over the *Wolfgang Zee*. Under the cloudless sky the slightest of waves made its way delicately and determinedly toward the shore. He let the terry cloth robe fall away from his body and shivered slightly from the western breeze. It was an alpine August and the days for swimming were numbered. On the opposite shore stood the village of St. Wolfgang, and beyond it the *Schafberg*, the climbing of which was a University scheduled activity this Saturday. By now the students would have reached the "Stairway to Heaven," the path to the top—so named because that would be the destination if one slipped off it. At this distance, he could see the tiny snow pack at its peak, an aroused nipple on a rounded, dusky breast.

He was alone.

The placid warmth of the surface split beneath his arched body to reveal the chillier depths below. Rik allowed the water's buoyancy to lift him to where he could survey the expanse in front of him. As he treaded water, he could feel his pores close and adjust themselves to the circumstances in which they had been placed.

Gradually he eased over on his back and struck out toward the center of the lake. Behind him he could see the buildings of the *Sommerhochschule*—the boathouse, the classrooms, the recreation hall and dining room, the dormitories—fading into the distance. And as he watched, they seemed to take on the form of other schools, colleges, and universities, one after another. And then there was nothing above him but the clear, blue mountain sky.

HIROSHIMA 1964

Trailers for sale or rent
Rooms to let...fifty cents.
No phone, no pool, no pets
I ain't got no cigarettes
Ah, but... two hours of pushin' broom
Buys an eight by twelve four-bit room
I'm a man of means by no means
King of the road.

Rik switched off the music as he turned on to Washington Street. He was right. The noise was in the engine, not the radio—the water pump, he guessed. The Mercury Monarch, with its sleek bathtub curves, was thirteen years old. In its younger, speedier days, Lynne had nicknamed it *Hermes* after the winged messenger/thief Greek god. But the gods are immortal; now time and again *Hermes* was just an aging organ away from the automobile graveyard. He'd have to hope the pump lasted the month, or that the garage would give him till the end of the month to pay. At least the car had had the grace to grow old before becoming worthless. Not like him.

From Washington Street he turned left on to Great River Road, which doubled as Iowa Highway 92, and across the bridge became US-61. If he went straight ahead and the pump didn't fail him, he could be across the Mighty Mississippi in minutes and be in Chicago in three hours. It was autumn and the end of another lousy Cub season, but the Bears would be in Wrigley Field, and they'd won the NFL championship last year. Downtown there would be State Street and the Art Institute on Michigan Boulevard. The theatre season had begun, and the Lyric Opera, Fritz Reiner and the Chicago Symphony—the aquarium, the Museum of Science and Industry, the Natural History Museum. Life!

The car rolled up to the stop light at Colorado Street. Beyond it Rik could see the bridge towering above the river. It was an engineering joke. Begun simultaneously on both the Iowa and Illinois sides of the Mississippi, it failed to meet in the middle. A third of the way across, just as one picked up speed, mesmerized by a blinding sun above or confused by a moonless night, the road took a sharp 45-degree turn in search of its brother from the neighboring state. The angle had been the undoing of many an unwary driver more concerned with where he was going than how he was getting there. Two photos hang on the wall of the *Muscatine Journal*. One from 1906 shows a buggy hooked in the railing with a horse hanging from its harness over the river. The second from 1955 shows an 18-wheel semi-trailer in the same position—both embarrassing, neither fatal. Of the less amusing fatalities there are no pictures.

Rik contemplated the possibilities. The turn in the highway was reinforced now. Still, if one hit it hard enough, the railing might be penetrated. The Mercury Monarch—the salesman told his father back in 1951—was capable of a mile per hour for every one of its 112 horsepower. He'd never driven it that fast, but he'd come close. If the water pump held out, it would probably be all over at the railing, except for the photos in tomorrow's *Journal*. Or there might be that moment of breaking through, that sensation of flying as the Big Muddy reached up its welcoming arms to engulf him.

An impatient car horn sounded for the third time as the

image of the river dissolved into the green of the traffic light above him. Rik gunned the Mercury and, wheels squealing, made a sharp left onto Colorado Street, heading for the Junior College.

*****

On the first stair landing Lynne paused, breathing heavily. The Laundromat being just two blocks away was one of the selling points of this apartment (as was the $65 a month rental). But today the basket seemed heavier and the stairs steeper, as she struggled to complete a battery of Monday morning chores before facing three consecutive classes in the afternoon. The blood pounded in her ears, and through it she could hear another sound, a phone ringing from the floor above her.

Lynne burst through the door and tossed the keys on the kitchenette table. Why had she bothered to lock it? There was little worth stealing. Until their first paychecks had liberated their belongings from storage they had slept on a mattress on the floor with their coats as blankets, eating off paper plates and drinking out of plastic cups from Henry's Drive-In. The second paycheck had brought the telephone, whose insistent demands filled the space on the other side of the living room. As she crossed the sagging floor, Lynne reflected briefly on Rik's claim that it was possible to dip out of sight when navigating the distance between the two walls. (Not true— although there was a spot near the front door where you could stamp your foot and make every door in the apartment swing open.)

"Lynne?" The voice on the other end of the line was striving for control. "She's gone, Lynne. My baby's gone."

"Marti?" Lynne tried to simultaneously catch her breath and reassure her sister-in-law. "Who's gone? Annie? Oh Marti, I'm so sorry!"

"We brought her into Mercy Hospital last night. Michael and I were with her all night, until he had to go home to milk the cows. I called him, but he's either in the barn or on his way here. So I called you. The boys are staying with Mom. I haven't talked to her yet. I don't know to tell her. She loved Annie so."

Lynne jammed the phone between her shoulder and her ear, and fumbled in her purse for her cigarettes. Her hands were shaking. "Tell me what happened, Marti. We'll find a way to tell your mother."

The other woman wasn't listening. "She knew I was there, Lynne! She was awake—almost to the last. She loved me; she didn't want to leave me. I held her little body and played with her little fingers and the little purple nail beds. She was three years old and only weighed *fifteen* pounds. That wasn't right. That wasn't fair! Her skin was almost as blue as her eyes. She was beautiful, but she wasn't *right!*"

Lynne searched frantically for an ash tray within reach of the phone cord. "It was Cyanosis, Marti. Annie was a Blue Baby. You knew this would happen someday."

"Why? Why did it have to happen at all? She was talking now; did you know that, Lynne? We sang little songs to one another. Michael would play peek-a-boo with her. I was teaching her patty-cake. The boys would carry her around. She waited every day for them to come home from school."

"Listen." Lynne adopted a calm she didn't feel. "There has to be a doctor or nurse there somewhere. Have them call Michael again. I'll stay on the line until he gets there. Then I'll call Rik at the JC and we'll drive straight up to Wisconsin."

"No, don't do that." The voice on the other end of the line was more sober now. "You and Rik both have classes to teach, and I know that Rik is directing a play. We'll be all right. There's nothing you can do. There won't be"—Marti's voice cracked and then recomposed itself—"*services* until Saturday, probably. Come up on Friday afternoon after school. I'll be all right."

"You're sure? I know they'd let us go."

"I'm sure."

There was a long silence, and for a moment Lynne wondered if they'd lost the connection.

"Lynne?" The voice was almost a whisper now. "There's something else. I can't tell Michael, but I've got to tell somebody."

Lynne watched a column of ash break off and fall onto the living room rug. "What," she asked?

"They know what caused it. Why my baby couldn't get oxygen into her system."

"Why?"

"It was nitrates. It gets in the water and joins with the blood protein, and then the blood won't carry the oxygen."

"Nitrates?"

"It's from the pesticides, you see? We put it on the fields, and it gets into the water table and we drink it. And if you're little you can't fight it off and it takes over your blood! That's why I can't tell Michael. If he thought he'd hurt his baby, it would kill him, don't you see?"

"Marti, you can't know what the cause was." Lynne tried to sound reasonable. "Annie was probably born with a defective heart. You can't blame yourselves."

Her sister-in-law's voice was insistent. "God wouldn't let us hurt our own baby, would He? He wouldn't do that, would he, Lynne?"

Lynne bit her lip as the coal of the cigarette burned her fingers.

"No matter how bad we've been, God wouldn't let us do that. Would He?"

*****

The inside window of the Office looked out on the student lounge. The Dean sat behind his desk with his back to the window. Legend had it that he did so because if he saw what happened in the lounge he might have to do something about it. Behind the Dean and to his right sat a large man in a white suit. He was horizontal to the window, and with a flick of an eye could observe the lounge, the Dean, or Rik, who sat immediately opposite the desk.

Through the opening in the blinds, Rik idly watched the people in the lounge—some in groups, some alone, some grabbing an early lunch or scurrying to or away from a class, a few sprawled insolently on couches, and others almost desperately trying to avoid notice. He recognized many of them, although their names often escaped him. A 20-year-old with a sly smirk and an outdated DA haircut was trying to impress a high school girl with his masculinity. Rik had hired his father to fix the used refrigerator in the apartment, only to have him take the handle with him on a two week drunk, leaving Lynne with the only Maytag closed by a tourniquet. The girl trying to make the Coke machine work was just beginning to show. The school system frowned on unmarried pregnancies, even at the JC level. Pregnant teachers weren't allowed at the high school—in fear that students would find out where babies came from, Rik guessed. The thin boy gesturing animatedly to a friend had stopped him in the hall, begging for a draft-avoiding passing grade in rhetoric—which might have been easier achieved by attending class.

"And it's precisely for the sake of the students that we can't let this play go forward." The voice of the Dean cut through Rik's reverie. "We are responsible to their parents for their moral environment, and something like this reflects badly on the reputation of the school. There are high school students who take classes here, and I don't propose to expose them to this language, or the college to the criticism that would result from producing such a play."

"It's an American classic."

The man in the white suit stirred almost imperceptibly,

but the Dean seemed to sense the movement and responded quickly. "There is profanity in it! There is adultery in it! There are racial themes in it, and it will not be done in this school. You need to understand where your responsibility lies. I don't care how long you've rehearsed it. From now on the Administration will pre-approve any play you're thinking of doing. If you want to produce a classic, why not direct Shakespeare? Nobody objects to that."

"That's because nobody knows what's happening."

The Dean flushed. "This isn't a debate, young man. You haven't been here very long and you don't seem to understand what your job is. Mine is to make this school run smoothly, and that includes the face we show to the public. Right now you're a zit on that face, mister, and until you're ready to clean it up, we'll have to clean it up for you."

*****

Rik paused outside the office door, and then turned on his heel to head back in. His fingers were on the doorknob when a strong hand grasped his arm above the elbow.

"Why don't you come with me instead? I'll buy you a cup of coffee."

Ed Favor led the way from the coffee machine to a table in the television room. Above the darkened screen a banner spread the breadth of the room: "Watch America in the Tokyo Olympics, 6-10 p.m. October 10-24." The English professor they called "Farmer Favor" eased carefully into a chair opposite Rik. He did, in fact, share a dairy farm with his brother west of town, but his shambling gait had less to do with straddling a furrow behind a walking plow than with taking a German bullet in the hip during the Battle of the Bulge.

"So you were blessed with the presence of the Great White Whale."

"Do they call him that because of his looks?" Rik was quizzical. "I never met him before and never heard of a college where the Superintendent of Schools was in charge. But he was. He didn't say a word, but I had the feeling the Dean was talking as much to him as he was to me."

Favor snorted. "Oh, he was! And the Great White Whale's the reason your play was shut down. (Don't be surprised. Bad news travels fast.) You don't think the Dean ever read *Of Mice and Men*, or cared enough to censor it?"

Rik scowled as he sipped his coffee. It was stale as usual. "So what is this guy—a theatre critic or a preacher?"

"Neither. He knows less about literature than the Dean, if that's possible. In this town the JC is grades 13 and 14 of the system, and in every school there's someone who carries tales to the Superintendent. Here it could have been a student counselor, but my guess would be Mrs. Van Buren, the Dean's Secretary. She would have had access to the script, would be most likely to have been upset by the language, and goes to the same church as the Superintendent. Did the Dean give you the 'zit on the face of the organization' speech?"

Rik blinked. Was this guy in the room or what?

The man across the table laughed. "He does that whenever he wants to sound tough. He's not from here, and the Superintendent doesn't trust him. The Dean thinks that if he squashes you, the Great White Whale will let him alone for a while. Do you know how he got that nickname?"

"Who—the Superintendent?"

"Yeah. It's not the way he dresses, or even his bulk— although that's a clue. Look at those sagging pectorals and bulbous arms. The Great White Whale is an ex-swimmer. That's what happens when you exercise certain muscles intensively, and then stop exercising at all. Everything turns to flab. He's an ex-athlete and all of his toadies are ex-athletes."

"How do you mean?" Rik had the sense of being initiated.

Ed Favor leaned forward. For him this was not a new speech. "For example, there are four junior high schools in his district. Every principal was a star athlete at the JC, and they all commuted 35 miles to the University of Iowa to get their bachelor's degrees, and they all studied educational administration. That way they couldn't be corrupted by the atmosphere of the University, or anything they might learn in a class. That's true for two of the three student counselors here as well."

"And the third?"

"That would be Webber. He taught psychology here for years, until they realized he was going through all the texts and cutting out anything that had to do with the human reproductive system."

"So they made him a counselor?"

"So they made him a counselor."

"Wow." Rik leaned back in his chair.

Favor patted his pockets in search of the gum he habitually chewed to ease the pain in his hip. "Years ago, the Superintendent told me he tried never to hire teachers who were too smart. He said the students wouldn't be able to relate to them. I used to believe he was worried that people who think ask questions and challenge hierarchies, but really it's just never occurred to him that he might be wrong. He's not even a villain; he's just the way things are."

Rik resisted the temptation to leap to his feet and run out. "How do you do it? How do you put up with this year after year?"

Favor spread his hands with resignation. "I have the farm. I see things grow. I have my kids. They grow. Even my students grow—the Great White Whale's wrong about some of them. I teach them literature and to express themselves." He grinned. "It's the ultimate subversion. If I don't fail too many ballplayers, they leave me alone."

"I don't know if I can do that. I teach eight sections of the same course. Sometimes I can't remember where I am."

"I know." Favor's grin was sympathetic now. "Last week you taught the same lesson in the same class two days in a row, and none of your students said a thing. (I told you bad news travels fast.)"

Rik suddenly felt dizzy. "It's like high school, isn't it? The jocks run everything, and the administration covers its ass. Only you never get to graduate. It's permanent limbo. I'd be better off dead!"

"Nobody's ever better off dead." Ed Favor's voice carried the certainty of a survivor. "Once you know where you are, you can always find a way to keep your mind alive. Some of the students will surprise you. Your own resilience will surprise you! You don't have to be here forever, but you'll never build a future unless you're running toward something rather than away from it."

*****

Lynne replaced the delicate Japanese teacup in its saucer, a wave of nausea unnoticed by the others in the room passing over her. In a living room corner the longcase clock struck the quarter hour, momentarily halting Ellen's nervous chatter about her daughters, Barbara and Susan, who Lynne frequently minded when Ellen had to take their father to the hospital. Rik seemed distracted, and the gaunt man in the recliner, who they had ostensibly come to visit, hadn't spoken since they entered the room. She found herself studying the side handle teapot, decorated in silver gray glaze with the embossed figure of a bird of some kind. The pot was perfect in every detail except for its lid whose fine lines had melted into one another like the dough of a poorly formed biscuit.

"It's a crane," a voice rasped from across the room. "To the Japanese the crane is a symbol of longevity and fidelity. In legend they live a thousand years and are always faithful."

Ellen shifted uneasily in her chair, but Lynne looked up hopefully, glad that their host had the energy to include himself in the conversation. "Yes?" she prompted.

The skin over the man's veins and facial bones was stretched as tightly as waxed paper and his reply came with effort. "I got it in the Aki ward, close to Ujina Harbor."

"Where is that, Harry?" Rik asked.

"Hiroshima. They sent a contingent of us from Los Alamos that September."

"Nineteen forty-five? They sent you in that soon?"

"Yes. There were some people left. They were friendly." The gaunt man rested for a moment. "The Project needed a record of what happened, the diameter of ground zero, a measurement of the radiation. We had to see how successful our 'Little Boy' was." Lynne detected a touch of irony in the rasping voice. "'Fat Man' was a relative failure, you know. Missed the target. Fog over Nagasaki. Not nearly as effective as the firebombing in March. That wiped out a quarter of Tokyo—right where they built the Olympics Stadium in Yoyogi Park. We sent teams everywhere. I got Hiroshima."

"That was before we met," Ellen interjected.

"That's right." A wan smile crossed Harry's face. "I came home from Los Alamos that Christmas and never went back. I went to work in my father's button factory, and never again got closer to nuclear energy than teaching physics part-time at the JC. Dad thought my education had been wasted, but I'd learned everything I wanted to know. We met the next June when you came back from your freshman year at Clark."

Ellen returned her husband's smile. "I never went back either. We were married August 6th. I was nineteen years old."

"And you've kept the teapot ever since?" Rik asked.

"Kept it?" The gaunt man gave a snort which evolved into a cough. "I had to smuggle it out of Los Alamos! It was part of the scientific evidence. You see the lid?"

Rik looked puzzled, but Lynne nodded.

"The pot was on a stool just inside the open window of an elementary school in the Aki ward, its lid just visible above the frame. That's how we knew the bomb went off at the proper height! The radiation from the blast melted the lid and burned its outline into the blackboard on the other side of the room."

Another wave of nausea swept over Lynne, and when Harry looked across the room, it was into a face as pale as his own.

"What happened to the children?" she asked.

*****

The following Saturday, Lynne was putting a tray of cookies in the oven when the phone rang. Ellen had to take Harry to Muscatine General Hospital. Could she watch Barbara and Susan until they (or she) were able to come home? Minutes later, on a glorious afternoon made all the more precious because the weather could not last, Lynne was walking catty-corner across the back of the East Tenth Street lawns, returning the smiles of elderly men basking in the routine of tending the last of the summer flowers to the radio call of a University of Iowa football game. On the rear steps of Harry and Ellen's house, their arms filled with an astonishing variety of dolls, two solemn little girls sat waiting for her. Usually on their walks together, Barbara and Susan skipped with excitement, chattering about school and friends. Today they were so close to Lynne that she was able to walk with a hand on each of their shoulders and had to be careful not to step on them.

Lynne stood in the kitchen doorway for a moment, watching the girls playing in the space she had cleared in the living room: seven-year-old Susan, immediately lost in the adventure of her dolls exploring the caverns beneath the cushions of a battered couch; nine-year-old Barbara imposing rows of order on every Raggedy Ann and Andy under her command. Back in the kitchen a bread board on the counter awaited the cookie sheet from the oven. Lynne removed a frosting tray from the refrigerator, automatically reaching for a cigarette and switching on a radio habitually tuned to Iowa City's WSUI. The familiar voice of Milton Cross filled the room.

"—and now the audience files back in for Act III of Texaco's Metropolitan Opera broadcast of Richard Strauss' *Die Frau ohne Schatten*. The curtain rises in a grotto beneath the realm of the Spirit King, where the Wife is haunted by voices of the Unborn Children rising from the cooking fire. The Dyer, her husband, searches for her, regretting his attempt to kill her for giving away the shadow which symbolized her childbearing.

Scene two finds the Empress and the Nurse before the Temple of the Spirit God, father to the Empress. The Empress enters the temple, hoping her father will let her remain human. The Wife and the Dyer arrive in search of one another: she to die at her husband's hand; he to forgive her and hold her in his arms. The Nurse, having previously tricked the Wife out of her shadow, now deceives them both, sending them in opposite directions. However, the Messenger of the Spirit God has seen her sin and condemns the Nurse to wander alone in eternal exile between the Mortal and Spirit Worlds.

Inside the Temple in Scene three, the Empress begs her father for forgiveness and a place amongst those who cast shadows. Without speaking, the Spirit God shows her the Emperor, almost turned to stone, and a Voice urges her to drink from the Fountain of Life and claim the Wife's shadow for her own. But the Empress refuses to steal the happiness of the Dyer and the Wife and become human by robbing humanity from someone else, singing 'I will—not!' This act of renunciation frees her; she receives a shadow, and the Emperor is restored. As the setting changes to a beautiful landscape, the Dyer and his Wife (who has regained her shadow) are reunited. Both couples sing in praise of humanity and their Unborn Children."

"Lynne, are the cookies ready yet?"

"What kind are they?"

Lynne snubbed out her cigarette, switched off the radio, and turned to the two towheads in the living room doorway. She put on a very serious face. "Well, if there were some plates on the table, we might just find out what kind of cookies there are."

Susan scrambled to open the sideboard, and the more careful Barbara distributed three plates around the kitchen table. In its center Lynne placed a tray of gleaming gingerbread cookies, some decorated with yellow pigtails and fringed skirts, others with Dutch boy caps and wooden block shoes, all with dabs of bright blue frosting eyes. The little girls squealed with delight, reaching across the table.

"Wait!" Lynne interrupted them in mid-reach. "You can't eat somebody you haven't been introduced to." She picked up two of the little figures, and holding them opposite one another, began speaking in a sing-song voice. "Hi! I'm Charley Cookie... and I'm Cindy Cookie. We're the Cookie Kids and we're looking for our mommies."

Barbara and Susan squealed again.

"We want our mommies, but we're afraid our mommies don't want us. Do you want us?"

"Yes," the two little girls screamed in unison.

Lynne's eyes were wide. "If you want us to be your babies, you have to promise not to eat us! Do you promise?"

"Yes," came the response.

"Well, I guess it will be all right then." Lynne reached across the table and handed one cookie to each girl. Susan triumphantly bit the head off her little boy figure, giggling as she spit crumbs, but Barbara hesitated and looked at Lynne.

"Lynne, if I eat my baby, can I ever have another one?"

*****

His appearance, as he settled into the comfortable desk chair, was just short of sleek. His fashionably Ivy League cut hair tapered down to within a hand's width of the professional gown, which touched the top of his white collar and hung casually open as he leaned back. A modestly colored silk tie, held in place by a fraternity pin, perfectly split the gap between the gown's buttons and its buttonholes. He was clean-shaven and handsome without quite being pretty, a model in reality for what Richard Chamberlain in *Doctor Kildare* pretended to be in art. Aware of the authority he possessed and they did not, the others in the room waited for him to speak.

"To begin with, this happens often, at least in one out of every five or six cases. It's usually some chromosomal abnormality, maybe when the zygote went through the division process, or it could be related to lifestyle—smoking, drug use, too much caffeine, or exposure to radiation (although, of course, that's not likely here). It's easy to tell when it's happening—nausea, abdominal pain, dilation or effacement of the cervix, rupture of the membranes. That sort of thing will continue until curettage is performed."

He paused, waiting for a response from the young woman on the other side of the desk. Her face was tense, and her hand gripped her husband's arm so tightly, the knuckles were white, but she did not speak.

"The best thing to do is to go in there right away and fix whatever we can. We need to stop the bleeding and prevent infection with a D&C. We can't guarantee anything, but if we can clean out the area and find the right combination of drugs to prevent fever, there's a good chance we can avoid permanent damage."

The young woman opposite him looked confused. "And will that save the baby?"

"Save the baby?" The doctor snorted in disbelief. "My dear young lady! At this point I'm only hoping I can save the womb!"

*****

There was a chair next to the door outside Lynne's room, but Rik chose to stand. The medical staff was preparing her; then she would be taken upstairs for the surgery. He would be allowed to ride up in the elevator, but it was strongly suggested he not be present for the prep, and, of course, being in the operating room was out of the question. Gradually, he became aware of a pair of orderlies, indistinguishable in age and garb, lounging casually against the opposite hallway wall, waiting to move the gurney.

"Watcha gonna do this weekend," queried the taller man on the left?

"Are you kiddin'," the other responded? "Tomorrow night's the opening ceremony of the Olympics. Why do ya think I just got a color TV? Come on over and watch it with me. Bring your own beer though. I'll be damned if I want you sucking my refrigerator dry."

"Can't," the tall one replied. "My weekend to pull the Saturday night shift."

"Tough. You still up on the fourth floor?"

"Four months now."

The shorter one gave a look, which probably passed for him as thoughtful. "Why do ya suppose that they put the ICU and the maternity ward on the same floor?"

"How the hell should I know? Maybe they wanna even out the numbers. You know—win one, lose one? I'll tell you one thing though. I sure as hell prefer working on the ICU side."

"Why's that?"

"It's a lot quieter. They just lie there. Half the time they're not even awake. In the maternity ward they're always screamin', and when they're not screamin', they're whining—always making such a big deal about things!" The tall man's face brightened. "Hey, you know the difference between the maternity ward and the ICU?"

"Is it a joke?"

"Kind of. In the maternity ward, the doctor and the patient go into the operating room and three people come out. In the ICU, the doctor and the patient go into the operating room and one person comes out."

The shorter man looked puzzled. "I don't get it."

Rik's right hand grasped the top of the chair as he stepped toward the orderlies. Maybe some extra time in the ICU would improve their senses of humor. Just then a hand touched his left arm.

"Your wife is ready to be taken up to the operating room, Mr. Temple," a nurse said softly.

Rik looked down at Lynne's face as the orderlies expertly guided the gurney down the passageway. Her eyes were closed, but he couldn't tell if she was conscious or not. There was a tension about her mouth, as if she were in the act of denying something. He didn't know if he was allowed to touch her, or if she wanted him to.

He switched his attention to the elevator at the end of the hall. The arrow on the floor indicator was coming down, as if the lift were the bearer of a Rapture come to summon them. The group of attendants paused, a stretcher's length from the elevator door, which opened to reveal its mirror image ending its descent even as they prepared to rise: an occupied gurney, guided by orderlies, flanked by medical personnel in scrubs, and trailed by a mourner.

It took a moment for Rik to recognize Ellen, who, eyes wide open and unseeing, moved toward them with the blind assurance of a Lady Macbeth. In front of her laying on the gurney, his face matching the color of the sheet covering his body, was Harry. Rik studied his former neighbor's features, which reflected neither pain nor peace, but merely absence. Then the two entourages passed one another without acknowledgement, headed, for the time being at least, in opposite directions.

*****

"How is she?"

Rik looked up from the chair outside Lynne's room to see Ellen standing in front of him, as neat and unassuming as ever, and holding a cardboard box.

"She's fine," he said standing, and then corrected himself. "She's not ready for visitors, I'm afraid," adding awkwardly. "How are you? I'm sorry about Harry."

"Thank you. I'm fine." Her response had an auto pilot sound, as if it had already been made too many times. Then she switched to the purpose of her visit. "Look, I know I can't go in tonight, but would you take a walk with me out to the garden for a cigarette?"

"I don't smoke."

"I know you don't, but I do." She repeated herself with a touch more urgency: "Will you go with me?"

"Of course."

Visiting hours ended early on Saturday nights and the hallways were nearly empty. Out of the corner of his eye, Rik studied the woman walking beside him. She seemed lighter, more buoyant somehow, as if a great weight had been momentarily lifted from her. She was still young, he realized, mid-to-late thirties, perhaps a dozen years older than Lynne. Harry must have been about that age when he came back from Hiroshima. He had started over in this town. Could Ellen?

She slowed her pace slightly. "How did the operation go? More important, how is Lynne taking it?"

Rik chose his words carefully. "Very well—and very badly. The operation was a success. They cleared out—what had to be cleared out—but the uterus is intact. If we wait a while, we could try again." He stopped at the door of the inside garden, suddenly helpless, pleading for understanding. "We didn't plan this, Ellen. It was an accident, and now it's gone—she's gone, a little girl—and that was an accident too. We hadn't even picked any names. I don't know what to say, and she won't talk to me. She just sits there, watching the Olympic ceremonies on television, and she doesn't even like sports."

"That's okay," the older woman soothed him. "You can have the post-baby blues—even when there isn't a baby. Let's go into the garden."

The inner garden was on the side of the hospital away from the streets, with the building surrounding it on three sides. With paths firm enough to support wheelchairs, lined with carefully trimmed hedges and flower beds, and sheltered by stately elms, it was a favorite of families needing relief from facing the fate of those they had come to visit, and, inevitably, of smoking patients in the act of ensuring that fate would happen.

It would be dark soon and the garden was unlit except for the windows of the hospital rooms which surrounded it. Ellen chose a bench near the center, and they sat, but instead of lighting up, she looked down at the cardboard box and began to speak.

"He knew what was going to happen to him, Harry did. He was one of the first physicists at Los Alamos to figure it out. He guessed it when he was at Hiroshima in September of '45, and though it took years to prove, he was right. Harry guessed that as many people would die of the radiation as died of the blast, and that not all of them would be Japanese. When he figured out that they were going to continue making bombs at Los Alamos, he just walked away and never looked back. But he brought the radiation with him, and he knew it. It took nineteen years to show up, but it was always there."

She looked up at him, and Rik found himself unable to turn away. Her voice was steady, descriptive not accusatory. "I was the one who wanted to get married. He was twice my age, but he was so full of life." She paused for a moment, searching for the right word. "Focused, ya know—as if he didn't have time for anything but life! He told me what he thought was going to happen, but I didn't care. I thought I'd have more life with him than I'd get from a hundred years with anyone else. And I did! It was about ten years ago when the first signs of anything else appeared. One day we looked at one another and we both knew without saying that there was only one way for that life to continue. And the next year we had Barbara, and two years after that, Susan. And now I'll have Harry forever."

Ellen's fingers fumbled with the cover to the box. She was in the shadows now, but her eyes still gleamed in the fading light. "Harry wanted Lynne to have this—and you too, of course." Looking down into the box, Rik could see what appeared to be a twisted piece of ceramic. Reaching in, he retrieved the side handle teapot, with its still-faithful crane etched into the glaze and the radiation-melted lid firmly screwed into the top.

"Harry could see you weren't happy at the JC, but he thought that was because you didn't understand that you can't run away from what's wrong in the world. You'll always carry it with you, and that the important thing was not the cards you were dealt but the way you played them. And Lynne—he knew Lynne knew what was important when she thought past the radiation, past the teapot, and concentrated on the children. It's a great teapot, Rik! What it was exposed to, we can't even imagine, but it didn't break, Rik. That's why Harry wanted you and Lynne to have it. It's a little beat up, but it makes a hell of a pot of tea, Rik! You can still do with it what needs to be done."

*****

The room was in semi-darkness when Rik re-entered it. Lynne sat up on the bed, her knees tucked up under her chin. The light of the cathode tube flickered on her face, and her eyes, dull and unfocused when he left the room, were lustrous and glowing, fixed on the television screen. Rik turned to see what she was looking at.

Through the open gates of a magnificent stadium a young man dressed in white top and white shorts trotted into view. In his right hand he carried what appeared at first to be a fencing foil, gripping in his fist the pommel beneath the guard, with the blade pointed vertically toward a cloudless sky. The top of the metal reed was blunted, and a flame glistened where there should have been a point. Like the youth who carried it, the torch was slender, handsome, and steadily moving forward.

The volume on the television was down, but Lynne provided the commentary.

"His name is Yoshinori Sakai, he's nineteen years old, and he's the last of the runners to carry the Olympic torch. All the other runners were born after the War, so the Japan they know is all new, you see. But Sakai wasn't born *after* the war; he was born on August 6th, 1945—in *Hiroshima*! In the midst of all that death, he came to life. He is straight and strong, and full of hope! Isn't that wonderful? That life goes on?"

She reached out her arms to him, and he sat on the bed next to her, and she curled herself into his chest.

"We'll have another baby, won't we, Rik? It'll be a little girl and we'll call her Annie after Marti and Michael's Annie. And she won't be blue; she'll be straight and strong, and she'll run in the sun and we'll see her shadow. And Barbara and Susan will come over and babysit with her. She'll wait for them after school, and I'll make cookies for them. That's what will happen, won't it, Rik? That's what life will be like, won't it?"

*****

At the top of a stadium's steps on the other side of the world, a handsome young man was lighting the Eternal Flame.

*****

A month of nights, a year of days,
Octobers drifting into Mays;
I set my sails as the tide comes in
And I just cast my fate to the wind.

I shift my course along the breeze;
Won't sail upwind on memories.
The empty sky is my best friend,
And I just cast my fate to the wind.

DANTON ON THE KAW

Georges Danton was a leading figure in the early days of the French Revolution. After engineering the slaughter of the aristocrats and the overthrow of the monarchy in August 1792, Danton became minister of justice and virtual head of the Provisional Executive Council. In July 1793 he left the Committee of Public Safety, advocating a conciliatory foreign policy and an end to the Reign of Terror, and attacking the dictatorship of the Committee. On March 30, 1794—six days after guillotining the extremist Jacques Rene Hebert and his faction—the Committee arrested Danton and the Moderates (whom they termed "Indulgents"). When it appeared that Danton's powerful oratory at the trial might turn the Convention against the Committee, it ruled that dissent against the Court was "counterrevolutionary," a capital crime. Danton and his followers were executed April 5th. He was not yet 35 years old. Maximillian Robespierre, who succeeded Danton as leader of the Committee of Public Safety, followed him to the guillotine three months later.

The play *Danton's Death* was written early in 1835 by Georg Buchner, a German medical student who was in hiding because of revolutionary activities inspired by the anti-establishment uprisings of 1830. Composed on a basement dissecting table in his physician father's house, *Danton's Death* was Buchner's only literary work (which included the plays *Leonce and Lena* and *Woyzeck* and the novella *Lenz*) to be published in his lifetime, although it was not performed until 1902. Buchner received his doctorate in Strasbourg and was teaching at the University of Zurich when he died of typhus in February 1837. He was less than 24 years old.

*****

"I pounced on the globe and rode it bareback like a runaway horse, I gripped its flanks with my legs, I clutched its mane, my hair streamed above the abyss, I shouted in terror: And woke."

--Danton's Death, Act II, Scene 5

10:38 p.m., April 20, 1970

The light flickered on the screen a few feet away and then resolved itself into the image of a white horse racing across a prairie field toward the camera. It was a half-length away when the camera angle suddenly changed, and the viewer found himself sprinting parallel with the horse, in tandem but growing closer and closer until seemingly nothing separated the two. It was thrilling, and the adding to the picture of hoof beats that increased in speed and volume, the closer the camera got would only make it more so.

Thrilling—but wrong! Rik sighed and rubbed his eyes. Above the camera, light flickered inexplicably on the ceiling of old Flint Hall, the home of the University Film Department. He had the room and the editing equipment for the evening only because a TV production graduate student had sneaked him in. The use of multimedia in his stage production which had seemed daring as an idea looked clumsy and obvious on screen. The scene wasn't about a horse; it was about Danton's subconscious recognition that he was being carried along by forces of history outside of his control. The use of a literal image only cheapened the theatrical moment. The time and a fair portion of the already small production budget had been wasted. Rik remembered a parody he had once written of an old poem from grade school.

"Listen my children and you shall hear
Of the midnight ride of Paul Revere
On the eighteenth of April in Seventy-five
Hardly a man is now alive
Who remembers that famous day and year:

When out of the past
Came the thundering hooves
Of the great horse Silver
The Lone Ranger rides again!

The wall turned white in front of him and the finished film slapped noisily against the spinning rear reel. Rik clicked off the camera, and rubbing his eyes again, looked up. Light continued to flicker on the ceiling, and he found his gaze drawn toward the high window on the far wall. The night sky was alive with glints of red and yellow.

On Jayhawk Boulevard, the shouts that the stone walls of Flint Hall had muffled swept over him in waves. In the distance an ever nearer siren and belching horn marked the ascension of a fire engine up the curving streets of Mt. Oread. Smoke and flames could be seen through the windows of the upper two levels of the Memorial Student Union. Some people were already emerging from the building carrying furniture and works of art, while others, uncertain as to their role, grouped in the flickering shadows that surrounded it. Instinctively, Rik moved toward an open doorway. A uniformed security guard rose up in front of him.

"Don't even think about it!"

Rik hesitated. "I'd like to help," he said.

The guard sneered at the bearded young man in a T-shirt and cutoff jeans. "Help yourself, you mean. We've got a pretty good idea of the kind of help your kind is. Just move back and you won't get hurt."

Rik suddenly saw himself in the other man's eyes. Frustrated, he stepped forward. "You're going to need as many hands as you can get." He could sense as much as see a mirthless grin spread across the cop's face, as he slid a side-handle baton off his belt.

"C'mon," he said in a low, challenging voice.

Rik stepped forward again. A hand gripped his right arm above the elbow.

"Let the piggy go play in the mud."

He turned. Silhouetted in the headlights of the fire truck was a young woman in a muslin blouse and skirt made almost transparent by the harshness of the light behind her.

Her features were lost in shadow, but the mane of fine hair on her head seemed as much aflame as the Union itself. Rik followed her back to the sidewalk, and when he looked over his shoulder, the guard had melted back into the building.

"This is terrible," he said.

"It's no worse than they would have done to us," she answered with a phrase so melodramatic that Rik wanted to laugh. Her gaze was intense, and her eyes seemed to change colors in response to the flashing lights around them.

"You can't be serious."

"Yeah? Tomorrow morning the *Journal-World* will blame this fire on the students, just like this morning they said the protest at Allen Fieldhouse proved we had no respect for education! Well, they're right about that! Whatever it is that they're trying to teach us, we've got no respect for it."

Rik stared into a face framed by high Slavic cheekbones which he knew, even in this light, was flushed with anger. "Who's they?" he managed.

She looked at him, amazed. "Amerika, with a capital K! The ruling classes who buy bullets with our money and wash their ideas down the world's throat with our blood. They start a war every time their power is threatened, and the media convinces the young and the poor to fight it. Three birds with one stone! They get the world's raw materials and use up anybody who doesn't gain from it. Haven't you ever read *1984*?"

Rik struggled to simultaneously absorb the attack and deflect it. "What's this got to do with burning down the Student Union?"

The girl drew back, her voice suddenly cold and judgmental. "How old are you?"

"Thirty-one."

She sneered. "That explains it. Forget the beard! You're one of *them* now, waiting for your nice little secure teaching job. Tenure in five years. A cabin by the lake in twenty-five. Do you know who's in hock to the CIA? The National Council of Churches, the National Student Organization, the American Newspaper Guild, and the American Friends Service Committee! And when my brother kicks open the door of some hooch in Nam and wastes a mama-*san* and her baby, they'll all say it's because they didn't want to be free. And if he raises a stink about it, they'll make *him* take the fall. Or maybe you get your war information from *Beetle Bailey*?"

A second and a third engine had joined the fire fight on the hill. A police cordon was forming around the Union. Rik felt the pressure to fall back along the street, and when he turned his back to the fire, the girl was gone.

"EVERYONE WHO IS NOT PART OF THE OFFICIAL EMERGENCY RESPONSE TEAM, PLEASE VACATE THE AREA!" A bullhorn overrode any human response. "ANYONE WITHOUT AN OFFICIAL REASON TO BE WITHIN THE ESTABLISHED PERIMETER WILL BE SUBJECT TO ARREST."

Out of the shifting waves of people retreating down the

hill, the white-gowned figure momentarily re-emerged.

"Hey Rik," she called. "What time is rehearsal tomorrow night?"

*****

"Shall spiritual nature be more considerate in its revolutions than physical nature? Shall we not expect an idea to destroy what opposes it as well as a law of science? Shall an event take place which revolutionizes the entire shape of moral nature and shed no blood?"

--Danton's Death, Act I, Scene 12

"I just don't think you get this play."

Rik sat in a chair facing the desk in a University office, in what was the latest in a seemingly endless line of being called to account. "That's possible," he ventured.

The office was spacious. Eight-foot bookshelves faced one another the length of the side walls. In the rear, a window stretching from waist-high to the ceiling was framed by a coffee table and a coat rack. A slim, bespectacled, man approximately his own age paced self-importantly in front of it.

"It's about Revolution! It's about the necessity to destroy a state apparatus which will only allow those who unconditionally believe in it to live. It's *1984*, and even the meaning of words has been undermined. It's a metaphor for America's narcissistic, capitalistic, imperialistic, horseshit foreign policy."

Rik shifted uneasily in his chair, glancing at the academic comfort which surrounded him. He believed in stage action; metaphor was something critics drew after the fact. Fred Espinoza was the faculty advisor on Rik's play, his rising academic star based on two items—his editorship of an anthology of Latin American plays (thus satisfying the

Department's need of visible "diversity"), and his direction of an evening's worth of scenes from American drama which had drawn the ire of everyone from Bob Dole to the local branch of the John Birch Society. In Espinoza's defense, the Students for a Democratic Society and the College of Fine Arts had locked arms in a rare unified defense of academic freedom— the SDS because its grip on the anti-war movement was slipping away, and the CFA to prove its relevance beyond the classroom. Everyone needed a Fred Espinoza to point to with either pride or venom.

Everyone but Rik. State-supported rebels seemed a contradiction in terms for him. Espinoza was often absent from campus, attending conventions which padded his resume and pleased a Department priding itself on the contacts generated. His classes were packed with his acolytes, and seemed to reflect attitude more than substance. Rik doubted that the assigned papers were ever read. He knew they were never returned.

The truth was that he didn't care much for Espinoza's *magnum opus*, *Amerika in Stages*, either, not because of its alleged obscenity and anti-Americanism, but because it was badly constructed and poorly paced. Rik was no lefty, but Mao's Little Red Book was right on that one: "Works of art which lack artistic quality have no force, no matter how progressive they are politically." Any production that could put Clifford Odets, Arthur Miller, and Sam Shephard on the stage and have you glancing at your watch every five minutes was doing *something* wrong.

And yet who was he to argue aesthetics? His production of *Danton's Death* glistened with flop sweat. He could read in his actors' eyes their dismissal of the play as a pointless exercise, could see in their movements resistance to the exterior discipline he tried to impose in place of the internal motivation he was unable to inspire. The charge of "irrelevance", as damning as "Communist" would have been 15 years earlier, was made, proved, and punished in the bored reaction to every rehearsal note.

"That could be," Rik admitted, "but what do I do now?"

"You don't believe in Revolution, do you, Temple? You're a thinker, not an actor." The late afternoon sunlight framed the man behind the desk. "It took Robespierre 12 days to kill Danton. You've been working five months on this play and it's deader now than it's ever been. And that's because you're trying to dissect an idea, not bring a movement to life. A play has to *do* something! I'd shut down this production now, if I thought the University was still going to be open on the day the play is supposed to open, and I'll tell you something else."

"What's that?"

"You intellectuals think you've done your part by attending a Coffee and signing a petition. You imagine that Power's going to pay attention to you because you put your baby in a stroller and take your pretty little wife on a protest march? It might as well be the Easter Parade. Danton died because he wouldn't stand up and fight. There's a New World coming that has to be bought and paid for. And you've got nothing to spend on it but time, and you're wasting that. You've been living off interest so far, but pretty soon you're going to have to decide how to use your principal."

*****

"We know very little of each other. We are thick-skinned creatures—we stretch out our hands, but what is the use of rubbing our hides together?—we are very lonely."

--Danton's Death, Act I, Scene 2

The house was far away from the University—on the east side of town in a working-class neighborhood. In point of fact, the word "working" was something of a misnomer. Unemployment was endemic on this side of the river.

According to Simone, who lived next door, for the thirty-eight children in her son's third grade class there were only two fathers living at home. The only obvious numerical advantage the people there had over the residences that climbed the hill toward Academia was in their variety of skin pigments. White, Black, Indian, Hispanic, Asian—no street went more than a half block without some change in accent, eye slant, or color.

Lynne loved it here. It reminded her of the "Bloody First Ward" in Tripp Lake where she'd grown up, in a house on the edge of town "with a cornfield on one side and a graveyard on the other." She had made a home in the middle of the block, and knew everyone from one end of the street to the other. Taking out the trash, Rik would often find himself greeted warmly by a total stranger, operating only on the awareness that he was Lynne's husband. Nowhere was she known better than at the second-hand furniture store across the street, which supplied many of the discards that came to life again in the rooms she had re-imagined and redecorated. The value she had added to the house was even appreciated by their landlord, who occasionally ignored the deadline for a payment that was already amazingly low because—as he explained to Rik—he "didn't want to rent to niggers or spics."

As he came up the steps she met him at the door, a finger to her lips. Beyond, in the gathering shadows of the living room, Rik could see their daughter, Annie, a blonde replica of her mother, asleep on the couch. Lynne quietly closed the door and led him to the porch swing in front of the picture window, through which she could see the child.

"I'm sorry I'm so late," he apologized. "It was the only time Fred could see me. And I can't take long. I have to go back for rehearsal."

"You can sit down for a minute, can't you? She wanted so badly to stay awake long enough to see you, but she was so worn out she fell asleep right after I fed her." There was tension in his wife's voice and in the hand that drew him down next to her.

"What did the new doctor say?"

"She's going to order tests." There was a catch in Lynne's voice, and she spoke faster, without raising her voice. "I like her, I really do! At least she's kind—not like Dr. Cook. She's not jumping to conclusions either—not like he did about the retardation! She says it could be a hearing problem, or at worst an operable tumor of some kind. That would explain her withdrawal and why she's so slow in developing speech. There'll be x-rays, of course. The doctor's going to clear a place on her schedule day after tomorrow. It won't take long to find out. You can go with me, can't you?"

Even before she had finished, she could see in his face the reluctance to commit. "I don't know. Is it in the afternoon? That's the day I teach. And I have production meetings beginning at three. I'll try."

Lynne's eyes flashed. "I think this is more important!" Then she recomposed herself, and looking through the window at the sleeping child, spoke more calmly. "Sit with me for a moment, please, and then I'll put your supper on. There'll be an extra helping of pork and beans. There was a five-gallon can dented over at the Van Camp's outlet and it was taken off the line. Todd up the block shared it with everybody on this street. You'll be so tired when you come home. I want to talk with you now."

She paused and Rik tried not to look at his watch.

"Yes, I could take Annie to the doctor by myself, or Simone could go with me. But that's not the problem! We've been telling ourselves that Annie would outgrow whatever is happening to her. But she won't—it's something, and soon, hopefully, we'll know what it is. And then we'll have to deal with it. We don't know if anything can be done, and if it can, we don't know how long it will take or how much it will cost."

Rik interrupted, impatient. "I know all that—"

"Please!" She raised her hand to his chest. "Let me finish.

I've been thinking about it ever since we got home from the doctor's office. We've got the student insurance from the University, but if that gets used up, all we've got is your teaching stipend and the little I get from grading papers from the University Extension course. And that's been barely enough to take care of us week to week. I could look for a full-time job, but we'd still have to pay somebody to look after Annie, and she's upset easily right now."

She paused. Rik looked at her expectantly, but her next subject caught him off guard. "Have you done any work on your dissertation lately? Because we may not be able to live like this much longer."

Rik felt himself flush in the semi-darkness. "You know I haven't. We agreed on this! I'm writing on documentary theatre at Stoke-upon-Trent in England. I've got an internship there beginning a year from now. I'd be there already if I'd found a way to bring you and Annie with me!"

Lynne raised her voice. "You may have to find something else! Something that doesn't require going overseas. What if Annie needs long term treatment? How are we going to pay for that? If you found another subject, if you quit the play—it's not going well, you said so yourself—if you start writing now, you'd be a solid ABD by fall. You could get a teaching job, you did before. Maybe not exactly what you wanted, but—"

"What I had before?" He was standing over her now. "What I had before is why I came back here now!"

From the depths of the living room a piercing wail ascended into the night sky. Instantly Lynne was past him and through the doorway, emerging a moment later clutching to her breast a red-faced child struggling for the breath to release yet another terrified shriek of the abandoned.

The mother sat in the porch swing, rocking vigorously back and forth, alternating kisses with coos of comfort. "It's all right, baby! It's all right. Mama's here. She didn't go anywhere. She was right here all the time. She wouldn't ever leave you alone!"

*****

"We all have pleasure in something—in bodies, in pictures of Christ, in flowers, in playing games... the longing is the same... the people who get the most pleasure have to pray the most."

--Danton's Death, Act I, Scene 4

Marianne sat in a plush chair in the green room, pensively studying her script. Her feet were pulled up underneath her and the long skirt of her white lacy dress dipped emptily over the chair cushion and down to the rug. She held the book in both hands and the bell sleeves of her scoop-necked blouse fell away from her shoulders, while colorful fabric bracelets led the way up one arm to a psychedelic-painted index fingernail paring away a page from its fellows, and a brow-high flowered headband struggled mightily to hold a mane of red-brown hair clear of a pale broad forehead.

From across the room Rik studied her intently. At first glance she was innocence personified in her formless and concealing white dress. A step closer, however, and the innocence became more studied. The extended skirt clung lightly to the drawn-up legs and the curve of a hip stressed the otherwise loose fabric on the side closest to him. The restrained hair had an intensity all its own and the shadowy present breasts behind the embroidered neckline drew more attention by implication than they would have by open display. As he watched, a sensuous lower lip protruded forth in response to her concentration on the lines, and he became aware that his observation of her was simultaneously intrusive and distancing—a cognitively dissonant blend of Pre-Raphaelite purity and pornography.

In that moment Rik knew why he had cast her.

154

They sat opposite of one another: Marianne, less confident with the script than she was toward any man; Rik, grateful for a text which allowed him to express himself fully, if not openly.

"Why do I have to play all three women?"

"For the same reason that all the crowd scenes are done as puppet shows, some of the characters are introduced through magic lantern daguerreotypes, and some scenes are just voiceovers on top of projections. It's an experimental production in a small theatre. Every actor doubles except Danton and Robespierre. You just happen to triple because none of the three main women characters are on stage at the same time. Even the street women in the puppet shows are played by men."

Rik paused to see if the explanation was sufficient. It was not.

Marianne frowned. "What about Marion? The prostitute? She was a young girl, she had a lover, and he committed suicide. What's the point of that?"

"The point is that being a prostitute doesn't make her guilty." She looked at him quizzically and Rik chose his words carefully. "She came of age sexually, and that was the defining aspect of her existence." He rose and moved to the rear of her chair, leaning over her shoulder, searching for a line in the text. An unfamiliar scent invaded his nostrils, and it was a moment before he could find the place in the script. "Read here."

She bowed her head to the task.

"Then, one year... spring came, and there was something happening all round me, in which I had no part... but I had to breathe in the strange atmosphere of it that nearly smothered me. I would look at my body... I felt torn in two and melted together again. A boy used to come to the house. He was pretty, and said foolish things. I never knew what they meant, but they made me laugh."

Rik leaned forward, until his face was next to hers. "Now read here."

"I was like a sea, which swallows everything and drags it deeper and deeper. There was only one thing that I could feel—all men melted into one body. It was my nature. How can you escape yourself?"

"Now here!"

"Other people have Sundays and working days, six days for living and one for praying, they feel something on their birthdays and when the New Year comes. I don't understand that. I feel no change, no holidays, I am one thing always, an endless longing and grasping, a fire, a stream, a hunger. My mother died of horror... people pointed their fingers at me... that's stupid... we all have pleasure in something—in bodies, in pictures of Christ, in flowers, in playing games... the longing is the same... the people that get the most pleasure have to pray the most..."

"And Danton says: *'Why can't I hold all the beauty of you inside me?'"*

She turned to look at him. *"Danton, your lips have eyes."*

*****

"The Revolution is offering me retirement, though rather differently than I imagined."
-- Danton's Death, Act III, Scene 1

There had been a spring rain the night before and the neatly trimmed turf of Memorial Stadium was beginning to show muddy scars from the feet of the crowd which milled aimlessly around the platform and microphone at the center of the field. Rik moved from group to group, making mental notes of student comments.

"They ought to have scheduled a football game so the team would know what it's like to play in front of a crowd."

"If they close down the University, will I lose all my spring semester credits?"

"My folks have been after me to play it safe and come home, but when they see my GPA I'll really be in danger."

"Is the chancellor really going to come out and take the vote?

"I'm from Sedgwick County, and our sheriff is running for attorney general. He promised to 'jump feet first into the drug-ridden KU hippie communes.'"

Rik was contemplating following up the last statement, when he felt a tap on his shoulder. It was Stan Stawiki, a law student who had unexpectedly shown up for *Danton* auditions and had been rewarded with the role of Robespierre.

"They tell me that today's crowd numbers 15,000, which should make it the summer's most popular on-campus event prior to opening night of *Danton's Death*.

"Why, is the National Guard coming?"

"If they finish their training at Kent State in time."

"Somebody was just talking about the sheriff of Sedgwick County."

"Vern 'Law' Miller? 'The Super Sheriff?' Why he's the talk of the Law School. Mostly disbelief that he ever got his J.D. But he's not our problem yet."

"What's that? *Danton's* Committee of Public Safety?"

"Pretty close, actually. The Board of Regents. Have you ever heard of Henry Bubb?"

"Sounds like a cartoon character—a cousin to Elmer Fudd?"

Stan responded with a sound halfway between a laugh and a snort. "'Kill the Wabbit. Kill the Wabbit!' You're pretty close again. He's a Board of Regents member who has come up with a solution to campus problems which brings together the students *and* the National Guard.

"I'm afraid to ask."

"As well you might be. Regent Bubb thinks that every student should be made to attend classes—at the point of a bayonet, in necessary. Wait a minute. Who the hell is that?"

Rik turned around to see a towering young black man mount the speaker's platform and take the microphone in his hand like a rock singer, quieting the crowd with the sheer command of his presence.

"My name is Jacob Jefferson," he began. "Some of you know me by my nickname, 'Tiger,' and some of you know me as the President of the Black Student Union. What you may not know is that I've lived in Lawrence all my life. And while most of you are here because of the Vietnamese War—I won't say the war <u>in</u> Vietnam, because the war is being fought right here on campus and on a thousand other campuses around the country—I'm here to fight another war. A war that will decide where I can go eat, where I can swim, where I can go to school, and where I can live. It even decides if I'm a football player—which I used to be—what position I can play and whether I can see on the sidelines a cheerleader the same color that I am."

The young black man paced back and forth on the speaker's stand, working his audience like a veteran preacher. "You may be sympathetic to my situation or you may not. But chances are you think your opposition to the Vietnam War is different from my experience of racial prejudice. It's not. For young black men like me Vietnam is just another example of racial prejudice—not just prejudice against the Vietnamese, but prejudice against me. You think of Martin Luther King, Jr., as a Civil Rights martyr, but Dr. King realized that Vietnam was a Civil Rights issue. He said the war effort takes 'the black young men who have been crippled by our society and sends them eight thousand miles away to guarantee liberties in South Vietnam which have been denied to them in Southwest Georgia, East Harlem,' and, though he didn't say it, in Lawrence, Kansas."

The crowd roared in appreciation. "So I'm not asking to stop opposing the Vietnamese War abroad or at home. I'm asking to remember you're fighting alongside of another group of Americans who too often have been invisible to you—to remember that the ideals you're trying to uphold in Vietnam also need to be upheld right here in Memorial Stadium.

Now, let's take a vote." With that, Tiger Jefferson wheeled around toward the opposite side of the field, where a double cordon of black young men escorted a man in a rumpled blue suit some of the crowd recognized as Chancellor Lawrence Chalmers.

"I was hoping he wouldn't actually come," Stan Stawiki said gravely.

"Who, Jefferson?" Rik was astonished. "He wasn't just articulate. He was magnificent!"

"No, Chalmers," Stan answered. "If he stands up there and lets the students decide whether or not the University stays open, the Board of Regents will never forgive him. His ass will be grass."

*****

"She has blessed me with a baby girl."
"Wrong! She has given the Republic a daughter."
--Danton's Death, Act II, Scene 2

Rik stood at the rear gate which opened from his yard onto the alleyway and watched his three-year-old daughter race from one end of the yard to another—from the sandbox to the back porch to the brick grill. She stopped, looking up at the chattering squirrel in the tree above.

She seemed happy enough, paying no attention to her solemn father. Exhausted, Annie had slept all the way home from Kansas City. Her mother had carried her into the house, while Rik walked down the back road as far as the Black Student Union and back, trying to shake the mood the trip had left him with.

They had gone to the University of Missouri in Kansas City, which had one of the finest hearing centers in the country. Lynne had gone in with Annie to have her hearing aids fitted, leaving her father to pass the time with an intern who, whatever his height and his expertise, was probably younger than Rik.

Nervous, he had made some comment about Annie's sweetness and pliability.

The young doctor flashed a thin smile and leaned backward, looking down his nose:

"You realize, of course, that she'll never go to a regular school."

He never relayed this assessment to Lynne, who was already making plans to enroll Annie at the hearing clinic of the University of Kansas.

Rik looked up from his place at the gate to see a smiling Lynne crossing the lawn to pick up Annie, both of them entranced by the equally curious squirrel looking down at them. Lynne turned toward Rik, and Annie, seeing her father, squealed with delight and held out her arms. Lynne walked over to him and Rik took Annie in his arms. The girl twisted around and pointed, eager to share the squirrel with everyone.

"You should have seen her in the house," Lynne said. "She wanted to listen to everything. I switched on the radio and she was amazed by the music, and when I turned on the vacuum cleaner she jumped and then laughed. She could hear the refrigeration when I opened the door, but my favorite was when I held Cleocatra in my lap and Annie listened to her purr.

You never saw such a smile.

"She came outside about fifteen minutes ago. It's a shame you weren't here to see her. Where did you go, anyway? She's been running from one corner of the yard to another, listening to birds, an airplane going over, anything! I don't think I ever paid any attention to that squirrel until she noticed it.

"Isn't it wonderful?" Lynne's face glowed. "I was worried that there would have to be an operation at the very least, and *that* might not work. And all we needed was a pair of hearing aids, and now everything is fine. She'll have a normal life. Won't she?"

*****

"But, back there, in people's minds, 'my memory' is still alive. It is kicking me to death. Me or it?"
--Danton's Death, Act II, Scene 4

"Ham" Smith had an excellent resume as a student actor: Puck in *A Midsummer Night's Dream*, Ariel in *The Tempest*, Tom in *The Glass Menagerie*, Jerry in Albee's *The Zoo Story*, plus a couple of other scenes in classes that Rik had heard about. So naturally Rik was relieved when Ham showed up for *Danton* auditions. He seemed like the perfect Camille, the young friend who was a bridge between Danton and Robespierre. But as the auditions went on and no obvious Danton made an appearance, he moved Ham up to the lead role, where he showed a command of the language and an understanding of the character.

Recently, however, he seemed distracted, and Rik wasn't surprised or too worried when Ham asked to talk with him after rehearsal. In the building of a character, the good actors usually followed a pattern of three steps forward and two steps back, while the great actors take three steps forward and *one* step back. Rik had never worked with a great actor.

However, when Ham slumped down in the chair opposite him, Rik was instinctively aware that his actor's problem was personal, not artistic.

"Do you really think this play's going to open?"

Rik paused. "Call it existentialism, but I'm acting like it will."

"I'd feel a lot less guilty if it didn't." His voice was so low that Rik leaned forward to catch the words. "I mean, it's about the French Revolution. Who even cares?"

There was an edge of bitterness in Rik's voice. "In the words of Mario Savio, 'I'm tired of reading history. I want to make it.'"

"I don't even know who that is."

"Look it up. When are you leaving?"

"Tomorrow."

"Then you're here to say goodbye, not to discuss what would be required to make you stay. Well, thanks for giving me 21 hours to convince Orson Welles to move to Lawrence." Rik got up to go home.

Ham straightened up, his voice regaining some of its usual power: "Rik, I don't think you understand what I'm up against!"

"What *you're* up against?" Nevertheless, a wide-eyed Rik sat down again.

"As far as my family is concerned, I'm here on parole. Now they want me to come home, go to school there and get a degree in business."

Rik struggled to process the information: "Parole? Where's home—and why business?"

Ham impatiently explained the obvious: "Because it's respectable in the community and in the Church. Oh, and they want me to get married as soon as possible."

Rik's blank face was its own question.

Too far along to let the subject go, Ham started again. "I'm Mormon, and home to me is Logan, Utah. That's about 80 miles north of Salt Lake City. Utah State University is there, but I convinced my family that KU had a great business school—which it does—and then I only took theatre courses. I thought I could get away with it because—thanks to my mission—I was over 21 and didn't think my parents would have access to my transcripts. They want me to come home because they think I'm gay and that getting married will cure me."

Another blank look. "Okay, there was a Mormon corporal in my platoon, and he told me what a mission was, and asked me if I wanted to know more about the religion, and I didn't think I did, so I never got to what 'gay' was and how marriage cured it."

"Look it up!" Ham was impatient again, but quickly relented. "Oh, never mind. It's a guy who prefers men to women. It's all because of what happened on my mission. It was in Northern Minnesota where the winters are very cold. Nothing would have happened, but my companion and I had a room with poor heating and cracks in the wall, so we shared a bed. There still wouldn't have been a problem, but my companion got cold feet and that's why we were sent home."

Rik was dazzled by the mixing of metaphors. "I'm still confused by the business degree and the marriage cure."

"Well, my family thinks that business is more masculine than theatre—no offense—and there's a place for me in the family business—plumbing and heating, if you believe it. The Church believes that homosexuals can never go to heaven, and Logan is a big community theatre town, so if I can find a girl who's interested in theatre, maybe I can have the best of both worlds." Ham looked hopefully at his former director. "By the way, my real name is Hyrum, not Hamilton like I told everybody."

Rik stood up slowly and held out his hand. "I apologize, Ha-Hyrum. I *didn't* understand what you were up against, and, it *is* bigger than anything I have to deal with.

"The best of luck, you'll need it."

A grateful smile on his face, Hyrum Smith was out the door before Rik could put the chairs away.

*****

"The city's quiet, the lights are out-- There's a child crying, somewhere near."

--Danton's Death, Act II, Scene 5

The ringing of the phone only added to the pounding in Lynne's head. She was suffering from being the "designated adult in the room." She could do anything, and she was paying the price. Rik had called earlier to ask her to come out and look at the *Danton Death's* costumes. He knew that something was wrong, but couldn't explain it to the costumer—and Lynne could.

This was the Rik who yesterday didn't have time to accompany her on Annie's first trip to the University of Kansas Hearing Center—very probably the worst day in Lynne's life. Annie had cried all the way through the lesson on "voiced" and "unvoiced" sounds—wildly searching the space for her mother, who was sobbing behind the one-way glass in the booth on the far side of the wall. That evening during the bath which had calmed both mother and daughter, Lynne discovered that Annie had in fact taken in the information her nurse had tried to give her. She tried to share her joy with Rik when he came home from rehearsal—a Rik who pitched forward face down on the bed and fell asleep in the middle of her explanation.

The next call that morning had been a plea from the kitchen committee of the "End the War in Vietnam" committee. Could she please take over the cooking for Saturday's fund-raising rally? They'd just become aware that no one who had volunteered to do the cooking actually had a *kitchen*! And after all, Lynne had promised to supply the food that was to be used at the rally. This way she wouldn't have to move it.

Before she could hang up the phone, the one opposite to hers was passed to another committee member, who reminded Lynne it was her turn to mind the fund-raising booth in the mall Sunday. Ordinarily, considering how much of a load she was taking on with the cooking, Lynne would not have been asked to fund-raise as well, but then she always did so well in one of these public events. The committee chair supposed it was because the shoppers in the mall could identify with a middle-class mother in a way they couldn't with fresh young college students.

Lynne bit her lip, about to explain that success depended upon choosing the right place to set up the table and arranging the exhibit in such a way that the shoppers would want to stop and see what was going on—all of which she could easily teach even a fresh young college student. By this time, however, the other woman was already apologizing for being too busy to talk to her and hung up.

The calls of a three-year-old came from the crib in the other room. Lynne poured herself another cup of coffee, noticing that her hand was shaking, and wishing that she had not given up smoking earlier in the year.

The phone rang.

She contemplated pulling it off the wall, but the remembered difficulties of not having a phone when they were graduate students a few years earlier countered the impulse.

"Lynne? Are you there?" A reassuring voice blurred by too many cigarettes was on the line. It was June Lane, her neighbor from Iola, Kansas, where Rik had worked as a community theatre director. The second of fifteen children, she had demonstrated sense enough to limit herself to three— and one of those three was Lynne, who as an only child was initially ill-prepared to be a mother. "I came up to Lawrence to get those government foodstuffs my sister's been hoarding all these years and bring them over to you for the anti-war rally."

They were the only words she got out before Lynne cut her off with a rush of summaries of Annie's hearing problems, her husband's indifference, and her urge to declare war on the "anti-war committee." She paused in mid-sentence as Annie pressed against her leg. (She was getting too big for the crib.) On impulse she dropped to one knee and held the phone to her daughter's hearing aid-plugged ear.

A calm tone greeted mother and daughter. "It looks like this might be a good day for me to do what I've wanted to do for weeks. Why don't I come over to the house and take Annie to the park for lunch and to enjoy the playground? I can bring her back and put her down for her nap, and if you get from your errands on time we'll be able to talk."

A broad smile spread over Annie's face: "Unie," she squealed!

*****

"Somebody once told me about a sickness that makes you lose your memory. Death ought to be like that. With any luck it might be even more serious and make you lose everything. —If only it could!"

--*Danton's Death*, Act I, Scene 9

University of Kansas College of Liberal Arts and Sciences
John Arnold, Interim Dean

May 11, 1970

To: Assistant Instructors
College of Liberal Arts and Sciences

In response to the edict of the Office of the Provost, all classes taught by Assistant Instructors of Liberal Arts and Sciences will end as of 5 p.m., Friday, May 15. Teachers will be compensated for the semester according to the contracts signed, and student grades will be due by the dates specified in the University Calendar.

Assistant Instructors who wish to do so may offer their students **Alternative Courses** to fill out the rest of the semester. All such courses must have the written approval of the Chair of the Assistant Instructor's department and his or her advisor.

*****

"You're telling me that this is your alternative class?"

"That's right."

"What do you call it?"

"The Fifties."

Marianne stood with her back to the classroom window, with the late afternoon sun framing her red-brown hair. Rik marveled at her instinctive actress ability to find a back light which put the focus on her.

"You mean the *Nineteen-Fifties*?"

"That's right."

She shook her head disdainfully. "Who cares about the nineteen-fifties? All that phoniness—*Lassie, Leave it to Beaver*!"

"There was more than that," Rik protested. "What about Korea? Civil Rights and school integration—Rock n' Roll?"

"Nobody cares about Elvis either. He sold out years ago!"

"Just hear me out," he pleaded. Don't make up your mind before you listen to my pitch." Rik moved behind the table at the front of the classroom. Encouraged by the May weather, some of the Alternative classes had moved outdoors, but he felt that would only give whoever showed up an excuse not to pay attention.

Marianne surveyed the items on the table. "Okay, you've got a cassette recorder and a couple of tapes, plus what looks like a clothing box." She reached out a hand. "Can I open it?"

"Not yet. Let's hear the tapes first. You know how everyone always says, 'if older people would just listen to us, they'd understand the way we think and would change the way they act?' Well, I've a got a theory: Before we can change their minds, we have to understand *why* they think the way they do—and the only way to do that is to study what influenced them."

Marianne waved dismissively. "But what they believe doesn't make any sense!"

"That doesn't mean they don't believe it, and unless we can change their minds about the war at home, we'll never stop what's happening in Vietnam." Rik put the first tape in the recorder.

Marianne shrugged her shoulders. "Like Johnny Carson says, 'If you buy the premise, you'll buy the bit.'" She sat down in the front row. "Show me what you got."

Rik pressed the "On" button, and the tinny voice of Gene Autry filled the room.

People say that I'm a bit old-fashioned.
Just the same, I'm gonna have my say.
If we all believe in God and country,
Ev'rything will be OK.

With the Bible on the table and the flag upon the wall,
Neighbors, that's the answer to it all.
They're the backbone of the nation, and we'll always find
*   salvation,*
With the Bible on the table and the flag upon the wall.

If a man has neither God nor country,
What a price that man has had to pay.
If he had his life to live all over.
You can bet that he would say:

With the Bible on the table and the flag upon the wall,
Neighbors, that's the answer to it all.
They're the backbone of the nation, and we'll always find
  salvation,
With the Bible on the table and the flag upon the wall.

"And that was from the Fifties?" Marianne was incredulous. "I don't know which was worse—the sentiment or the music! Let's look in the box." Before Rik could object, she had ripped the tape off the container and opened it to reveal the contents.

"What in God's name are these things made of—rubber?" Her hands shuffled quickly through an assortment of vintage undergarments as though afraid the material might stick to her fingers.

"Nylon," Rik answered, "but not as fine as in your stockings." He separated the garments and laid them out on the classroom table: a corset, girdle (with attached garters), and finally, a long line bra with padded bullet breasts.

"You're telling me people wore these things."

"I'm telling you that there are women in your family who are still wearing them. Look," he paused, trying to gather his thoughts. "The National Guard shooting at Kent State on May 4th—do you remember what people said about the girl student protesters?"

"I remember the sign saying the same thing would be happening in River City in four days. Or was that in *Harambee*?"

"Several middle-class women in the city of Kent were

quoted as saying, "You know that those girls weren't wearing any underwear."

Marianne looked disgusted. "What's that got to do with the shitty cowboy song? Sometimes I don't wear any underwear, and when I do you can't tell. That's the style. Are you telling me those women *resent* my freedom?

Rik snorted. "Yes, but there's more to it than that." He held up the corset, which extended from the breasts to below the hips. "Something like this acts as both a symbol and protection."

"Something like that is hot, and I don't mean that in a good way."

"You're not seeing the corset with the eyes of a 1950 nice young woman." Rik tried not to sound impatient. "The corset is so hard to get off that you can rule out spontaneous sex. It both protects your virginity and is a symbol of your virginity."

Marianne had an "ah ha" look in her eyes. "Whereas the most important thing in their lives—virginity—is meaningless to us because we have the pill. Which means that 1950 women can simultaneously see us as satanic sluts, and be jealous because we can break the rules without earthly consequences. Which means that the women of Kent might see the National Guard mowing us down as punishment from God." Her jaw dropped at the audacity of her own conclusions.

Rik was awed. "Brilliant. Now tell me how this lesson applies to *Danton's Death*."

Marianne chewed her lip momentarily. "There is only Good and Evil in the world. The Proletariats are Good and the Nobility is Evil. If—like Danton—you're no longer interested in eliminating Evil, you are Evil. The friend of my enemy is my enemy. Enough of that, what's the other tape?"

"Pretty unnecessary at this point." Rik took on a wry grin. "It's a 1952 radio broadcast of *I was a Communist for the FBI*. A bunch of college students at a county fair destroy a Communist literature booth because it's Un-American."

"Great." Marianne was happy again. "Let's schedule that for the next anti-Vietnam rally, only we'll put the Board of Regents in the booth."

*****

"You roared wonderfully, Danton. If you strained yourself like that earlier, we'd not be in this state now."
--Danton's Death, Act III, Scene 7

Rik fought to clear his head of the bad dreams of the night before. Atypically, once he did fall asleep, a pitying Lynne had left him there while she and Annie went to the grocery store. Now Stan Stawiki was on the phone, making no sense at all.

"I'm telling you to get your ass in gear and meet me down at the County Courthouse, *mach schnell*!"

"That's not even Polish. Can I have breakfast first? I haven't even showered."

"I needed a second language for my minor. You can eat afterwards. Nobody cares how you smell, and if you want to do your play without a Danton, go back to bed."

Rik was suddenly wide awake. "Where's the County Courthouse?"

"111 East, 11th Street—just around the corner from Massachusetts. And get here *tout suite*. (That's my third language.)"

Rik hastily dressed, and just as he entered the driveway, Lynne returned with Annie and the groceries. It took ten minutes from the carrying in of the groceries to reach the end of Massachusetts Street. The VW "hippie bus" skidded around the corner through a yellow light and into the Courthouse parking lot. A moment's panic because of an uncertain set of brakes, and the vehicle was in a space reserved for court officials.

"Ten o'clock court date!" he yelled at a startled uniformed

attendant, and sprinted toward a frantically waving Stan Stawiki waiting at the Courthouse main door.

"Now here's what you have to do." Stan's voice was low, but urgent. "When I poke you, you stand up and say to the judge: 'your honor, I'd like to offer the defendant the opportunity for community service.' Have you got that? Now let's go in."

"What's community service, and who's the defendant? What's it got to do with replacing Danton?

"Shhh!" Stan was already headed down the aisle. A black-robed figure was headed to the podium from somewhere in the left rear of the courtroom. Down front Rik could see a familiar back being spoken to by someone he guessed was a lawyer or public defender. He sat down next to Stan in an aisle side seat halfway to the back.

The judge opened the session.

"Is the defendant Jacob Jefferson present?" Rik looked inquiringly at Stan, who answered under his breath. "You said yourself that he was a magnificent speaker."

Both of the men down front rose, and the white man replied. "He is, your honor."

"The defendant has been charged with malicious mischief in fomenting the takeover of the University of Kansas Memorial Stadium at a time when a key vote concerning the future of the University was in progress. He has offered no defense for his actions and must now be prepared to accept the consequences. The Court sentences the defendant to thirty days in the County jail and a fine of seventy-five dollars."

Stan poked Rik sharply in the ribs, and he leaped to his feet.

"Your honor, I like to offer the defendant the opportunity for" (he paused for a desperate second) "community service."

The two heads down front snapped around, and the judge raised his eyebrows. "Would the gentleman please come down front?"

Rik came down to the area left and below the judge, followed closely by Stan. An anxious public defender and a glowering defendant took the spot to the right.

"And you are, Sir?" The judge was looking at Stan.

"I'm the gentleman's legal advisor, your honor."

The judge returned his gaze to Rik. "Would you be so kind as to explain the manner of the community service you're proposing for the defendant."

"Yes, your honor." A trickle of sweat ran down behind Rik's ear as he looked at a stone-faced Stan for confirmation of his assumptions. "I'm the producer of an event at the University and I believe that the defendant would be of inestimable value in the carrying out of that event." He could see Stan relax.

"And where would this event take place?"

"In Murphy Hall, your honor."

"And what time frame would be involved?"

"Adding up the time for preparation and the presentation itself, I'd say about thirty days, sir."

A deep voice interrupted from the other side of the podium. "Say, judge, I don't know anything about this community service thing and I'm not sure I want to go off with somebody I wouldn't know from Adam!"

The public defender was speaking into his client's ear in a stage whisper Rik could hear across the room: "Look, Tiger, unless you want to spend thirty days in jail, or you have someone else with a similar proposal, I suggest that you at least listen to these guys!"

Tiger Jefferson shrugged off the white man and turned his six-five frame towards Rik and Stan. He spoke low, but it was through clinched teeth. "All right, I'm gonna listen to what you ofays have to offer, but it better be good. I've been in the clink before, and I'd rather go back than be made a fool of."

*****

"When I was a child. All that effort to feed and clothe me, keep me warm, just to make work for the gravediggers."
--*Danton's Death, Act IV, Scene 3*

Rik felt his irritation rise as he hurried down the steps in Murphy Hall—a guest for dinner that Lynne didn't know, and he would be late again because Fred Espinoza decided this was the only time they could meet. At the foot of the stairs, he looked down the hallway and saw a familiar figure emerge from Espinoza's office.

For a moment a mane of red-brown hair caught the light from a ceiling lamp, and then a young woman slipped into the shadows to adjust her skirt.

"Couldn't wait to share our little bombshell with our esteemed advisor, huh?"

Marianne was unaccountably flustered. "What? Oh hi, Rik. No, he already knew. I just came here for..." She trailed off in mid-sentence, and Rik suddenly put two and two together. The mussed skirt. The coffee conferences on the plaza. Marianne's new political opinions, her change of classes, *and* her change of advisors.

He felt a tinge of jealousy but tried to keep it out of his voice. "Are you sure you've thought this through?"

"I don't know what you're talking about."

"I think you do. He's been married twice. Doesn't that ring any bells for you?"

"Nobody cares about marriage anymore. Some of the most interesting men I know are married. *You're* married!"

In the shadows Rik flushed at her ability to point out his weakness, but persisted. "I know guys like Fred. He'll make a career move soon. Will he take you with him?"

"Would you?" Marianne pursued her advantage. "One, I don't think we've got to that point. And two, I don't think it's any of your business. Now, if you'll excuse me, I have laundry to do. And that's not a metaphor!"

Rik listened to her heels clack up the stairs. Then he turned and knocked on the office door, which opened immediately to reveal its angry occupant.

"What the hell have you done now?"

*****

An hour later Rik climbed the step to his own porch, listening to his empty stomach growl. Lynne met him at the door, a finger to her lips. Tiger Jefferson sat on the couch, his long legs pulled up to his chin, and his attention focused on the floor in front of him. There sat Annie, gravely introducing her dolls to her new audience, naming them one by one, and adding any details that came to her mind.

"Daddy," the little girl squealed and ran over to her father to be picked up. Tiger stood as well, uncertain if he was to be guilty or embarrassed. Annie pointed at her new friend. "I show Tiger my babies."

"We already ate, Hon. Annie was getting hungry, but I can warm up the stew." Lynne reached over and took the little girl into her arms. "Now I think it's time that this young lady was in bed."

Annie wriggled around toward the living room. "Want Tiger to do it," she commanded.

Both parents turned inquiringly to the startled figure by the couch.

"I don't mind if you don't mind."

A few minutes later Annie was in her pajamas and snug in her bed, the doll of her choice rewarded with a place on her pillow. "Want Tiger to sing to me," she pleaded.

Lynne intervened hastily. "I don't think Tiger has time..."

"That's okay. I can do it." Almost immediately the big man began to sing softly.

"Hush little baby, don't say a word.

Papa's gonna buy you a mockingbird.

And if that mocking bird don't sing.
Papa's gonna buy you a diamond ring.

And if that diamond ring is brass.
Papa's gonna buy you a looking glass.

And if that looking glass shows a frown.
You'll still be the prettiest girl in town."

Annie was entranced. "Do you have a little girl at your house?"

"No, I was the oldest of five boys. But I always wanted a sister." Tiger looked thoughtful. "Would you be my little sister?"

"Yes!" Annie answered with a smile as wide as her pillow.

*****

Rik tore into his second helping of stew with almost as much enthusiasm as he had devoured the first. Lynne sat across the table from him, a Coors bottle in her hand, and looking more relaxed than he had seen her in weeks.

"I'm so glad you're working with him."

"He has a reputation as a troublemaker. He's doing community service with me on a misdemeanor charge. Thirty days with me, or thirty days in the county jail."

"You're missing the point." Lynne leaned across the table and took his free hand. "Someone sang that song to him— taught to him! And I'll bet he sang it to his brothers when they were little. And someone taught him to be gentle with small children. Anyone who was raised like that, I'm glad you're working with."

*****

"He redeemed them with his blood. I redeem them with their own. He had the ecstasy of pain. I have the torment of the executioner. Who denies himself the more, he or I?
--*Danton's Death, Act I, Scene 6*

ROBESPIERRE: I say to you, he who stays my arm when I draw my sword is my enemy. His motives are irrelevant.

DANTON: Where self-defense ends, murder begins. I see no reason that compels us to go on killing.

ROBESPIERRE: The social revolution is not yet over. Vice must be punished, virtue must rule through terror.

DANTON: I do not understand the word 'punishment'. You and your virtue, Robespierre! You take no bribes, run up no debts, sleep with no women, always wear a clean coat and never get drunk. Robespierre, you are abominably virtuous. Is there nothing in you, not the merest whisper, that says to you, very softly and very secretly, 'You lie! You lie!'

There was a smile on Rik's face as he called for a break. "Okay, let's take a look at this scene. What does it say to us today?"

The actors looked at one another, and Stan Stawiki cleared his throat.

"In their separate ways, both characters are saying that 'the personal is political.' Robespierre justifies the deaths he causes as the 'birth of a virtuous society,' but because the deaths are literal and virtue is just an idea, he has to embody virtue so that the people will know what it looks like. And since Danton believes in letting people be who they are, he doesn't have to 'embody' anything and suspects that Robespierre's killings are only to cover up his own weaknesses."

"Okay, that tells us about the play. What does it tell us about society?"

Stan looks at Tiger, who gives him a "keep going" smile.

"Well, the real question is why the people allow the Committee of Public Safety, led by Robespierre, to keep killing people. Are they just afraid of the Committee, or is it that the Committee has given them an enemy in place of improving their terrible life styles?"

"So, you've answered your own question. Can you bring it closer to home? Tiger?"

"Well, if Stan is right, we have to ask *why* the people can't see who their real enemy *is*. One possibility is that the enemy keeps changing—as in *1984* when there are three main empires and the country is always at war, and when they change opponents, the media immediately goes to work to help the people forget who they *used* to be fighting. Another possibility is that the enemy *never* changes. What are the last three countries where America has been at war?"

Stan counted off on his fingers: "Vietnam, Korea, and Germany—no, Japan!"

"They're all Asian." Rik had given up as a neutral observer.

"Let me correct you," Tiger gave a tight grin. "They're all *yellow*! Korea was the first modern U.S. war where black and white troops were integrated. And Vietnam? Both of you were in Memorial Stadium a few days ago. What did Dr. King say about Vietnam?"

"What *you* said was that blacks were sent there to ensure that Asians got rights they couldn't get for themselves in America."

"Precisely! And what is our favorite American term for Vietnamese people?"

"Gooks," Rik admitted.

"The only way America could get Blacks to fight for them was by painting them as a color more sub-human than they were."

"So what you were saying at Memorial Stadium was not that black people were invisible, but that the *system* that assumed they were sub-human was invisible."

"Precisely! And Blacks in America—and here in Lawrence—have to keep pointing that out again and again until the system is changed! Do you know how the best restaurants in Lawrence were integrated?"

Rik and Stan looked blank.

"When Wilt Chamberlain was the best college basketball player in the country, and *the* University of Kansas basketball program, bigtime newspaper and network reporters would come from the East to interview him. Wilt would arrange for the big-shot reporters to meet at a segregated restaurant—and rather than get a bad national review, the restaurants would give them service fit for a king, and pick up the tab."

"When I was on leave in '61, and Lynne and I came to visit KU, there was a "Wade In" by a young black man at the municipal swimming pool. It was a Monday. Blacks could only swim on Tuesday and Thursday, after which the pool was drained."

"Langston Hughes lived in Lawrence. In his autobiography he said: 'Misery is when you find out your bosom buddy can go in the swimming pool, but you can't.'"

"And what happens when you block off a football stadium so you can make a speech?"

"You get thirty days for malicious mischief, which you can only work off by taking part in some ofay's ridiculous theatre project. Har de har har!"

*****

"The earth has a thin crust. You could fall through a hole in the middle of the street. One must tread carefully."

--Danton's Death, Act II, Scene 2

Maxwell Street on the Near West Side of Chicago is one of the city's oldest residential areas, and one of its oddest business areas. The birthplace of the Chicago Blues, the Maxwell Street Market is an eclectic mix of handmade projects, resale houseware, and clothing. It has also been imitated all over the United States, including Lawrence, Kansas.

Lynne Temple had turned homemaking into an art form. She made clothes not only for her own family, but for all the offspring of her prolific friends. She was known for stretching a Christmas turkey to a Valentine's Day feast. The rebirth in her hands of the secondhand furniture from across Pennsylvania Street would have been the envy of a baptismal preacher.

However, even Benjamin Franklin needed the occasional spark from the Heavens, which is why one early summer Saturday, Lynne and Annie were on Massachusetts Street taking part in a "Maxwell Street" sale. At first the little girl stayed close to Lynne's legs, but soon the colorful surroundings attracted her interest to the point that she became impatient with her mother's dawdling over half rolls of fabric and incomplete sets of cooking utensils, and looked around to fulfill her own interests.

As for Lynne, each new second-hand table and clothes rack that flowed from the sidewalk into the street carried possibilities for new beauty in her home. She could even see seven months ahead when she discovered a tiny electric Christmas tree, which given a little wiring and a new bulb, would fit perfectly on the tiny dresser in Annie's room. And her ear was delighted by a local band's cover of one of her favorite songs, "You and Me March to the Beat of a Different Drum," by Linda Ronstadt and the Stone Poneys. The only problem was that the drum, however powerful, was not quite in sync with the band. When she looked around, she realized the drumbeat was coming from a group of black-clad marchers up the street. They were carrying what appeared to be a coffin. She also realized that Annie was nowhere in sight.

Lynne dodged from one side of the street to the other, looking behind a J.C. Penny rack where she'd paused before, under a frozen dairy truck where Annie had made a plea.

"Annie!"

Caught between their own shopping concerns and the sound of the ominous approaching marchers, no one paid any attention to her.

Having exhausted every exhibit she could remember, Lynne raced down the sidewalk looking in the windows of whatever stores were open. The marchers were almost abreast when she looked back toward the street—and saw Annie, standing head and shoulders above the crowd.

The bystanders scattered before the drive of the slender mother, who scooped her daughter from the table on which she was standing. Annie ignored her, remaining determinedly focused on the marchers in front of her.

"Hi, Tiger!"

The fierce face of the lead marcher melted as his head turned to the left. "Hi, Annie. Lynne," he nodded—not noticing the gratefulness on the face of the woman who was so happy to be in the presence of someone taught to be gentle with small children.

*****

"The Revolution is like Saturn: It devours its own children."

--Danton's Death, Act I, Scene 5

Entering the dressing room after rehearsal, Rik was surprised to see a young black man and a much older black woman obviously waiting for someone. He turned back to see

Tiger Jefferson coming in after him.

"I didn't mean to spring this on you this way, Rik, but I barely got to rehearsal on time as it was. This is my grandmother, Mrs. Lulu Howard, and this is my brother, Isaac. I thought it was only fair to you to explain what was going on."

Rik stepped forward to shake hands and murmur something appropriate. Both of Tiger's kinfolk looked at him with polite, but obvious, suspicion. A nervous Tiger gestured everyone to sit.

"Isaac here has gotten into a little trouble with the cops—a family trait!" He gave a short laugh, which Rik interrupted.

"I don't think I could justify another community service deal, Tiger."

"We're not asking for anything like that. It's just that you're going to find out about everything sooner or later, and I figured sooner would be better." He gestured toward his brother. "Isaac was one of the brothers who delayed the chancellor coming in that day so that I could speak. The next night I was arrested, and he was pissed off—and went and did something stupid!"

"They didn't have any right to arrest you! You were just a student expressing an opinion. They never would have done it to a white man."

His brother raised a hand to be allowed to continue. "He went up on campus and threw a brick through a Watson Library window, and then ran away. Somebody who was at Memorial Stadium saw him and told the campus cops it was me. Ofay can't tell one black man from another. By the time they figured out that I couldn't have done it because I was already in jail, the cops had gone to our house with a search warrant. They broke in and found Isaac reading a book he grabbed through the broken window."

"*The Autobiography of Malcolm X*, and I only got halfway through it."

"At his court date, the same judge who farmed out me to you, offered him a deal too—two years or three. He just turned nineteen; he could go to jail until he's 21, or he could sign up for three years in the army. Frankly, I don't know which is worse, but he decided he looked better in khaki than in stripes."

"How do I figure in this?"

"I was hoping he might hang around backstage until it's time for him to go. It'll keep him out of trouble. He can move furniture, help Amy with the props. I got him a paperback copy of *Autobiography*. He can finish it in here." Isaac stirred uncomfortably.

"When does he leave?"

"Not before the baptism." Grandmother Howard spoke for the first time, but forcefully. "That will be three weeks come next Sunday at the African Methodist Episcopal Zion Church. Where this boy will be going, we don't know. We do know the Good Lord will be looking after him, but being washed in the Blood of the Lamb will make that certain."

"The play opens later that week," Rik mused.

Lulu Howard fixed him with a stern eye. "In that case, young man, you'd better be there too. I've read the play my grandson is going to be in, and you both are going to need all the help that God can give you."

*****

"Stop thinking altogether if thought's going to turn straight into speech. There are some thoughts that must never, ever be heard."

--*Danton's Death, Act II, Scene 5*

Marianne dawdled over her coffee long enough for Rik to be certain that the casual part of their conversation was about over.

"What do you think of Fred?"

"Why ask me? I may not be neutral on the subject."

She gave a surprisingly relaxed smile. "You may not—and let's just say that I have a hunch as to why. But I've never had a director who was so good at analyzing a character as you are. So let's just pretend that Fred's a character in a play—*Danton's Offstage Life.*"

"Wrong title to begin with. Fred is no Danton. Danton believes in the revolution so much that he would sacrifice himself rather than let it violate its own principles. He could have escaped, but he wanted this showdown more than the Committee of Public Safety did. He knew they couldn't destroy him without revealing their own corruption. That's why Robespierre only survived Danton by three months—and was guillotined upside down so he had to watch the blade fall."

Rik's smile was not as relaxed as hers. He leaned back: "Now you tell me. Do you think that Fred wouldn't have saved himself if he had the chance, or after executing Danton wouldn't have skipped town to Brazil?"

Marianne flushed. "I didn't know the Brazil thing was common knowledge."

"I don't know if it is or not. But the other night when the protesters were at the Military Science Building next door, I was drafted to patrol the floors of Murphy Hall with Fred and Jack Becker. Amazing what you learn if you keep your mouth shut."

"Okay, this time I have two questions for you." Her voice took on more of an edge. "One, can you see the appeal of someone who knows how to survive? Don't you think Julie, Danton's wife, would have preferred a live husband, and not having to commit suicide herself? And, two, do you know what Fred is going to do in Brazil?"

"One, sounds great—until he's put in the position of having to decide who to sacrifice, him or you. Two, haven't the faintest."

"He's got a grant to study censorship."

Rik let out a snort. "That's rich, considering what censorship did to him."

"What did it do? If you mean that tenure block, it was reversed a month later."

"Yeah, did the Board of Regents reverse it for the Law professor who was taking part in anti-war activities? But no, that's not what I meant. You didn't hear about the UNESCO offer?"

"No!" Marianne was perplexed at being out of the loop.

"There was a job open for an educational theatre advisor at the State Department, and Fred was supposed to be first on the list.

Marianne was indignant. "And they cut him out because of those hick objections to *Amerika in Stages*! All of that 'obscenity and anti-American' bullshit!" She suddenly focused on Rik. "No, I can see it in your face. You bought into it too! Tell me, was it jealousy or just stupidity?"

"Neither, I'd like to think. It wasn't the material— Steinbeck, Odets, Miller, Shepard, or any of the songs—and I wasn't trying to suck up to anybody. Fred Espinoza is just not a theatre guy." He watched Marianne's eyes widen, then narrow in disgust.

"He's a director and a scholar. What have you ever done?"

"Nothing, but I know the difference. Fred was hired as a scholar on the basis of two major publications: *Four Latin American Plays* and *Theatre PhDs and their Dissertations*. Fred put the four plays together and found a publisher, but he didn't translate them, and his introduction is as routine as they get. And the other publication is just a bibliography."

On an impulse Rik reached across the table and took the girl's hand. "And then there was *Amerika in Stages*. Can you honestly tell me that was a good production? It wasn't that the material was challenging; it was just that Fred either couldn't meet the challenge, or made no effort to. Ask the people who were involved with putting the show on. Steve Bowdoin wrote the linkage between the scenes, and when some of the scenes had to be replaced because of 'hick objections,' they were directed by Ira Levers.

One of the actors told me that Fred "had no theatre discipline." He never scheduled makeup rehearsals or tried to acclimate the actors to the many different spaces they had to play in. In a two-month tour from Zagreb to Budapest, he never carried any of the 14 bags the company had with them. In Bucharest he missed his own production, going to a Yiddish play at a different theatre."

Marianne looked as if she had been slapped in the face. She withdrew her hand, paused, and made one last effort. "There are a lot of people in his graduate seminar that think he'll be a chair in a big department someday."

"How many of those people would you like to work with— or go to Brazil with?"

Sobered, Marianne stood up. "I asked you to tell me the truth, and you did—as you saw it. Maybe I won't go to Brazil, and I can't go wherever you're going. But wherever I go, I won't be going alone." She turned on her heel and was gone.

*****

"You'd have no trousers at all, if men didn't take down theirs with your daughter. We work with all our parts   Why not *that* part?"

--*Danton's Death, Act I, Scene 2*

"Okay, I know that this is an experimental production in a small space, and using puppet shows reduces the size of the cast we need, but why don't we just eliminate them altogether? Aren't they basically comic relief?" A long rehearsal was nearing its end, and Bobby Harvey, who doubled as Camille and Thomas Paine, was having trouble with the women's voices he'd been assigned.

Rik thought for a moment. "In a way you've just answered your own question. The first puppet show is the second scene in the play. We don't attempt to hide the puppeteers. They're in plain sight. When you come on as "the wife" after being Camille in the first scene, the audience knows to expect double casting. Second, the characters in the puppet shows are the proletariat. They're the swing vote and the majority. They live in misery and they're looking to blame someone for keeping them there. Both the COPS, the Committee of Public Safety" (an actor snickered) "*And* the 'Indulgents'—Danton and his friends--need to keep the proletariat on their side if they want to keep their heads. Now, let's try it again."

2ND CITIZEN: "*They* told us 'Kill the aristocrats, they are wolves!' We hanged the aristocrats from the lanterns. *They* said, 'The King eats your bread.' We killed the King. *They* said, 'The Girondins are starving you.' We carried the Girondins to the guillotine. But who wears the clothes of the dead? *They* do! Our legs are still bare and we're freezing."

1ST CITIZEN: "Death to all who read and write!"

2ND CITIZEN: "Death to all who run away abroad." (A Young Man is introduced among the puppets.)

MULTIPLE VOICES: "He's got a handkerchief!" "An aristo!" "Hang him on the lantern." "To the lantern!"

2ND CITIZEN: "He doesn't blow his nose with his fingers! To the lantern!" (A lantern is lowered.)

YOUNG MAN: "Mercy!"

1ST CITIZEN: "It's only a game! A twist of rope around your

neck for a second. We have mercy, you do not. You murder us for all our lives, murder by work. We hang on the rope and jerk for sixty years. But now we're cutting ourselves free. To the lantern."

Rik raised a hand to stop the action. "Okay, two things. One, when Danton starts to fight back at the end of this act, he knows exactly where to go. He's on a Christian names-basis with the commonest of people. 'The tarts are running at his heels, the crowd hangs about whispering every word he says.' Two, this is the only scene where a live actor makes contact with puppet show characters. That's Robespierre. What does Robespierre have in common with the proletariat that Danton doesn't? The proletariat don't enjoy life because of their poverty. Robespierre deliberately doesn't enjoy life. His virtue is that he would destroy those who make the proletariat aware of their poverty. Danton enjoys life. His virtue is his recognition that killing others won't make your life better." Rik gestures for Stan Stawiki, who plays Robespierre. "Come over here, Stan, and give us that last speech."

ROBESPIERRE: "Poor virtuous people! You do your duty, you sacrifice your enemies. Only by your own self-destruction can you fall. Your enemies know that. But your legislators keep watch. Their eyes are infallible, they guide your hands, and from the hands of the people there can be no escape. Come with us to the Jacobin Club. Your brothers will open their arms to you, we will put your enemies on trial for their lives."

Rik clapped his hands. "Thanks, Stan. That's it for today. Remember when you leave here that your leaders may be more concerned with their own welfare than yours. Right and wrong may not be determined by local values, but personal danger may be."

*****

"My life has no beginnings, no endings. All I know is an endless longing and grasping, an endless fire, an endless river."

--Danton's Death, Act I, Scene 5

Marianne paced back and forth, snapping her fingers, gearing herself up to begin the scene. Then she stopped and turned to Rik. "Before we start, I've got a question. Does Danton love his wife, and if so, why does he go to Marion?"

Rik hesitated, always reluctant to be a man giving a character analysis to a woman. He looked at Tiger, who was searching for the answer on the ceiling.

"Since they're both being played by you," he said facetiously, "how could he resist?"

She punched him in the bicep. "Get away from my lamppost, Sport. You're bad for business!"

Tiger rubbed his arm good naturedly. "Well, what are you doing New Year's Eve? It's going to be cold out here."

Rik intervened. "Charming as this all is, suppose we treat Marianne's question seriously."

"Thank you very much!"

"Everybody remembers Marion from *Danton's Death*, even though she has only one scene and Julie has several. But go through those several scenes and see how similar they are. They all express the centrality of Danton in Julie's life, from her first line—'do you trust me?—to her final scene when she takes poison because he's been sentenced to death: 'It's lovely to say goodbye. I've only to pull the door behind me.'"

"But Marion is different. She loves Danton, and yet they both know that he can never fully satisfy her. She gives him something that Julie never can—a goal beyond his reach: 'Why can I never quite hold your beauty, never entirely embrace you?' In that way she is like the revolution to him, something he understands but cannot control."

He stopped for a moment and looked at his actress: "Did you know that for the 18th century French the name 'Marianne' symbolized 'liberty, equality, and fraternity.'"

She looked at him, struggling to find words.

"Never mind, do the big speech."

Marianne paused, lowered her head and began to speak, gaining confidence as the scene evolved: "Spring came. All around me I felt something going on I had no part in. I was lost in my own world, a strange feeling, there was a strange atmosphere around me, it almost choked me. I'd lie on my bed and look at my body, I'd feel like I was double, then I'd merge back into one.

"Then a young man came into the house. He was good-looking, and he said extraordinary things. I didn't understand, but he made me laugh. My mother invited him a lot, and that suited us both. In the end, we said, 'why sit side by side on two chairs, when we can lie side by side between two sheets?' I enjoyed that much more than his conversation, and if the greater of two pleasures is yours for the taking, why not take it? But I began to change. I became a sea, devouring everything, moved by tremendous tides, even in its depths. All men's bodies merged into one, his or any man's. That's how I'm made, can we help how we are made?

"At last he realized. One morning he kissed me as if he wanted to choke me. Then he let me go and laughed. He said he didn't want to spoil my fun. My body was all the finery I had. I'd need it, it would be torn and dirty and worn out sooner than I knew. He left. That evening I was sitting at the window, staring at the sunset. I'm very impressionable. I don't think, I feel things. I was lost in the waves of golden light. Then a crowd of people came down the street with children dancing before it. They were carrying him past in a basket. The light shone on his pale face, his curls were damp. He'd drowned himself. I cried. All of me wept with a terrible longing. Then it was over. Other people have weekdays and Sundays, they work six days and pray on the seventh, they celebrate their birthdays, they make New Year's resolutions. That way of living means nothing to me. My mother died of grief over me, people point their fingers at me.

"They're stupid. Only one thing matters, what gives you pleasure? It may be bodies, pictures of Jesus, flowers, children's toys. It's all the same. The more pleasure you get from life, the more you say your prayers."

Tiger stepped in as Danton: "I'd like to be part of the ether so I could bathe you and flow over you, and break against every wave of your body."

"Danton, your lips have eyes."

Impulsively he leaned forward and kissed her, a long, deep, exotic kiss lasting until he had to hold Marion (Marianne?) to keep her balance.

Amy Powell, the stage manager, leaned forward to identify with the movement. "Wow," she said. "I don't recall you blocking that in, but it sure looked good."

Rik gave a wordless nod.

"And real!"

"It sure did."

$$*****$$

"Bread not heads, wine not blood! The guillotine's a bad flour mill, Samson's a rotten baker's boy, we want bread, bread!"

--Danton's Death, Act 3, Scene 10

At his front door, Rik meet his three-year-old daughter coming out—riding on the back of a long-haired young person of indeterminate sex.

"Hi, Daddy. We go sand box." The duo were halfway across the lawn before Rik realized that Annie was wearing one of her nicest frocks and urging her steed along with a pair of her shiniest black shoes.

"Hey, kid!" The young person turned on a dime to Annie's delighted encouragement and ran in place while taking her father's orders. "Make that the swings. She's already dressed for church."

"Okay, Mr. Temple," replied a surprisingly deep voice. Rik shook his head and entered into the kitchen

It was a hot summer day, but Lynne, the epitome of the cliché of a happy woman in the kitchen, was putting a large bread pan in the oven. A longhaired girl (he guessed this time) was at the table, beating the mixture in another bread pan into submission. A third longhair was wheeling in a stack of packets with U.S. government markings through the back door. If either of them noticed Rik, they gave no sign of it.

Fittingly, it was Lynne who saw him as she straightened up from the oven. She raced across the room and kissed him on the cheek, but before he could speak, was back at the table. "That's okay, hon. I'll take over here. You go help Bernie get the other food packets out of the truck. You know how he is about lifting." The girl at the table obediently followed "Bernie" out the back, and Lynne took over at the table.

"Where did Reece go with our daughter?"

"Out to the swing. I told him to keep her away from the sandbox."

"Good. Annie can be insistent." Rik was at the refrigerator. "Not the lemonade on the top shelf, hon. That's for the rally. There's a pitcher on the bottom shelf for the family. Listen, if you think Annie can't out talk Reece, you should have seen her over in the mall this morning."

"The Mall?" Rik was getting a glass out of the kitchen sink cabinet. "What was she doing in the mall?"

"*She* was just playing with her dolls in the shade in front of that new Walmart store. *I* was minding the anti-war literature table, just like I said I was going to do at breakfast.

There was one of those government men over there taking pictures. I don't know why they don't come right out and introduce themselves. Nobody else wears those little hats anymore. Anyway, he took some pictures of me, and then he decided to take a close up of Annie."

"Did he scare her?"

Lynne laughed. "Not in the least. She wanted to introduce him to her dolls, but he wouldn't give his name. By this time they probably all have FBI records."

"I'll give odds that you do." He poured another glass for Lynne, who sat down at the table with him.

"Probably. At least the FBI (until they pick you up some dark night) are more polite than the PTA."

"They were there too?"

"In droves. Accusing me of trespassing. (I had a permit.) Accusing me of corrupting teenagers visiting the mall. (It was Sunday morning; why weren't they in church?) Accusing me of creating an America where my little girl wouldn't be safe. (Would she be safe in a country where she was always lied to?)" She reached across the table and took his hand. "I don't have to tell you. You hear it every day."

"Yes, but for me it comes from people who think I'm too chicken for the revolution. Where'd you get the government goods? From June Lane's sister again?"

Lynne's face lit up. "No! From Simone's mother—well, actually from Simone. Her mother died last month. The government had been giving her supplemental food for years that she'd hoarded. Simone got a kick about Government Issue being used for an event that 'challenged' the government. (She still can't say "anti-war.") You never know where you're going to find a hidden revolutionary."

"I think I already know the answer to this question, but are you coming with me and Annie to Isaac's baptism?"

She squeezed his hand. "No, and you know why."

"Do I?"

"Yes, because somebody has to use public property to help the public. Because somebody has to give teenagers something to believe in that they can't buy in a mall. Because somebody has to use Government Issue to change the Government. And because somebody has to build an America that doesn't lie to my daughter.

"Now go change your clothes, and I'll go find out if Annie talked her way into the sandbox."

*****

"Moses led his people across the Red Sea and let the old, corrupt generation die out before he founded his new state. We do not have the Red Sea or the desert, we have war and the guillotine."

--*Danton's Death, Act 2, Scene 7*

Who's that young girl dressed in white?
(Wade in the water)
Must be the children of the Israelite
Oh, God's gonna trouble the water."

As the choir wound down and the parishioners sought their seats, the tall man assumed his place in the pulpit, his dark suit framed by the pointed arch behind him and his wide shoulders mimicked by the forward tilting cross above his head. For a long moment he surveyed the kneeling figure before him, a young man wrapped in a robe, his shaven, now born-again head still shiny from the baptismal waters.

Reverend Washington knew the Jefferson boy by sight, knew his whole family, and knew as well that he had not requested the baptism. For both men it was a favor to Isaac's grandmother, Lulu Howard, the solidly built, white-haired woman who sat stoically in a center seat of the congregation. She was a pillar of the African Methodist Episcopal Zion Church, and a calming influence in the community and in her family. This grandson, like his brothers, had withdrawn from the Church after the rock throwing mob incident in which the stained-glass window above the oak front doors was smashed. As they had thought to protect the Church, she now sought the Church to protect him. To please his grandmother, Isaac Jefferson had presented himself for baptism even as he prepared to leave to a Vietnam-focused army.

Rik stirred uneasily in his seat. He'd been in plenty of black churches, but this occasion was different. For one thing it was Sunday, but the pews were half empty. There were tensions between the town and campus black and white communities, tensions that went beyond last spring's *Kristallnacht* episode. Some parishioners blamed the Jefferson boys for stirring up trouble; some blamed whites in general. Rik was the only white man in the building.

The minister cleared his throat and began to speak.

"Brothers and sisters, we are met together in a time of great joy! The flesh has been submerged in the waters and a soul has emerged, clean and born again. But remember, my brothers and sisters, the journey of the soul is long, its way perilous, and its destiny by no means certain."

As Rik drank in the spectacle before him, a Greek theatre history lesson formed in his mind: The area that framed the ministerial platform was the *orchestra*, and the deacons and deaconesses exuding rhythmic "wells" and "amens," were the *chorus*. The baptized young man was slightly above them in "the speaking place" or *logion*. Still higher, the minister instructed them from the *theologian*, or "the speaking place of the gods." He himself was in the *Theatron*, "the seeing place," or more accurately translated, "witnessing place."

Can I get a witness?

"I take as my text today the Book of Deuteronomy from the Old Testament, Chapter 34, Verses 1 and 4: 'And Moses went up from the plains of Moab unto the mountain of Nebo. And the Lord shewed him all the land of Gilead, unto Dan. And the

Lord said unto him. This is the land which I swore unto Abraham, unto Isaac, and unto Jacob, saying, I will give it unto thy seed: I have caused thee to see it with thine eyes, **but thou shalt not go over thither.'**

But why was this, my brothers and sisters? Why was the last Prophet to see God face to face denied the right to enter the Promised Land? And why were the Chosen People of God forced to wander for 40 years in the desert when they were just a mountain away from the Land of Milk and Honey?"

Rik found himself watching his little blond daughter, Annie. Without a crowd filling up the Church, she had turned the seat area between them into a baby bed for her doll, Hope, who she tucked into a towel as a blanket, fretted over and hushed into silence. Hope was black. Rik had tried to talk Annie out of bringing her, afraid that churchgoers might be offended, but those who noticed her were either friendly or merely curious. As for Annie, she searched the face of each dark man who entered.

"Where Tiger?" she whispered to her father.

"When the Israelites first came to the border of Canaan, Moses sent twelve spies into the land, who returned with stories of its fertility, but also told of the violence they had encountered there. The Israelites were afraid. Some rebelled against God and His Prophet. Others asked to be returned to bondage in Egypt. Moses was angry and concluded they were not worthy to receive the Promised Land."

Annie adored Tiger. She growled in imitation of him, giggled when he called Hope his "little sister" and "sang her to sleep," and demanded that Tiger be present at her bedtime when he visited the house. She never feared him the way others did—those who saw him not as a "tiger," but as a "Black Panther," the face and voice of racial rebellion at rallies and on television from his time in high school to his present position as the president of the Black Student Union.

"My brothers and sisters, Moses realized that the old

people with their old ideas could never enter into the Promised Land. It would take a whole new generation with faith in themselves to take up the challenge that the New World would offer. The Milk would be there, but the cattle must be tended; the Honey harvested, but the hives must be protected. Forty years is not too long to strive for an Eternal Heaven. We are at the border now, my brothers and sisters. Are we to cross into Canaan or return to the Wilderness"?

As the minister paused, the great oak doors beneath the patched stained-glass windows burst open. The congregation turned in one anticipatory move, and froze as if captured in a snapshot. Framed in the late afternoon sunlight was a tall, powerfully built young black man, dressed in black trousers and a white shirt mostly covered by a leather jacket. On his head was a black beret, and standing next to him was a blond woman in the equally iconic garb of a flower child.

From a pew halfway down the aisle came the delighted cry of a little girl.

"Look, Daddy. It's Tiger and Mommy!"

*****

"You women, you can trick a man into falling in love with a lie. We'd have to crack open the tops of our skulls to really know each other, tear out each other's thoughts from the fibre of the brain."

--Danton's Death, Act 1, Scene 1

Lynne and Annie got a ride home with a parishioner who was a member of the Peace Action League. Lynne had come to sit with them, but despite Annie's fussing, Tiger had stood at the back until the congregation stood up for the last hymn, "Lift Every Voice and Sing," and then left without speaking to anyone.

Rik excused himself supposedly to check the sample

program at Murphy Hall, but actually drove around town to give himself a chance to think. Part of that thought dealt with Reverend Washington's sermon. What did he mean about "Old Ideas and The Promised Land?" The reference was familiar. Dr. King had recalled it the night before he was assassinated: "I've been to the mountaintop. I've seen the Promised Land. I may not get there with you. But I promise that we as a people will get to the Promised Land."

But what were the "New Ideas" and would he recognize them when they manifested themselves? Rik was what one of his teachers had called a "Whammy"—a white, heterosexual, American, male, a member of a group so privileged that they took being at the center of the universe for granted. He would likely only recognize a "New Idea" when the figurative waters of the Red Sea were closing around him.

Certainly Tiger and Lynne had shown great theatrical timing by entering just as the minister paused after asking where His People were headed. A black man and a woman— two natural leaders, who would only become "centers of the universe" through their own efforts: he with his physique and magnetism, she with her sensitivity and intellect. They had looked so perfect together standing in the doorway—as perfect as Tiger and Marianne had looked kissing in the Danton/Marion scene. Even Annie was hypnotized by Tiger's presence.

Was he the only one who didn't fit in any of these triangles?

Only then did he realize that he had driven his car into the Murphy Hall parking lot. A moment later he was climbing the steps and heading for the Experimental Theatre.

Something was wrong. The "Ghost Light" was on in the middle of the stage, but there was a dim light visible from the backstage dressing room as well. Rik quietly made his way through the theatre and looked through the dressing room door.

Two beautiful bodies, one black and one white, Tiger and Marianne, were interlinked on the large dressing room couch. Rik was struck by the *innocence* of their perfection—an innocence that came of their belonging together.

He eased himself out of the room. It was time to go home to Lynne and Annie.

*****

"Everything has the right to live. That gnat. That bird. So why not him? The stream of life should stop if a single drop is spilt. The earth should be wounded."
--Danton's Death, Act IV, Scene 8

It was dress rehearsal night, and fortunately Rik had left for the theatre early. The campus was crawling with National Guardsmen. As he pulled up by Allen Fieldhouse, he could see smoke blowing out from behind Murphy Hall. He started forward again, and immediately a National Guardsman appeared before the car, carrying an M-16 with an attached bayonet.

Rik rolled down the window. "Hey, Sarge, what's going down?"

"Access to campus is denied. Turn around and vacate the premises at once."

"I can't do that! I've got an appointment at Murphy Hall and I can't be late."

The soldier rested his bayonet on the car's window frame. "Unless the people at Murphy Hall are your pallbearers, I'd suggest you vacate the premise immediately."

"Okay, don't go all Kent State on me." Without waiting for a reply, Rik gunned the car backward, spun around and headed out to the first city street, turned right and headed up to Stouffer Place, where he and Lynne had lived in the early 60s. As he expected, the parking lot was full of students watching the events below.

"What in God's name is going on down there?"

A stocky undergraduate, with an arm around his equally pudgy wife, replied with absolute certainty: "According to a guy who walked across the field from down there, somebody set off a smoke bomb in the Military Science Building. No real damage, but it scared people real good."

"Anyone know who did it?"

"They saw a black guy running away. The money's on that Black Student Union president. Tiger what's his name."

Rik choked back a throat full of doubts. "Does anybody know for sure?

The stocky kid didn't like being doubted. "I don't know. I wasn't there. Somebody like him for certain. Where you going?"

Rik was headed down the driveway. "To the laundromat to pick up my clothes."

Fifteen minutes later he had crossed the darkened field and slipped from a shadow into the west door of Murphy Hall. He figured that if he ran into anyone inside the building, it would be a faculty member or graduate student on safety patrol (although he hoped to god it wasn't Fred Espinoza) and he'd be able to explain. But there was no one.

Inside the theatre, Amy Powell and Stan Stawiki were waiting on the stage. There was frantic activity in the light booth and a couple of the actors were out front. A pair of early audience members sat patiently taking in the unexpected drama.

"What's the head count?"

Amy glanced at her clipboard. "About half the cast and crew are here, and I called all but one of the others on the office phone. They're all going to try to get here."

"Who couldn't you reach?"

"Marianne." Amy looked grim.

Rik sighed. "How about Tiger?"

Stan stepped forward. "He's in the dressing room with Isaac, Rik. He won't let anyone come in."

"He'll let me in."

"Yeah, come in, Rik." Tiger Jefferson stood at the dressing room door. "You need to know what's going down."

Rik followed Tiger into the dressing room. "Did you know that some people think you set off that mess in the Military Science Building?"

"I didn't know, but I'm not surprised." Tiger pulled Isaac to his feet and shook him. "Look what you've done now! Don't you ever think ahead?"

Isaac pushed his brothers' hands away. "Not everybody wants to play the white man's little games!"

"Little games? You gonna win the Revolution by smokin' up a school building? What do you think you're gonna be doing in the army? Or maybe you think a brig will be more comfortable than the state pen."

Rik cut in. "Look, I don't want to get in the middle of a family feud, but I've got to get this "little game" onstage."

Isaac turned angrily. "*You* stay out of this. This is none of your business!"

Tiger spun him around and sat him down firmly on a chair. "That's right. It's yours and mine. Now listen to me! Did you wear your cap?"

"What the hell has that got to do with anything?

Tiger shook his brother by the arms again. "Answer my question! When you were running away from the Military Science Building, were you wearing your cap?"

"Yes!"

Tiger clapped his hands. "That's good! That's great! White man can't tell one nigger from another, but even they know the difference between a shaved head and a fro. Now listen to me. This is what we're gonna do. In my makeup kit there's a pair of scissors, a razor, and a can of shaving cream. You're gonna shave off that beard and mustache and get out of here.

The second you're outside of this building, you're gonna throw that cap as far as you can. Then you're going home. If anybody stops you, you just came up here to wish me good luck, but turned around when you saw the fire. Can you do that?"

Isaac nodded.

"Good. Now I'm gonna get into my costume and my Paul Robeson voice. Rik, you go out there and whip everything else into shape."

Rik stepped back into the theatre—stopping cold in front of a white-faced Marianne.

*****

"Life is just a more complex, a more ordered putrefaction than the simple rotting of death. But that's the only difference, complexity, otherwise life and death are one and the same."
--Danton's Death, Act 3, Scene 7

If the theatre legend that a bad dress rehearsal means a good opening night was true, the premiere was in trouble. The curtain was a good hour and a half late, but the entire cast and crew were there, plus fifteen or twenty stubborn audience members determined to enjoy themselves by denying authority's right to tell them where they could be or not be. Even the little touches which identified the production as experimental were well received: a trimmed script, actors playing multiple characters, the clichéd runaway horse, the puppet show crowd scenes, and—most surprisingly—the 18th century slide machine.

It was late in the rehearsal period when Rik discovered the historical existence of such an instrument, and immediately used it to solve his major technical problem: how to effectively but symbolically behead six men.

Rik assumed that few audience members would be aware of the machine's existence, so he took care to introduce it at the beginning of the play. In the opening scene the Deputies of the National Convention aligned with Danton make their individual entrances with a distinctive speech. Danton's wife, Julie, ran the slide machine that introduced each character with a flash of light that went dark, while another Deputy took his place. Having seen the introduction, the audience was prepared to see the same characters make a last speech before the guillotine, and then disappear into blackness.

Five victims knelt in front of the blade.

CAMILLE: "Witches! You'll quote the Bible in the end— 'Fall on us, ye mountains.'"

LACROIX: "You kill us on the day you lost your reason. On the day you regain it, you will kill them."

PHILIPPEAU: "I forgive you all. I hope your hour of death will be no more bitter than mine."

FABRE: "Goodbye, Danton. I die a double death."

HERAULT: "I can't joke any more. It's time."

Danton was the sixth fictional victim of the evening. That's where the police came in. Before anyone noticed, they were at both ends of the stage and in the audience.

"Give it up, Jefferson. This is the Law. Don't put any of these people at risk."

Danton paced back and forth on the stage like a caged tiger.

"We've got witnesses, Jefferson. Don't make it any worse than you have to."

DANTON: *"We had to do it, it was self-defense. The man on the cross took the easy way out. 'It is impossible but that* offenses will come—but woe unto him through whom they come.' Who can curse the hand on which the curse of necessity falls?"

"We found your cap in the dressing room, Jefferson. People at the fire site described it."

DANTON: *"Let the scum who accuse me come here, and I will heap shame on them. They are my prosecutors and my witnesses. Make them show themselves! Besides, what do your verdict matter to me? The void will soon be my sanctuary."*

"Calm down, Jefferson. Make it easier on your family. Don't you care about your Grandmother?"

DANTON: *"What composure can there be from me when I find myself slandered and calummied? I am a revolutionary. You cannot expect a cool and modest defense from my kind. Men of my stamp are beyond price to the Revolution; the genius of liberty shines from our brows."*

"There are five guns trained on you, Jefferson! We ain't gonna be patient much longer."

DANTON: *"I am not arrogant about what I have done. Fate guides everyone's arm. But only a mighty personality can be fate's instrument. Let my accusers appear. I will tear the mask from these villains and hurl them back into the darkness, from which they never should have crawled."*

"Take him, boys!"

Cops moved in from the opposite wings, with the squad commander reaching the center of the stage first. But Tiger was already gone, leaping over the guillotine model in an attempt to reach the aisle in front of it—and catching one foot on the raised blade. He sprang to his feet in time to take two police-issue bullets in the back. He paused, then moved forward as if unhit, only to receive two more bullets in the chest from a crossfire by the two cops in the audience. He put one hand on an aisle seat to steady himself, then turned to the stage to face the squad commander—who took careful and shot him in the forehead.

In a flash a beautiful woman in an 18th century gown and a mound of red-brown hair piled upon her head appeared in the aisle and threw herself upon her lover's body.

"There is a reaper name of Death
Who draws breath
From Almighty God.

Dear cradle who rocked my love asleep.
You suffocated him under your roses.
You passing bell, your sweet tongue sang him to his grave.
(She sings.)

Men and women, short and tall
Countless thousands fall
Down before your scythe."

"Come with us, Miss. We'll see that you get home."

Marianne straightened up from the floor. "Long live the Revolution," she screamed.

"The kid's cracked up. Let's get her out of here."

*****

"Only one thing matters, what gives you pleasure. The more pleasure you get from life, the more you say your prayers."

--Danton's Death, Act I, Scene 5

It was a foolish waste of time, but when you're headed off on a drive of hundreds of miles, what does another hour mean? Certainly, Annie was happy enough at the playground, and he'd left Lynne sitting on a park bench reading *The Bluest Eye*, a novel by somebody or other. Rik would be driving the yellow rental truck, and Lynne would follow with the VW hippie bus, with Annie playing in the open back seat space.

They were leaving Kansas for probably the last time, and it was the end of May when Mt. Oread was covered with cherry blossoms. Every year, Rik had promised himself that he would take his Super-8 camera up the hill and film them in all their pristine beauty. Nineteen seventy-one would be his last chance.

Except that it was already too late. The closer he got to the top of the hill, the more it was clear that he had missed the peak of the blooms. Overall, the shininess had faded, and some of the flowers on the lower branches were wrinkled, even turning brown.

Rik sighed, unpacked his camera and began to film. If anyone else saw the results, he would tell them it was a metaphor for his career as a graduate student.

There was a winding path down the hill between the blooming bushes which gave him a natural point on which to focus. As he was setting up the framework for the path, Rik was surprised to pick up a pair of feet coming toward him. On an impulse he held the camera in place, as the approaching figure revealed more and more of an exquisitely tailored flower child skirt.

Too exquisitely tailored. Nine years of living with a costume designer had taught Rik the difference between an adaptation believable at the distance of a stage and the real thing—and the difference was inevitably money.

"Are you just going to take pictures, cowboy, or are you going to say hello to a girl?"

Rik jerked the camera to an eye level, revealing a familiar

face no longer framed by a red-brown mane, but by hair cut by a hand as skilled as the one who had constructed her clothing. With one hand still clutching his camera, Rik awkwardly embraced Marianne, attempting to murmur something appropriate, but coming out with "that's different from the outfit you were wearing last year."

"Do you like it?" She stepped back, taking a shop window style pose. "Neiman-Marcus! Trust a Texan to turn the revolution into a style, but it goes with the hair." She broke the pose with another enthusiastic hug. "And speaking of clothing styles, I didn't see you at graduation the other day."

"I didn't graduate. I'm 'ABD.'"

"Sounds like a disease."

"It is. More people catch ABD than come down this hill with a PhD, although I'm told there is a cure for it in Minnesota."

"Cold climate. Nothing to do but study." Marianne approached this next subject more carefully. "I'm doing some traveling too."

Rik's response was just as careful: "Oh, has Fred prepared a nest for you in Brazil? I understand he isn't coming back."

"That train has already left the station—on a one-way track. I understand that my tutor has found a new student."

This time Rik was more genuinely concerned. "I'm sorry, I guess. You know I tried several times to visit you when you were in the hospital."

Marianne laughed. "You call it a hospital? I'd call it an asylum. I expected every day to be delivered in a strait jacket to Dr. Frankenstein. Besides, Dwight didn't like me to have visitors. He thought the excitement would slow my recovery."

"Who's Dwight?"

"Dwight Raymond, a member of the Board of Regents. He took up my case not long after the shooting. He convinced the police to drop the charges because of my mental state. (It goes without saying that there were no charges filed in the police shooting.) And as soon as the charges against me were dropped, Dwight decided that my mental state was improving and got me released from the hospital."

"Quite an uptick in influence over Fred."

Marianne was grim. "In some ways Dwight *is* Fred, with way more power and way more understanding. That's where I'm going—to his summer house in Puget Sound. He has a yacht. We'll probably sail south when the weather cools."

"So the train has left the station, but the ship has yet to sail." Rik plowed doggedly forward. "You must have told Tiger about Fred. What do you think he would have thought of Dwight?"

For the first time he saw in her eyes a familiar mixture of pain and determination.

"I loved Tiger! No, I never told him about Fred. He's dead! I'm not!" Her face softened. "How did Annie take it—Tiger's death?"

"Well, Lynne and I went to the funeral. It was at the AMEZ Church. Everybody knew the truth about what happened that night. Isaac must have told them. He'd already reported for duty. He's in Vietnam now. Ironic, isn't it? When we got home, Annie was 'playing funeral.' I don't know where she learned the basics, but she got them down pretty good. Simone's daughters are her babysitters. I suspect they taught her."

"Who was Tiger?"

"Hope, the only black doll she had. I haven't seen Hope around for a long time." Rik smiled painfully. "Annie takes her metaphors pretty seriously. Maybe living in a new place will revive Hope."

Marianne spoke carefully. "And Lynne?"

"Lynne is sad about being in a world that has one less person who knows how to be gentle with small children." Rik smiled more cheerfully. "She's thinking about having another baby.

"I see. Will that make it harder to find a place for you all at Stoke-Upon-Trent?"

Rik shook his head negatively. "I'm not going to England. I'll write about English documentary theatre, but the sources will be all newspaper articles, magazines, and whatever response I can get from letters. And it will all be written in Minnesota."

"You're doing what you think you have to do," she said. "And so am I."

Rik was about to protest, but Marianne quieted him with a finger to her lips. "I know what you're going to say, and it's already been said better in *Danton's Death*. I'm in the habit of being taken care of by men. I know that can't last. Marion's first lover tells her 'he doesn't want to spoil her fun. My body is all the finery I have, I'll need it, it will be torn and dirty and worn out before I know it.' But I *will* know it, and when that time comes, I will get off the ride—train or sailboat, whatever it happens to be—and not look back."

She took his hands. "Look, I can't come with you to Minnesota, right?" Rik looked into her eyes and gave a slight nod." "You *could* come with me to Puget Sound. I could tell Dwight you're my brother or my doctor, and we might have a few glorious days. But you're not a man of impulse, and that's why I trusted you so much."

Rik tried to speak, but failed.

"So I suggest we get off the ride right now. There are two paths down this hill. One leads to the playground, the other to a taxi stand. Let's leave and never look back."

Hypnotized by her, Rik began to turn.

"Wait!" Marianne commanded. She pulled his face down to her and kissed him. In an instant he had seized her firmly and returned the kiss. Then she was gone, down her own path.

For a moment Rik stood still, not looking after her, but not moving either. Then he started down the other path, and as he walked, he gradually picked up his pace.

Lynne and Annie were waiting for him at the bottom of

Mt. Oread.

BLACKOUT

It is 9:31 p.m. E.D.T., July 13, 1977. The bottom of the sixth inning at Shea Stadium, with the Chicago Cubs leading the New York Mets, 2-1. The thunder of a jet airliner passing overhead in a landing pattern for nearby LaGuardia Airport drowns out the public address announcement of the Mets' leadoff man, but everyone in the ballpark recognizes third baseman Lenny Randle, New York's only .300 hitter. Two months ago, that wouldn't have been true. In spring training, Randle had been a Texas Ranger. When Manager Frank Lucchesi gave Randle's starting job to a rookie, Lenny confronted Lucchesi in the dugout and sucker-punched him. The manager got plastic surgery, and Lenny got a thirty-day suspension and his release. It wasn't until Memorial Day, when the Mets named their washed-up third-baseman Joe Torre as manager, that Randle was inserted into the starting lineup.

"Joe told me," Lenny explained later, "that the 1973 Mets were in last place at the end of August and still got to Game Seven of the World Series. This team was just one player away from being that good, and I was that player. He told me I could change my life and the future of the Mets at the same time, and I believed him!"

Ray Burris, the Cubs' lean right-hander, picks up his sign,

as Lenny glances down at Torre in the third base coaching box. There was no signal, he had a green light to hit, but the look on his manager's face says it all: "Now is the time to turn it around."

Burris has good control, but he isn't overpowering. Twice already tonight he'd gotten Lenny in a hole with a first pitch sneaky fastball. Surely, he won't try it again. Burris goes into his motion and the ball leaves his hand—a slow curve, coming toward the plate, big and round and white. Lenny leans into the pitch and unloads.

Then everything went black! "I think the Good Lord is calling me," guesses Lenny.

*****

Miles away at West 65th Street in Lincoln Center, Rik Temple watches a highly touted production of Anton Chekhov's *The Cherry Orchard* by the Romanian director, Andrei Serban, from a stage right orchestra seat at the Vivian Beaumont Theatre.

It is Act Two of four acts. The bespectacled student Trofimov speaks passionately to an enraptured Anya: "Believe me, Anya. Trust me. I'm young, but I've had my share of hardship. In wintertime I'm always half-starved, ill, worried, desperately poor. Yet always, every moment of the day and night, I've been haunted by mysterious visions of the future. Happiness is coming, Anya, I feel it. I already see it!"

She gazes up into his face, as the stage lights slowly dim down.

Up in his ninth-row aisle seat, Rik Temple is puzzled. "Revolutionary production, hell," he thinks. "He cut ten minutes off the end of the Second Act."

From a small feminine body on the darkened stage comes the trained, powerful voice of actress Marybeth Hurt: "We're not *done* down here!"

He can hear the house doors opening, and as his head swivels, his consciousness registers the absence of the safety lights on the steps and of the exit sign at the top of the aisle. Reacting more quickly than the rest of the audience, Rik rushes up the stairs and out into the night air of a singularly absent New York City. Looming above on all sides are silhouettes of massive buildings, like towering monsters utilizing an occasional, oddly placed, generator-fueled eye to seek out their prey. For a moment an image from *War of the Worlds* flashes in Rik's mind, as if the Aliens vanquished by Orson Welles nearly forty years earlier have returned by the light of a Full Moon to once again challenge Mankind.

*****

On Ninth Avenue he sees his first bus. It stops for him in the middle of the street, a clear sign that all rules are off. It is crowded with people who are laughing, exchanging jokes and anecdotes, stories about where they were when everything stopped—people who have been jogged out of their normal behaviors, people who are simultaneously riding on public transport and acknowledging the existence of one another—in short, people who are no longer New Yorkers.

Rik pokes his head into the open bus door and questions the driver: "How far downtown are you going?"

The driver, the Sword of Damocles schedule no longer hanging over his head, is as relaxed and amiable as his passengers. He waves away Rik's proffered change: "How far you wanna go?"

"I live in the Village."

"Most of these folks want me to cut over to Seventh Ave, so I'm going that way. I can get you as far as Bleecker Street. Can you make it from there?"

"With my eyes closed."

The driver laughs. "Good! Do me a favor, will ya? Hang

out the window behind me and call out any street names you can see, so that people know where to get off."

Like a guard dog on a stagecoach, Rik leans out the window into the night breeze, straining to identify an unfamiliar succession of normally familiar streets: the joining of Central Park West and Central Park South in Columbus Circle, a Times Square at 47th West and Broadway that in the moonlight resembles a badly faded black and white postcard, the New York and New Jersey Port Authority at 34th Street. (Will it be possible to escape New York? No one knows.)

Someone taps him on the shoulder, and Rik turns to face a vaguely familiar young Latina woman with long, beautiful dark hair.

"Excuse me for bothering you, but I saw you at the play. Did I hear you tell the bus driver you wanted to get off at Greenwich Village?

Rik nods wordlessly.

"I live near East 8th. Would you mind if I walked with you until I got to my neighborhood. This may not be a good night for a girl to be alone."

"How do you know you're safe with me?" Rik meant it to be a compliment.

Her reply is direct, but not playful. "I figure anybody who goes to see Chekhov on a Tuesday is not going to attack a woman on a street corner, and you're big enough so that anybody who would might at least think it over first."

The bus driver cuts in. "I don't mean to eavesdrop, but if you wanna go to East 8th, you better get off at Sheridan Square, and that's coming up."

*****

As they step down from the bus onto Christopher Street, a man in a jacket and a Tyrolean hat is climbing on. He looks at Rik's companion with appreciation: "Ihr schwarzes Haar ist schon."

The Latina responds with a fierce burst of street *calo* which Rik can't translate, and of whose meaning he has no doubt.

"All he said was that he liked your long, dark hair."

The girl crosses the Square with angry, extended strides that Rik finds himself hard-pressed to match. "Well, he better not get used to it, because tomorrow it'll be short and blonde."

"Why? You look like Jaclyn Smith."

The Latina swings about to face him, the contempt in her voice almost hiding the touch of fear. "Yeah, you like to watch some masturbation substitute jiggle, but you should be watching the news. Don't you know that every girl he's shot had long dark hair?"

"Who?"

"The Son of Sam! Seven of them, all over the city. And four guys who were them. That oughta get your attention!"

She resumes walking, but more slowly now, as they pass Gay Street and approach Greenwich Avenue. It's obviously a subject she's thought a lot about, but hasn't talked through with anyone. "I heard a guy call into a radio talk show this morning. He said they probably had it coming, that if Valentina Suriani wasn't a slut, she wouldn't have been parked on the dark side of the street with her boyfriend. The host cut him off the air, but a lot of men think just like that—that if they're not gettin' any, it's the girl's fault. That a woman doesn't have a right to enjoy her body unless they say so. Why is that? Why are you so threatened, what do you think is *changing*?" The dark-haired girl is angry with Rik again. She needs him at this moment, but that only makes her angrier.

Rik tries to change the subject. "Were you at the play alone?" he asks, and is immediately certain that he's made a mistake, that he will be perceived as questioning her independence—but the Latina only laughs.

"You really weren't paying attention, were you? I was your

usher, I pointed out to you where your seat was." She stops and turns toward him, lifting her hair off from her shoulders with both hands and momentarily piling it on her head. "Yeah, you know me now, I can see it. So much for the Jaclyn Smith look catching your eye!" She lets the hair fall.

"So you've seen *The Cherry Orchard* before?"

She's walking again. On the south side of 8th West, one business is open, lit with a kerosene lamp. She stays on the north side, quickening her pace as they pass. "Yeah, thirty times! It plays every other night with *Agamemnon*, that show where they kill the girl so the gods will let them win the war. Can you believe that?"

"What did you think of the play?"

"*The Cherry Orchard*? What do I think of people who won't do anything to help themselves, even if they might lose everything? Hell, everybody I know is like that! Why do you think I left Spanish Harlem? I won't be like that! If I ever get a chance, I'll help myself. I'll take whatever I can get away with."

She comes to a stop near the corner of 8th East and University Place. "Look, you're a nice guy and all that. But this is as far as you go, okay? I'll be safe from here on, and I'll feel safer if you don't know where I live, okay?"

Rik nodded.

She smiles suddenly, and leans forward and kisses him on the cheek. "Hey, you married?"

"Yeah."

"I thought so. I didn't see a ring, but I thought so."

"I lost it seven years ago."

"Uh huh," she nodded. "Well, that's why I picked you, that and the way you watched the play. You got no idea how many guys show up there, they're not interested in the play at all. They're just cruising—you know what I mean—sometimes for girls, sometimes for other guys. The actors up on the stage, they're working, they're givin' their best, but to these guys it's just a place to make a pickup. You weren't like that, you watched the stage like a hawk. Kids?"

"Two. A girl and a boy. They're back in the Mid-West with their mother. I'm here for a seminar at NYU."

"Well, you teach 'em how to take what's theirs, and remember—your wife has a right to get hers too, whatever it is." She smiled again, turned on her heel and headed north on University Place.

Rik looked after her for a moment, and then began walking in the opposite direction.

"Hey," came a voice from behind him. Rik turned, but the Latina had already melted away into the shadow of a building. "Hey," came the voice again. "If you're ever walking along the street up here and you see a girl with short, blond hair, don't be afraid to say hello, okay?"

Rik smiled. "Okay."

*****

On an impulse, Rik decides not to go directly down University Place to his room in the NYU Law Dorm, but to retrace his steps on 8th West to Fifth Avenue, so that he can cut across Washington Square Park. He's now on the same side of the street as the business with its kerosene lamp silhouetting the lettering on the window: "MOTHER BUCKA'S ICE CREAM PARLOR."

A man with rolled-up sleeves and an apron hails him from the interior. "Hey Mac, you want a gallon of ice cream?"

Rik pauses in the doorway. "What would I do with ice cream?"

"Eat it here or take it with you, it don't matter to me. I been givin' it away for an hour and a half, and I only got a gallon left. You like French Vanilla? It'll only melt if you don't take it. C'mon, I hate to waste it, and I'm kinda in a hurry."

Rik finds himself seated at the counter, the spoon in his hand dipping into the soft, unbroken surface. "You going to close up and head home."

The man scurries about the room, piling stools on table tops, lowering the iron grate in front of the windows. "I'm closing up, but I'm not heading home. Do you know what it'll be like in the East Village?" His voice was as excited as his movements.

"Where?"

"In the East *Village*! Weren't you here in '65?"

"No. I didn't live here then."

"Well, it was fantastic. Sharing candles, stories, glasses of wine. People got to know their neighbors. There was friendships formed that night that lasted till this day. No, not just friendships—love affairs! I know two guys who met their wives that night. And I know a lot of other guys who met women that they never saw again, but will never forget. Nine months later, the birth rate went through the roof! Haight-Ashbury may have had a summer of love, but New York had a night of love. Two lucky thirteens! The city went dark in thirteen minutes, and it stayed dark for thirteen hours. And that was November! Can you imagine what it'll be like on a warm night like this?"

"Pretty hot I guess." Ice cream eaten too fast had suddenly frozen a lobe in Rik's forehead. "Say, have you got a paper towel I could use?"

"Just behind the counter directly in front of you." The man in the apron finished the closing up activities and straddled the stool next to Rik, waxing philosophical. "Sometimes a city needs something like this. The Big Apple's had a lot of worms lately. What with losing all those factory jobs, the city's bankruptcy, the school system breakin' down, the race riots, that nutcase runnin' around shooting people, New Yorkers don't see how the city could really be. Somethin' like this slows everybody down. It's like the old neighborhoods. They get to know one another again. All the old barriers are broken down. Everybody changes their lives. *They start fresh*, ya know what

I mean?... Is that all you can eat? Gimmie the container, I'll throw it in the trash can on the way out."

*****

The full moon shines directly above the Memorial Arch as Rik enters Washington Square Park from Lower Fifth Avenue. It's quieter than he'd expected, although a trace of marijuana smoke still hangs in the air. He'd missed whatever celebration might have been there earlier, had swapped it for French Vanilla ice cream. Somewhere at an indecipherable distance, a tremulous violin plays Massenet's "Meditation from *Thais*," but the mournful melody is undercut by a closer, more static sound.

Eventually, to the left of the path and a few yards from the fountain, he makes out the circle of a soft, pinkish glow, emanating, on closer inspection, from a sterno can sitting on the ground in front of a park bench. The shadow of the light gives a cadaverous cast to the face of the young black man leaning back on the bench.

"Loose joints?" The man raises his voice over the news report on the portable radio beside him on the bench.

"Business good?" Rik sits down opposite the dealer, aware he's getting only partial attention from someone who is deeply inhaling a sample of the product he is supposed to be selling.

"It was until about a half hour ago. I guess maybe the news reports killed the buzz." He forces his words through the half-swallowed smoke, then slowly releases it into the air above his head.

"What news report?"

The dealer gestures toward the radio dramatically and turns up the volume.

"....insisted the power outage was an Act of God, and denied that Con-Ed had any responsibility for the subsequent black-out and the citywide consequences. Mayor Abe Beame called for a legislative investigation into what he called the power company's negligence in not providing an emergency back-up system, and promised prosecution for those complicit in failing to prevent this disaster. Meanwhile, waves of arson and looting are engulfing several boroughs of the City. A score of blocks along upper Broadway have suffered what one caller to the station described as 'blockbuster bomb-comparable damage'. Hundreds of fires have been reported in the Crown Heights section of Brooklyn, in Harlem, and, especially, in the South Bronx. Firefighters have experienced difficulty in reaching some of these fires because of debris barriers built up in the streets. Police have arrested hundreds of looters and demonstrators. We take you now directly to reporter Mark Moskowitz on the streets in the South Bronx. . .

"Stacy, I'm looking at a scene directly out of Dante. Both sides of the street..."

He switches off the radio. "Do you mind? I've heard this one before."

"How did this all start?"

"*This* all started," for the first time the black man sits up and waves the joint in Rik's direction, "when these folks got up this morning and turned on the tube and saw all these things they couldn't afford to buy, being sold by folks with faces that didn't look like theirs, in places where they wouldn't be allowed in. *This* all started last fall when these kids were enrolled in a school that *already* looked like it'd been hit by a bomb, being run by a School Board full of kikes who send their kids to private schools. *This* all started fifty years ago when these old men came up here from a place where they lynched you *quick* like 'Strange fruit hanging from the poplar trees', to a place where they strangle you slowly with a noose made of dollar bills and lost hopes."

Rik risks a question. "How will it help to burn down where they live?"

"*Help*?" The black man's unpleasant grin reflects the light from the sterno can's flame. "It won't *help anything*! These folks are gonna wake up tomorrow, and if they're not in jail, if where they live hasn't burned down, if their kids aren't dead, and if the power's on and the swamp cooler is working, they're gonna see that nothin' at all has *changed*! The Governor is gonna appoint a Commission. Some sociologist from NYU— not them—is gonna testify, and when it's over, absolutely *nothing* will change."

"What about the future? What about Civil Rights?"

"The *future*? Civil *Rights*?" The dealer is pacing now, passing in and out of the sterno can's rosy glow like a moth with second thoughts. "What do ya want these people to do— *March*? You see those women marching last month, for the— whatdaya callit—ERA? You really think those broads are gonna get *Equal Rights*? Did you see those faggots in the," he snorts, "*Gay Pride* march? For five years they've been trying to get a Protection Law from the City Council. They might just as well ask to paint Manhattan lavender. My people gotta whole *history* of marchin', and what did they ever get—fire hoses, cops on horseback (with and without sheets), and police dogs. The *future*? Man, there is no *future*! But just for tonight there is a *present*. My people are a *presence*! The suits that run things—the government, the television, the newspapers—they know we're here. They'll forget tomorrow, but tonight we are *alive*, and they have to *pay attention*!"

"So what's the answer?"

"The *answer*?" The dealer is incredulous. "I live the answer, and I'm selling it. You can buy in anytime you want."

"Pot?"

"Pot, blow, horse, speed—you name it! If it separates the mind from the body, if it helps you forget the past, and forget that you have no future, it's good. Take one "o" away from good," he blows a smoke ring into the glow above the sterno can, "and you got God. Now is as fine a time as any to start, bro. Two bucks for two joints?"

*****

Rik stands in front of the tall gray silence of the NYU Law Dorm. His key to the door beside the central glass entrance still works, but the elevator doesn't, and the stairwell is as black as a tomb. His was the eighth room on the eighth floor, and his chances of finding it in the dark unlikely. He turns around and walks out the door, crosses West 4th Street, and re-enters the Park.

The figure on the bench seems unsurprised to see him. "Decide to take those joints after all?"

"No, but I'll give you fifty cents for a package of matches, or two bucks for that can of sterno. Take your choice."

*****

Rik doesn't strike a match until the eighth floor, and is proud for having found the right level in the dark. That match lasts halfway down the hall, and before the second match flickers out, he is standing in the doorway of room eight. A spray of moonlight lay softly across the ledge of the window opposite him. He can hear voices, people in other windows, on fire escapes, etc. The topic *du nuit* (the moment of the blackout) has been exhausted, and now people are just talking because they don't want this feeling to end.

Rik doesn't either. What time is it? Does it matter? What if the power never comes back on? What if everything is changed forever? Conversely, what if nothing that happened during this millisecond when the Powers that Run the World are absent *mattered*? He stands there for a moment, the door key in his hand, then walks back out into the hallway and heads for the stairs. This time his target is the 14th floor.

*****

Her name was Thyme Wright. (Well, of course it wasn't.) Thyme Wright was her pen name. Once she told Rik that she chose it because she liked being compared to a spice. Once she said it was a word play on the years she lost in the nunnery. Once she said it was a pleasant *reminder* of the name she'd had as a nun, and once that it came from the label she'd put on the weed she sold to finance her Ph.D. studies at a well-known university in the South. Maybe all of them were true. Maybe none. She'd certainly led a life different from Rik's. She'd been a child actress in Chicago, an equity member, the star of her own radio show, and had given it up for her greatest role, the Bride of Christ.

Her book, *Twisted Sister*, was an account of her years in that role, and was once optioned (and dropped) by ABC-TV as a subject for a mini-series.

Thyme was a mass of contradictions, the frank acceptance of which only increased her charm. In appearance, she was the epitome of smiling, long-legged All-American Girl achievement, on the cusp of choosing between the PTA presidency and the boardroom. She gave up the World for the Church, which made her a biology teacher. She became celibate for Christ and fell in love with a novitiate. Because of her homosexuality, she left the Church, after which she married, had a child, and left her husband for another woman. She was a health nut who relaxed on tequila and marijuana. She left Catholicism to become a Wiccan.

Thyme was in the same NYU seminar as Rik, the first fellow student he met there. They were all college teachers in theatre or in English, mostly at small institutions or in entry level positions at state universities, attempting to gain a foothold on the next rung of the academic ladder, or—in Rik's case—to find new inspiration for a calling he could feel slipping into routine.

In a way their sex was an afterthought, the capstone to a

conversation about a play they'd seen or a political topic analyzed over drinks. To prolong the glow of shared ideas, they went to bed. It was a symbiotic relationship. Thyme's Ph.D. was in black theatre, and with Rik at her side, she could venture into uptown theatres where a lone white woman might have felt intimidated. The price that he paid was his participation in feminist conferences, his presence at gay rallies, and—speaking of intimidation—his accompanying her to lesbian bars. The Blackout would be another experience for them to share.

The fourteenth floor is easier to negotiate than the eighth. Candlelight is visible through the transom above one of the doors, and more important, high-pitched voices of ever-increasing decibels can be heard from the moment Rik steps from the stairwell into the hallway.

"You bitch! You tell me you're coming here to study, and I'm not here one evening, and I find a pair of jockey shorts under the bed! It's bad enough I have to put up with you sniffing around every tramp in town, but to come to New York and find you've gone back to *men*. . ."

"Jana, honey, it's not like that."

"Not like what? Not like you squealing like a stuck pig when some prick's dick is stuck into you? Don't forget, I know you! I know you!"

"What you don't know is what a dump this place was when I moved in. It hadn't even been cleaned after the last person moved out. I stuck a dust mop under the bed, but I must have missed the shorts..."

"You expect me to *believe* that! How do I know that bastard won't be back here any minute? Or is it *bastards*? How many of them are there? Why don't you just nail the toilet lid *up*? You can use it as a *douche*. You probably need it."

"Jana, don't say anything you can't take back. If I was going to do anything like that, why would I invite you here? Come here, baby. Come here."

For a moment it's quiet, and Rik backs slowly away to the head of the stairs, and as he turns, a chilling scene straight out of Bergman's *The Seventh Seal* unfurls beneath him. Winding up the staircase like some hydra-headed snake is a single file of people, hand in hand, led by a cloaked figure holding a flickering candle high above his head. *Totentanz*!

*****

The moon is down. Rik sits on his bed, moodily nursing his last Lone Star. Drink it while it's still cold, one part of his brain argues. You can't sleep anyway. "So what?" responds another set of cells. If warm beer could kill, there never would have been a British Empire. You think the electricity will be off forever? Even if you threw it out, at $1.06 a six pack, what does it matter?

Mostly, however, he puzzles over what Tom King said to him after class this morning. Tom, a professor of Languages at NYU, an expert on *l'theatre du panique*, among other things, leads the seminar in which both Rik and Thyme are participants.

"How many years have you been teaching college, Rik?

"Eight."

"How much of that is at the University level?"

Rik studies his professor's face, with its skin so taut that the bags under his eyes seem to be the totality of his body fat. The answers to the questions are readily available on the resume he'd submitted to be a part of the seminar, and wouldn't have required a private meeting. Tom's questions are a preliminary rather than an end in themselves.

"None, if you don't count four years as a graduate assistant.

"How old are you?"

"Thirty-nine."

"Really! You look younger."

"It helps to have a supportive wife—and kids." Rik attempts to shorten the process by anticipating the next round of questions, but to no avail.

"She's still back in the Midwest?"

"Iowa. She's teaching this summer." Rik neglects to mention the blistering heat that had caused the Federal Highway to explode, the rambling farmhouse with its lack of air conditioning, the necessity of balancing a job with the demands of two, pre-adolescent children.

Tom glances at his watch. "I'll get to the point. I've going to lunch in thirty minutes with Rosa Stein, the Chair of the Theatre Department at Brooklyn College. She has an opening for an undergraduate theatre history teacher. Whoever gets the job will need to have two publication specialties, and help out with the master's program in theatre history. You've got a book in contemporary British theatre, and a fair start in African-American Theatre—which is pointless to continue unless you have access to New York. I can't promise anything, but I'll recommend you if you're interested."

Interested! The seminar was on 20th Century avant-garde theatre, beginning with Pirandello. Guest speakers had included the director Andre Gregory, Lee Breuer of the Mabou Mines, the playwright Jean-Claude Van Italie, and Richard Foreman of the Ontological/Hysteric Theatre. They'd been introduced to the Olympians of Off-Off Broadway: Ellen Stewart, "La Mama" herself, Spalding Gray, and Robert Wilson of *Einstein on the Beach*. And Rik *understood* them! The work he was doing, the things he had become interested in on his own, was not so much different from they were doing. But—a metaphor flashed into his mind from his boyhood on the farm—*here* the soil was rich, supportive, accepting of the ideas he was trying to plant! Interested!

Tom was gathering up his things. "You don't have to make a decision today. All I have to do is tell Rosa that you're interested. Like I said, I can't promise anything, but they're in a tough situation. A faculty member had a heart attack on Sunday. This could be something temporary or it could be a career. Talk to your wife. I'd advise you to take a leave of absence from Osawatomie..."

"Oskaloosa"

"Whatever. Don't cut your ties until you're sure this will work out. Housing will be a problem. Think about taking something temporary, and leave the wife and kids in Iowa until you know the job is permanent. Can I tell Rosa to get in touch with you?"

"Yeah, of course." Rik thought about Lynne's having begun teaching again, her work with the Iowa Women's Political Caucus, his kids growing up across the street from the "Y," three blocks from the elementary school, two from the junior high.

"And Rik?" Tom stopped at the door. "You're thirty-nine years old. I know what the law says about age discrimination, but if you want to get in on the ground floor at a major university, I advise you to do it as soon as possible."

*****

Rik glances sideways at his new bride as they walk across the grassy field that separates married student housing and the University. It is one of those hazy Midwestern days, which manage to be both hot and oppressively humid. He can feel the sweat gathering in his armpits and under his waistband. Lynne walks silently beside him. The path, which he thought would lead to the campus, has become one of those faceless small town American main streets, dotted with closed businesses, faux counter-culture shops, and empty lots where grass fights its way through cement. They walk for what seems like hours, and Rik becomes more and more resentful of Lynne's awareness that he's taken a wrong turn. Her right hand is in his left, and Rik looks down to see that he has a hammer in his own right hand. The street is empty. He turns suddenly and drives the hammer down on her head, only to realize at that moment that it is the eraser end of a No. 2 pencil. Lynne takes no notice and continues to walk. After a time, she speaks.

"I'm sorry I haven't been a very good conversationalist. I have such a headache."

Rik lies on his back in the middle in of the night. Lynne sits straddling him, leaning over him, with her long hair hanging on either side of his face. "I will be with you always," she says.

*****

Rik wakes in the middle of the night, his bladder bursting, and staggers toward the bathroom. He curses. The toilet is another victim of the power outage.

*****

The Washington Square Park area takes three days to have its power restored. Sometime after midnight on Saturday morning, Rik awakes, entwined, not altogether comfortably, with Thyme on her narrow bed. Unable to return to sleep, he looks around, comparing her room with his. A night lamp with a colored shade casts a soft glow that blurs the room's harsh, functional dimensions. Bits of second-hand furniture carefully chosen and placed, covered with decorative table scarves, and even the odd, appropriate knick-knack give the impression of graceful curves, relaxed living. Six floors below, *his* room has the Spartan rigidity of a barracks. There is a radio on a window ledge, which also serves as a typing table for an ancient Smith Corona portable, still attached to the bottom of a carrying case. The only sign of humanity is a wall full of theatre programs, occasionally interspersed with a child's drawing. A crude calendar, marking the days off one by one, would not seem out of place here. Her room is a home. His is a prison.

A radio turned low emits soft rock music. Thyme cannot go to sleep without it.

They share the night with the Doobie Brothers.

"She had a place in his life
He never made her think twice
As he rises to her apology
Anybody else would surely know
He's watching her go

But what a fool believes he sees
No wise man has the power to reason away

What seems to be
Is always better than nothing."

Thyme turns over on her left side, and burrows into his chest. Rik cups his right hand around a breast, and receives in return a contented sigh.

"Are you awake?" she asks.

"No, I always try to cop a feel while I'm asleep. It upgrades the quality of my dreams."

"Do you know what I'm dreaming about? Autumn in New York."

"We'll have to find a different station. I think this one only plays 'Contemporary.'"

"I'm serious. I've got a post-doc here in the NYU English Department. I'm not going back to Little Rock. I was editing a community Gay and Lesbian newsletter, and they found a copy on the Xerox machine. They've been looking for a reason to fire me ever since, and sooner or later they'll find one. It won't stand up under scrutiny, but it won't be worth the fight. They think I'll turn their daughters into dykes."

"What about Jana?"

"I'll always love Jana, but I think it's over between us. I

don't like not being trusted."

Rik ponders the irony for a moment, feeling scarcely justified in making moral judgments. "When did you find out?"

"Last week. Tom told me. He put in a word for me."

"I might be here too."

"I know." Thyme makes a delighted sound. "Brooklyn!"

"Let me guess. Tom told you that he'd put in a word for me."

"No, I *asked* him to do it. I met a woman at the Brooklyn Academy of Music, and she told me about the professor who had the heart attack. I told Tom and he agreed to recommend you. He saw it from your point of view."

A wave of bitter recognition washes over Rik. "Did he by any chance have the same point of view I have at this moment when he agreed to recommend me?"

Thyme stiffens. The physical distance between them cannot be more than an inch, but it has become a chasm. "Maybe you better go back downstairs," she says.

"Well, what am I supposed to think?"

She turns over to face him. They are eye to eye now in the semi-darkness, and the warm puffs of breath from her words drive their meaning into his understanding. "You have a right to think what you *want* to think. You have a right to think that I risked *my* opportunity to see that *you* got one. You have a right to think that I knew *I* was going to be here, and that I wanted *you* to be here too! You have a right to think how *important* that is to me, and then you have a right to ask yourself how important it is to *you!*"

He grabs her face with his hands and kisses her hard, following the kiss with a question whose answer he already knows. "Will you be here for me *alone*?"

"No!" she responds, and holds his gaze for a long moment before dropping her eyes. "You want me to change my life, but you don't want to leave Lynne. I want us to go on like before.

I don't want us to change! That's what you want too, isn't it? That's enough for both of us, isn't it?"

*****

One of the perks of National Endowment for the Humanities seminars at NYU is the free tickets. The events seen, of course, are the subject matter for many of the classroom discussions, but then the fact that what comes out of the oven is the subject matter for a class of chefs doesn't lessen its value to the palate. The last free tickets for Tom King's seminar on 20th century avant-garde drama are not, strictly speaking, for a 20th century play at all, but for Richard Schechner's production at the Performance Garage of Seneca's 1st century tragedy, *Oedipus Rex*, as adapted by the British poet Ted Hughes. Schechner is the Moses of the Experimental Theatre in New York, *The Drama Review*, which he edits, is his Ten Commandments, and the Performance Garage in the formerly industrial district of SoHo is his Wilderness. There, his adaptation of Euripides' *The Bacchae*, a 405 B.C. play about the need for balance between the intellect and the physical, became *Dionysus in 69*, a play about the position, not the chronology.

In the Sixties Schechner's Revelations were inspired by the theories of Antonin Artaud's Theatre of Cruelty—the need to break down the cultural barriers which stand between true communication by the senses. In the Seventies he has moved on to the Environmental Theatre of the Polish director, Jerzy Grotowski—the idea that all theatrical communication is determined by the physical relationship of the audience to the performance. With that in mind, Schechner tests the concept in previews by moving the spectators between acts from a balcony above the stage to the orchestra seating around it and vice-versa. After each performance, he leads a discussion on the effect of the watchers' point of view. This preview is on the night of Monday, August 2, 1977.

The story of Oedipus is too well known to require much explication. A boy is born to the rulers of Thebes. A prophecy says he will kill his father and mate with his mother. He is abandoned on a mountainside, rescued, and carried to another land where he grows to be a man. Hearing the prophecy for the first time, he leaves what he believes to be his home to protect those he believes to be his parents. At a place where three roads meet, he is accosted by an older man and kills him. Arriving in Thebes, he solves the riddle of a Sphinx that is terrorizing the City, is named ruler, and is given the hand of the widowed queen. Many years later, seeking out the source of a plague that curses Thebes, he discovers that he is its cause, for having killed his father and married his mother, despite his attempt to prevent it. She hangs herself out of shame, and Oedipus gouges out his eyes, leaving Thebes to wander the world in darkness.

The most familiar version of the Oedipus story is by Sophocles, the great poet of Athenian Democracy. He preached the doctrine of *Sophrosyne*, moderation in all things, and the moral for his *Oedipus Rex* was taken from the shrine of Apollo in the sacred groves of Delphi, "Know Thyself." Sophocles lived to be ninety. He was born when Athens lived under the threat of Persian invasion, and died just two years before his City fell to the warriors of Sparta.

The Roman Seneca, born 400 years after the death of Sophocles in less optimistic times, was tutor to the Emperor Nero, who eventually ordered him to commit suicide. Seneca was a leading Stoic philosopher, one who believed fate preordained everything in life and that the wisest of men could only accept what fate imposed. The adapter of Seneca's *Oedipus*, Ted Hughes, was reviled and spat upon by some feminists in the Sixties for his supposed contribution to the state of mind of his wife, the poet Sylvia Plath, before *her* suicide. This play was his first major creative effort after her death.

$$\star\star\star\star\star$$

Schechner might have anticipated the inability of the audience members to separate their spatial points of view from their view of Oedipus himself. No matter how he attempted to bully each watcher into an alienated analysis of how his or her feelings were affected by changes in height, angle, and distance, the subject always returned to the viewer's identification with the King of Thebes. Distracted by his own choices, Rik paid little attention—until some rows away, Thyme Wright stood up.

Thyme is an effective communicator, an attractive, poised woman, familiar with the medium, and expressing herself in a lively, well-modulated voice. "I'd like to start by thanking everyone who is involved with this production. It was well-staged, powerfully acted, and brilliantly supported technically."

She leads the audience in a spontaneous round of applause, and as it dies away, begins to speak again. "At the same time, I'd like to raise some questions about the interpretation of the text. Oedipus, whatever his origins and crimes may have been, is an effective and highly respected ruler of the City. The people come to him because he has saved them in the past, and they are confident that he will do so again. And he *does*! He finds the killer who's unpaid-for murder brought the plague upon Thebes, and he punishes him and banishes him from the City. The City rejoices because *it* has been spared. All right, you point out, that's only fair because Oedipus *was* the murderer! But that's not the *cause* of the plague. Oedipus is not to blame. He acted in ignorance, in self-defense, and the gods did not punish *him*. They punished Thebes, because the City made no attempt to find the murderer of its king. Oedipus didn't need to pay for the sins of Thebes. He had the power, he could easily argue his innocence, but he *chose* to sacrifice himself to cleanse the City."

Thyme looks toward the actors who have gathered in a casual group at the edge of the stage. "I want to compliment again our Oedipus tonight for his thoroughness and his consistency. But I believe he violated a principle I once heard Lee Strasburg expand upon. 'You don't play the end of the play before you get to it.' Yes, Oedipus is guilty, but the action of the play is the discovery of that guilt. Without that action, the play is pointless. Our Oedipus tonight was guilty from the beginning, and his self-sacrifice at the end of the play causes no one to rejoice because he is not a *worthy* sacrifice. Unless the City is saved, the play is not a tragedy."

"That would be true—if the play's Oedipus had been written by Sophocles, or if he were the Jesus of the New Testament." Rik is on his feet and speaking almost before he realizes it. "But this is the Oedipus of Seneca, or probably more accurately—I don't know—Ted Hughes. This is 1977 A.D., not 427 B.C. Nobody dies *for* us anymore. You're right that the Oedipus we saw onstage tonight was guilty from the word 'go,' but there are reasons for that. You look at Oedipus and see a strong and confident leader. I look at him and see a wounded child. *Oedipus*—the name means 'swollen foot'. His ankles were pinned together so that he couldn't crawl away from the place where he was put to *die*. How much of this does he remember? Who is going to have to *pay* for this? Yes, Oedipus knows that he is guilty. Unlike the rest of us, he was told at the beginning of his life that he wasn't *worthy* to live. Unlike the rest of us, he knows that the judgment against him is fair. At the beginning of the play, he carries guilt for a crime—he doesn't know what the crime *is*—but he knows that eventually he'll have to pay. At the end of the play, he is calm—even serene—because he has discovered the worst, and he has paid the price! No wonder the City is uneasy, no wonder it doesn't feel cleansed. Like Oedipus, it knows that it's guilty, but unlike him, it doesn't know of what, and it doesn't know if it *can* pay the price!"

Rik finds himself looking into the face of Thyme Wright. "The action of the play is not the discovery of Oedipus' guilt; it is the discovery of our guilt. This is not a god who dies for us, giving us Eternal Life. This is a man who dies for himself, for his own sins—he does so courageously, with dignity, seeing the truth with empty eye sockets—but he dies alone, as we all do."

There is applause, but he doesn't hear it. Thyme speaks, but he doesn't hear her either. He doesn't need to. She is saying, "Goodbye, Rik."

******

Continental Airlines Flight 7457 rolls to a stop on the tarmac of Des Moines International Airport at 4:11 P.M., Thursday, August 5, 1977—a rare on-time arrival. The passenger ramp is attached to the port side of the plane, and the exit door opens. At the bottom of the steps, Rik throws aside his carry-on and sprints toward the trio of figures which is running across the grass toward him. He sweeps up Karl with his right arm and crushes Annie (too big at ten to lift) against him with his left, leaning across her to kiss Lynne.

"Why is Daddy crying?" a little boy asks in wonder.

"Hush, Darling," his mother says. "He's just happy to be home."

*****

EPILOGUE

Midnight, August 2, 1977. Two blocks over from the Performance Garage on Wooster in Fanelli's Café on the corner of Prince and Mercer, Rik Temple sits contemplating his third bourbon and water. The water is extending his bladder, the bourbon seems to be having no effect at all. Tomorrow is a workday in New York City, and the crowd is thin. A news program with the sound turned down is on the television above the bar and Rik focuses on it as if it mattered. Someone slides up onto the bar stool next to him.

"Hey."

"Hey," he responds, turning to face a jeans and tee-shirt clad young woman, with freckles and a ponytail.

"My name is Maggie Phillips. I just wanted to say how much I liked what you had to say at the talk-back." She offers a hand. "The whole cast did."

He shakes her hand, which is surprisingly strong. "Why thank you, Maggie Phillips, although I don't remember you from the show."

"I'm the prop mistress, but the response from the company was pretty unanimous. Even Richard liked it, and if it isn't about him, he's hard to please."

"Schechner? I've had a long-distance bone to pick with him for a dozen years."

"You'd have a few more if you were closer. What was it this time?"

"Nothing important, really. I've liked a lot of his ideas—he's actually one of my heroes, but he has a way of making you feel like pond scum if you're not as far out front as he is. And most of the places I've been, they not only fire you for that kind of theatre, they might just jail you."

Maggie laughed loud enough to attract the bartender's attention. "Listen, lemme tell you a story. That ego sometimes has its drawbacks. What did you think of the set?"

"The sand pit? What were those things sticking up out of it—body parts?"

"Body parts, yeah. Half-buried remnants of half-forgotten crimes. I made plaster casts of whatever I could get the actors to stand still for. Ya see the distended belly?"

"Is Jocasta really pregnant?"

"That's Joan MacIntosh, Richard's wife. Yeah, eight months. When the baby comes, the play will have to shut down for a while. Anyway, one of the pieces—I don't know if you noticed—Richard demanded be included, was a penis."

"I didn't see it. Must have been too small."

"Richard would love that. He was the model."

"No kidding?"

"No kidding. He said no one else was suitable, although I don't know how he knew. So I had to make the plaster cast. Furthermore, he insisted that, since he was such a busy man, that it had to be done during rehearsal. So, anytime he felt he had to make a move while he was directing, I had to follow along on my hands and knees so that his dick wouldn't fall off."

"That must have helped the actors concentrate."

"Especially Joan. But wait, it gets better. Because he moved around so much, I didn't get the necessary grease on his genitals. So when we took off the plaster cast, all of Richard's public hair came with it."

Maybe it was that funny, or maybe it was the bourbon finally kicking in, but Rik lay his head face down, struggling for breath, as he pounded the bar with his fist.

"Remember," Maggie advised. "Your heroes may not only have feet of clay, they may have clay dicks."

Rik sucked in his breath, and was about to collapse again, when the television picture cut from a solemn-looking anchor to a frontal view of a parked Ford Fairlane, its front window pierced by two large bullet holes. For a brief moment the camera focused on the passenger side of the car, and Rik could see a head covered with short, blonde hair bent over behind the sunbeam-like perforation of the windshield.

Film at Eleven.

$$*\ *\ *\ *\ *$$

237

NEW YORK POST (August 13, 1977)

Statistical Summary of the July 13-14 Blackout

Stores looted in Crown Heights, Brooklyn: 75.

Blocks totally ablaze between Bushwick and Bedford-Stuyvesant: 2

Fires still burning on July 14th in Bushwick: 25

Blocks of Broadway destroyed: 35

Broadway Stores looted: 134

Total Stores reporting damage: 1,616

Fires responded to: 1,037

People arrested: 3,776

Damage cost: $300,000,000

Deaths caused: Impossible to calculate, as it would have to include everything from heart attacks in the Bronx to a drug dealer killed in Washington Square Park

*****

Shea Stadium, September 12, 1977. The game suspended with the visiting Chicago Cubs leading the New York Mets, 2-1, resumes with Lenny Randle at bat in the bottom of the sixth inning. Final Score: Cubs 5, Mets 1. (The Mets will go on to finish sixth in 1977. In 1978 they will finish last and Lenny Randle will be released.)

*****

Brooklyn Academy of Music, January 30, 1988. Rik Temple sits in a mezzanine seat overlooking the stage, awaiting the opening curtain of a highly touted production of Anton Chekhov's *The Cherry Orchard*, directed by Peter Brook. He flips idly through the program. Brian Dennehy as Lopakhin. His reviews had been great. Who would have thought that a movie and TV heavy could have re-made himself into a stage leading man? He had to find a way to get to New York more often. A well-dressed woman sits down next to him. The gray of her curly hair matches his beard, and her flesh, if more ample, is still firm.   Her eyes have lost none of their sparkle, and she kisses him as easily as if she had done it at breakfast. They are immediately at ease with one another.

"Thank you for inviting me. I've heard a lot about this production."

"Once I knew you were in town too, it seemed a shame to go alone. You had to miss the Serban production at Lincoln Center. Remember?"

"That's right! Jana was in town, and then the Blackout threw everything off schedule."

"How is Jana?"

"Jana? All right, I guess. Living in Florida, I don't see her often. We still own a piece of land in Arkansas, and every now and then we talk about building a cabin on it."

"Are you happy in Florida?"

"Pretty much. The students are bright, sometimes a little too rich, a little too self-satisfied. Maybe it's the weather. A Midwestern girl needs more of a challenge from her environment. Actually, that's why I'm in New York. I was upstate interviewing for a Dean's job at a SUNY school, and I took the opportunity to stop over on my way back."

"Congratulations! Did you get it?"

"No, actually!" Thyme smiles ruefully. "I was doing great, until a local newspaper caught up with my past."

"They wouldn't hire you because you're *gay*? In this day and age?"

"No, they seemed fine with that," she explains. "They didn't say it, but basically they wouldn't hire me because I'm a Wiccan. Even worse, an apostate Catholic Wiccan. A major donor apparently had kittens at just the thought of it. A word to the wise," she pats his cheek, "don't ever give an interview you don't want read back to you in court or at a job interview."

Rik leans back in his seat. "Don't ever change, love. Even

if I only see you once every decade or so, your life is exciting enough for both of us. When do I get to ghost-write that autobiography of yours? I want to make sure my name is in the index. I can dine out on that story for years."

"When do you want to start?"

"How about tonight? We could scribble on napkins over a late dinner."

A shadow passes over her face. "I'm sorry, Rik, I can't. I'm meeting a woman I was on a panel with at the MLA Convention."

"I understand."

"If only I had known that you were going to be here, I never would have made the arrangement. You know you'll always come first with me." She takes his hands and turns him toward her by force of will alone. "Did you know that when you were waiting for the taxi that last morning in New York, I was watching you from the lobby? I couldn't bring myself to come out to see you."

"Did you know that last morning in New York I wanted to come up to the 14th floor to see you, but couldn't bring myself to do it?"

"Did you ever wish you had stayed in New York?"

"Every day for a while. Not often now. I dream about it sometimes."

"Did Lynne know about us?"

"I don't think so. I hope not. I'm not ashamed, but she didn't deserve to be hurt. Were you happy in New York?"

"After a while. In the beginning I was just lonely. Do you know what I did that first morning after you left? I made an appointment at the Village Free Clinic to have my uterus scraped.

Rik is startled, solicitous, and ashamed in the same moment, but Thyme rushes on. "I hadn't been with a man for a long time. I wasn't using any kind of protection, and you weren't either. I couldn't take the chance."

"What about Tom?"

"What about him? You're my last man, Rik. I never had another. I loved you."

"Why didn't you tell me?"

"Because you asked. You never should have done that, Rik. You should have trusted me."

The house lights dim down, and the stage lights come up on *The Cherry Orchard*, a play once described to Rik as being "about people who won't do anything to help themselves, even if they might lose everything." Thyme squeezes Rik's hand as Brian Dennehy as a burly Lopakhin enters a stage that is bare except for a huge red rug.

Late in the second act Thyme leans close to his ear. "I have a title for our book," she whispers. "*Thyme on my Hands.*" Then she disengages her own hand from his, stands, and moves quietly down the row of seats toward the exit. He does not turn his head to see her go, but watches the stage like a hawk.

The bespectacled student Trofimov is speaking passionately to an enraptured Anya: "Yet always, every moment of the day and night, I've been haunted by mysterious visions of the future. Happiness is coming, Anya, I feel it. I already see it—"

How time flies!

HUNGER

It is eleven o'clock, and his wife Lynne is already in bed when the phone on Rik's desk rings. The woman's voice on the line has a raw coarseness that only three packs a day or a lifetime of tears can generate.

"Is this Rik—Rikart Temple?"

"Yes?"

"I'm sorry for calling you so late, but your number was in his notebook and since you're on West Coast time, I thought I'd take a chance. I hope it's all right."

"We're on Mountain time. Who is this, please?"

The voice is confused, her message unplanned. "I'm sorry. Grace—Grace Pluchinski. It was just that he talked about you so often. I'm sorry. Would it be better to call back tomorrow?"

"No—Grace? What is it? What are we talking about?"

"It's Gary! He's dead—three days ago. Oh god, I didn't mean to blurt it out like this! I'm just not thinking clearly. I was going through his notebook, calling all the numbers with names that I recognized. I figured you were so far away—that you wouldn't have heard!"

The spring rain on the study window picks up in intensity. Something in Rik's mind isn't processing clearly. "Where's Judi? Where's Callie?"

"Judi? Gone—divorced years ago! I'm Grace! I'm—I was—

Gary's wife. I don't know his daughter. He gave up custody; he always meets—met—her without me. Look, he shot himself! Okay? At his writing desk in the workshop. I found him Sunday night when I got home from the club. 'The Artist's Retreat.' Gary said you used to go there together. I'm a bartender. That's where we met."

Gary dead? Rik tries to sort the information he's just received into a coherent pattern, but images from 1971 of a young man his own age keep getting in the way. Judi gone? "But why? Why would he kill himself?"

"Why?" The voice is calmer now, the answer almost rehearsed. It is either true, or contains a truth with which she can live. "He felt that he had done all he could do. He said that several times lately. He'd done everything he had to do. There wasn't anything of meaning left to do."

*****

A reflection from the window in his office door catches his eye and he pauses momentarily, key in hand. A bespectacled academic with a graying beard, dressed in a clichéd corduroy sport coat and sixties turtleneck, looks back at him. The specter raises its head slightly to remove the shadow of an incipient double chin. Beside him in the glass appears another image—a face framed by a wedge haircut in the style Dorothy Hamill made famous and a pair of twisted gold hoop earrings.

"Professor Temple? Can I talk to you?"

Rik unlocks the door and holds it open. Jill Sullivan hesitates, looking down the hall. He follows her eyes to a girl who stands center, towering above her classmates of both genders. A local sports page picture flashes in his mind—Jackie Russell. She'd taken a class of his. The tall girl nods warily to one or the other of them, and in that moment, Jill slips by him into the office. For a moment, Rik is aware of her scent and struggles to identify it.

He looks inquiringly at her from the doorway. She stands a head shorter than he, but slim and athletic. At first glance a tomboy in jeans and a denim jacket, until the swirling hoop earrings drew one's attention in to Eurasian cheekbones and wide set eyes, half determined, half apprehensive. "No. Close it—please."

"Of course. Won't you sit down?" He finds himself closing the door almost stealthily, and makes a conscious choice to sit opposite her rather than go behind the desk. "What can I do to help?"

She pulls one leg up under her and perches on the edge of the chair. "It's my final paper. I've been thinking about what you said in class about how fast people's attitudes change sometimes, while other times people who want things to be different are crushed. You mentioned the integration of the military?"

"Yes, the Battle of the Bulge. When the Germans broke through the American lines, Eisenhower allowed black volunteers in white platoons. The studies showing how well they did gave Truman the proof he needed to support his 1948 Executive Order."

The dark head shakes impatiently. "That's interesting, but I want to write about personal relationships. About how people are kept apart by race and social class—stuff like that. Like Desdemona and Othello!"

"Desdemona was fascinated by Othello because he *was* different, older with experiences she hadn't had. Do you remember Strindberg's *Miss Julie*? Julie is seduced by her servant Jean, who can't get over the habit of calling her 'Miss.' He thinks that if they could escape to some other society, they could be equals."

"Exactly!" The wide-set eyes are excited now and the face-framing haircut has a life of its own. "Living what's true for them, not what society expects! 'The Personal as Political.' Only for your class, the plays would have to be American."

"There are dozens of examples! *Deep Are the Roots* came out at the very end of World War II. A young black officer returns home to the southern white girl he grew up with. They read *Othello* together as teenagers. Look." Rik strives to make his voice as disinterested as possible. "This afternoon the music department has the first run-through of their concert version of *Knickerbocker Holiday*, an American allegory about fascism. You ought to check it out. 'September Song,' where the old Dutch governor proposes to the young girl, is one of the best ballads in American musical history."

"I never heard of it." The girl retreats into the chair. "Jackie and I were going to a movie, but the yearbook is taking pictures of the basketball team. I still might go. *The Hunger* at the Spire?"

"The vampire flic?"

The dark eyes fix on his. "Oh, it's much more than that—much more! You ought to check it out."

*****

Lynne has taught three classes that day and exudes the desperate energy of the fulfilled as she strides in from the bathroom, wearing a fresh slip and rubbing lotion into her hands. Her return to teaching at the Catholic college across town the year before suits her. Her courses and her office hours are packed with young women who see in her an alternative to their exhausted, child-burdened, mothers and the celibate severity of the nuns—a vibrant professional whose marriage and children have not dimmed her interest in the world around her. Meanwhile, young pre-seminarians also crowd the classes, reconsidering their vocation.

Rik sympathizes with the male students, remembering the enthusiastic curiosity and bouncing ponytail that mesmerized him in a classroom a quarter-century ago.

"You see, he was arguing that this 'gay cancer' was God's

way of punishing immorality. So I asked him what the purpose of war was. What did God have in mind when children starved to death? What sin was malaria the punishment for? Or did God love mosquitoes more than people? Maybe—just maybe—this immune deficiency thing has to do with something other than who we love, or how. Maybe—just maybe—God would like us to show our love for Him by caring for his children. I don't know what world some of these priests live in! Surely the first job of a shepherd is to keep his flock alive!" From the closet she selects a blue skirt, then slips into a silk blouse. "Button me up, will you, Hon? Thank goodness you came home. I could hardly ask Gene to do it? Why *are* you home anyway?"

Rik knows the response before he makes the proposition. "I thought, with the kids away, we'd spend the evening together, have dinner, take in a movie, that sort of thing."

Lynne interrupts her selection of a belt for the skirt, quickly crossing the room to kiss his cheek. "Oh sweetie, that would be wonderful, but I just can't. I've got the Democratic Organizing Committee at four—we're having sandwiches brought in—and I go right from there to the anti-nuke meeting. They're the same thing, really! If we have four more years of Reagan, who knows what the result will be? 'Rocket Ron's' *1984* may make Orwell look like an optimist."

The doorbell rings, and Lynne hops out of the bedroom, donning a pair of heels in the process. "That'll be Gene." She stops at the front door and turns to him. "Annie's class won't be back from Mexico until Saturday afternoon, and Karl is sleeping over with David. Tomorrow's Good Friday, and he doesn't have school, but call Gina and find out if he has everything he needs. The rest of the salmon is in the refrigerator. You can handle your own supper, can't you?"

In the doorway stands Gene Roberts, the tennis playing public relations executive and congressional candidate. He takes in Lynne's appearance appreciatively. "Don't you look nice!" He waves to the man left behind in the living room. "Don't worry, Rik! I'll get her back home as soon as she's done saving the world!"

*****

The Spire is a dingy "second-run" theatre, with aspirations as an Art House. That reputation (and the Spire's profit margin) largely depends on weekend midnight showings of *The Rocky Horror Picture Show* at which the local punk subculture makes its contributions to the theatre's already sticky floor. The management has hopes that *The Hunger* might be another cult classic cash cow. A first feature by Tony Scott, the younger brother of the director of *Blade Runner* (itself a surprise Spire money-maker after a first-run flop in commercial houses), *Hunger*'s cast features erstwhile glam-rocker David Bowie, *Rocky Horror Show* survivor Susan Sarandon, and Catherine Deneuve from Polanski's *Repulsion* and Bunuel's *Belle de Jour*.

Rik looks around uneasily as he slides his money across the grimy counter. What does the jowly ticket taker see? A man in a raincoat, approaching middle age, attending an afternoon showing of a film whose salacious poster decorated the wall behind him. He has—he tells himself angrily—no reason to apologize for attending a vampire movie. Ten years earlier he'd directed the 1926 *Dracula*, and even made a scholarly contribution to the genre at Bowling Green University's Popular Culture Convention. He knows that the original Bela Lugosi film is a post-World War I metaphor for a corrupt Europe sucking the blood from innocent America, and that the Christopher Lee Hammer Films were a precursor to the sexual rebellion of the Sixties. He'd even speculated that the television miniseries of Stephen King's *Salem's Lot* was a reflection of the paranoia Reagan would eventually project onto the Soviet Union as the "Evil Empire." And, after all, wasn't the illicit exchange of bodily fluids the essence of most popular films?

Nevertheless, sitting in the deserted balcony, his unease grows. On the screen below him, a man sees himself aging rapidly before his still flawlessly beautiful wife. Rik finds himself building a pedantic wall between him and the events unfolding before him. Wasn't it Aurora, the Greek goddess of the Dawn, who pleaded with Zeus that her husband Tithonus receive Eternal Life—but forgot to ask for Eternal Youth? In the film the man cannot die, but the woman entombs him, undead, in a coffin in an attic full of coffins and moves on to a new love. The roots of *The Hunger* precede Bram Stoker, deriving from "Carmilla," the last story written by another Irishman, J.S. Le Fanu, in which an innocent girl becomes fascinated with a mysterious woman who is the incarnation of a portrait in the ancestral castle. Rik had quoted to his *Dracula* cast what the critic V.S. Pritchett said about Le Fanu's stories:

"It is we who are the ghosts. The secret doubt, the private shame, the unholy love, scratch away with malignant patience in the guarded mind, weakening the catch we normally keep clamped so firmly down, and out slink one by one all the hags and animals of moral or Freudian symbolism."

On the screen a young woman doctor, whose specialty is the aging process, appears at the door of a Manhattan townhouse to inquire after the husband who was her patient. In the balcony, a silent figure slips silently into the seat right of Rik. The light from the screen reflects from a twisted hoop earring and a wedge of dark hair is silhouetted against the shadowy background.

The exquisite blonde woman sits at the piano, gently playing. Behind her, the younger, red-haired woman sits, delicately balancing a glass of sherry.

"How do you spend your time? Are you lonely? I mean—

especially now that your husband's away. . . I like your pendant."

"It's Egyptian. . . You know it was a symbol of everlasting life?..."

A hand tentatively touches Rik's arm. Impulsively he raises it and drapes it over the girl's shoulders.

"What's that piece you're playing?"

"It's *Lakme* by Leo Delibes. Lakme is a Brahmin princess in India. She has a slave named Mallika."

"Mallika."

"In a magical garden they sing about how they follow a stream... crystal... gliding over the water."

Her hand is in his lap now, cool and firm, seeking out his much larger left hand. Out of the corner of his eye Rik studies the girl beside him. Jill's face is still. Her concentration on the film is total.

"Is it a love song?"

"I told you. It was sung by two women."

"Sounds like a love song."

"Then I suppose it is. . ."

She lifts her hand. As if by suggestion, his hand accompanies it. Inside of her blouse, there is no supportive undergarment, and it is not needed. The breast is high and warm. How long since he has touched a breast like that? "A breast that could fit a champagne glass," a long ago teacher in a less politically sensitive age had said.

"Are you making a pass at me, Mrs. Blaylock?"

"Miriam."

"Miriam."

"Not that I'm aware of, Sarah."

Rik's forefinger slowly circumscribes the areola complex, joining with his thumb to caress a nipple which seemingly grows beneath his touch. He can sense, rather than hear, a quickened rate in the girl's breathing but Jill's face remains resolutely focused on the screen, her lips parted. Light gleams from a bead of moisture forming at the corner of her mouth.

In the film before them, the younger woman's hand trembles, spilling drops of red sherry on her white blouse. Delibes' "Flower Duet" transmigrates from the calm precision of the piano into a passionate blend of soprano/mezzo soprano. A rush of blood invades Rik's scrotum. He leans forward, dizzy. A discord creeps into the music below. A great sadness sweeps over him—the pride in the capability of his aging body dissolving into the recognition that this young woman's passions would long outlive his ability to satisfy them. What has he in that moment given up? His marriage, his family, his home, his place in the community, the respect and trust of his friends, colleagues, and students? Who had he betrayed? Lynne, his children, himself—even Jill?

Rik looks up. The seat beside him is empty.

*****

Rik stands beneath the theatre marquis, hoping to outwait the rain before walking to his car. Across the street Jill emerges from the coffee shop, followed by the rangy figure of Jackie Russell. Oblivious of the drizzle, they stroll down the street toward the park. As they pass the bicycle shop, the taller girl takes the arm of the shorter one and draws her into the alley darkness beyond the prying streetlamp. Rik shivers. *Jack and Jill!* He might have known, had he paid attention. Rik turns up the collar of his raincoat and heads up the street in the opposite direction toward the parking lot.

*****

About eight o'clock the phone rings. Rik starts from a newspaper whose pages he hasn't turned in some time.

"Rik? Do you know who this is?"

How long had it been? Eleven years? Twelve? A thousand?

They had been young together. Rik and Gary running a department for the first time in a small Minnesota college, Lynne and Judi raising small children in their first mortgaged houses. There had been challenges then—challenges whose values they didn't question.

"Hey Jude."

"Is Lynne there? Have you heard?"

"No, she's at a meeting. Yes, Grace called last night."

Over the phone Rik hears a long inhalation. "Ah yes, the aptly-named Grace. They were both alcoholics, you know." The voice is a little sleepy, not in any way angry.

"Look, I know we're a long way away, Judi, but is there anything we can do?"

"Just talk to me for a little while, please." There is no demand in the statement. It is what she has to say to herself that the caller needs to hear. "Callie isn't home yet, you know. She was visiting my mom over the Spring Break, and she's driving her back. I think she'd stay away if she could. She blames me because she's got to blame someone. She thinks she has to point out my guilt to me, and she doesn't want to do it. She *knows* she has to represent the family at the funeral—everyone will be watching her—and she doesn't want to do that either. That's a lot of pressure for a teenager." There was a long pause and another sighing inhalation. "She's a real beauty, you know. My skin and Gary's red hair? Just pretty enough for older guys to give her the eye, and just young enough not to know any better."

Rik said nothing. If she was anything like her mother, that was likely. Gary used to say that Judi gave men headaches—not because she was difficult, but because they were always walking into doorframes when they passed by her: long dark hair with eyes to match, porcelain skin, slender waist, and legs all the way down to the ground—a small town girl in the guise of a hippie princess. He hadn't been immune to her beauty and doubted that many men were.

"I wasn't much older than Callie when I met Gary. Did you know that? Just seventeen! Washington State University! Seniors on the honor roll could take a class at the University. Gary was my teacher. Interpersonal Communication! Isn't that a laugh? The day grades were posted he stopped me in the hallway. He said he never dated his students, but now that class was over, he wondered if I would go out with him. When he found out I was still in high school, he asked when my birthday was and then just turned around and walked away. On the night of my eighteenth birthday, he called me. I don't know how he got my number. A year later we were married."

Her laugh segues into a cough. "Do you know what I'm doing?"

"Smoking something would be my guess."

She giggles. "That's right! Gary left behind all his stash when he moved out. He said he planned to do a lot of drinking, and he couldn't drink and smoke weed at the same time. I never touched it till now. Do you remember when he planted the patch of cannabis behind the house outside Cherry?"

"I remember when the deer ate it."

"That's right! Gary said his one contribution to the environment was that he had the most laid-back deer in Minesota. He said the only problem was that now he had to hide his potato chips because they all had the munchies." There was a long pause and she inhaled again. "He was always saying things like that. He'd been everywhere and done everything. He'd been a paratrooper; he even tried out with the Denver Broncos. Did you know that?"

"Yeah, he was a linebacker in college. Denver tried him at safety. He was too slow."

"He was the smartest man I ever met. . . The only trouble was that I hadn't met that many men." She sighed. "Did Grace tell you what happened?"

"That he shot himself?"

"Oh that!" She snorts, impatiently. "That was the 'Saddle

Bum Billy' stuff. You remember *Saddle Bum Billy*!"

"The one-man play that he was always trying to sell to PBS?"

"That's why he quit teaching, you know. He was going to write this series for Public Television about a North Dakota rodeo cowboy and trick shooter who became another Will Rogers. On 'spec'—isn't that what you call it? I don't know if he ever finished anything but the play. He did it for a few grade schools, community centers—that kind of stuff. Then one night he took Billy's .45 loaded with blanks, stuck it in his mouth and pulled the trigger!... Blanks! That's what really stinks, you know!"

"Why does Callie blame you?"

"Why? Who knows?... Because of *Cuckoo's Nest*, I guess."

"*Cuckoo's Nest*?"

The play—*One Flew Over the Cuckoo's Nest*. Gary was a big fan of Ken Kesey, thought he'd tapped into some kind of psychedelic American psyche. Identified with Randall McMurphy too, I think. A little crazy, a loner with a code. . . but Gary wasn't a loner. He needed an audience, someone to look up to him, cheers! He'd been an athlete, a military hero, a star student. He just never reached the next level. He didn't survive the first cut at Denver. There was no war when he was in the army, and when it did come, he didn't believe in it. Remember how he loved Jane Fonda?"

"Me too."

The voice is amused. "Yeah, but he loved 'Hanoi Jane.' You loved *Barbarella*. Remember when Lynne promised to get you the poster?"

"She never did."

"She wasn't stupid. She's been writing me the past couple of years. Did you know that? I always admired Lynne. She was the most understanding person I ever met. Passionate *and* understanding! It's a combination you almost never see. . . She seems a lot happier since she went back to teaching. She didn't need to be a star—not like Gary! She just needed to do something that meant something. She must have told you about Gary and me."

"No."

"Yeah?... Well, she probably had her reasons." A deep inhalation is heard over the phone, followed by a slow exhalation. The voice is sleepier. "I should have done that, you know. Gone back to school?... I don't think Gary wanted me to grow up. I was his last cheerleader. He was afraid I'd outgrow him. He thought his teaching career was in the toilet. He didn't go on to a big school—not like you did! He'd get like that even when you were still here. Stay out at the college, leave me here in this old house outside of Cherry with no one around but a motor mouth three-year-old? Cherry, Minnesota—the home of Bob Dylan, Bus Anderson, who invented the Greyhound Bus, and Gus Hall, the head of the American Communist Party. You'd think it'd be more exciting, wouldn't you?

"What happened with *One Flew Over the Cuckoo's Nest*?"

"Do you know he would come home and never say a word until he'd watched every possible news broadcast on television? Did Lynne tell about the time I cooked supper topless to try to arouse his interest?" The voice giggles. "If we ever get to know one another better, I'll show you the scar from the grease burn on my left breast. . . What did you say?"

"*Cuckoo's Nest*?"

"Oh yes! I guess he finally heard me—cast me in one of his plays—*Cuckoo's Nest*—the stage version, quite a bit different from the movie. I played Nurse Ratched. Gary brought in a professional actor he knew—a method actor! In the play Ratched picks on McMurphy because she has a repressed desire for him; he makes her feel weak, feminine. I told ya this guy was a method actor. Nobody had made me feel feminine for quite a while. Gary had the rest of the play on his mind. You can figure out the rest."

"Gary found out."

"Gary found out. Then the play was over, and 'Randall McMurphy' picked up his method and moved on to become somebody else."

"Gary moved on too?"

"Gary moved on too. He left me the house... and its payments. We got the house for no money down on the G.I. Bill. You and Lynne too, right? I got a job filing forms for an architecture firm, and eventually became the Office Administrator. Pretty good at it too! But I never went back to school. And I never went back on stage!"

"And Gary moved on to Grace?"

"He moved on to 'The Artist's Retreat.' He could be a writer there, talk about being a writer at least—'Saddle Bum Billy,' right? And everybody knows good writers are drinkers! To be fair to Grace, I don't think she was an alcoholic until she met Gary, just a girl who made bad choices in men. Besides, he was 'the smartest man who ever showed any interest in her'. When the Saddle Bum Billy thing didn't work out—and of course it didn't—she still stuck with him."

"But she wasn't his cheerleader anymore."

"She wasn't his cheerleader anymore. But that didn't mean that his life was over." The voice sighs and inhales again. "Did you hear my stomach rumble? Gary was right. This stuff makes you hungry. . . What is it about men? Why are your egos so fragile? You don't need to keep somebody from growing up to be a big man. People you don't let grow up are *dangerous*! I knew I'd done wrong! It didn't make him any less of a man. We could have worked it out—it was like he was expecting me to cheat on him! Like the play was a test, and I didn't *fail* it—I got exactly the grade he expected. Sometimes when I'd visit my grandpa's farm, I'd step in a cow pie. But I didn't throw away the shoe! I just wiped it off and went on! People are going to grow up whether you like it or not, and sometimes making a mistake is part of that growing up! Do ya understand? I've got to hang up and go to sleep now. Good night. . . God, I wish Lynne was there. She'd understand! She's a grownup, she's been there. I just wish she was here now and I could talk to her!"

"So do I, Jude. So do I. Good night."

YEMAJA

Lynne watched the argument from the other side of the room, curled up on the enormous davenport, balancing a glass of white wine in one hand and half-stroking, half-restraining a slender, blue-eyed Siamese cat with the other. Eennie was in heat, head butting and kneading in search of satisfaction, but she was no more predictable than the discussion of the two men at the built-in bar below the wall screen TV.

"*Belo Horizonte* is a city on stilts—literally and figuratively," the younger man said. "In this neighborhood life begins on the third floor. The city was built on the foothills to the mountains between here and Rio, and not that long ago! It grew up in the age of the skyscraper; only our skyscrapers start with a metal frame and not until we've cleared the hills do we install living space. A wonderful view, but available only to a privileged few and an enormous waste of space for a city of over two million people."

Lynne sipped her wine and contemplated the similarities in the two men. Their luggage had been lost somewhere between Miami and Sao Paulo, and her husband had borrowed a set of Julio's tennis whites. Rik was bearded, taller, and grayer than their host, but they shared a compact build, blue eyes, and dark, wavy hair. Except for how well they got along, it would be easy to mistake them for father and son.

Mercifully, Eennie had fallen into a catnap. Lynne mentally calculated the progress of the argument. It had begun with architecture, would inevitably segue into politics, and could not be complete without a series of the motion picture metaphors that both men loved.

Rik jiggled the ice in the *caipirinha* glass on the bar top. "According to the *Times* on the plane, that way of building is coming to an end—a condescension by Cardoso to steal some of the labor vote from Lula."

Julio laughed. "Oh yes, a law was passed! With the advent of Y2K in a few days there will be 'a new millennium in housing,' with the lowest floors made available to people with working class incomes. That's what I meant about "figurative" stilts. The law only applies to buildings begun *after* January 1st, 2000. All year contractors have been putting up metal frames for apartment buildings—to be filled in as wealthy customers become available. Didn't you notice them? It was bad enough in the winter, but now that the rainy season is here, we live in a city of lightning rods. I swear that during a nighttime thunderstorm if you looked out that window and saw those steel skeletons striding along the skyline, spitting sparks, you'd believe you were in the midst of an alien invasion from Orson Welles' *War of the Worlds*! No, my friend, there will always be ways in Brazil to keep the rich high above the poor, not matter the law."

Lynne anticipated her husband's response. "*Favors* and *favelas*, eh? Well then, perhaps you're referencing the wrong movie. Instead of *War of the Worlds*, you should be talking about Fritz Lang's *Metropolis*. After all, you live in this beautiful, two-floor apartment at the top of the building, with a black maid who comes in two days a week to clean, and the only lower forms of life you have to deal with are Eennie and Meannie—and Meannie hides most of the time."

Julio took on a look of patently false incredulity. "You want me to be like Freder, and descend from the Tower of Babel into the depths of the Underworld? You have no idea what lower forms of life I have to deal with as a tax lawyer—not the least the tax code itself, whose draconian Brazilian bureaucracy made owning this apartment possible. Lang's *Son of the Great Ruler* might have unified the workers and planners, but the real Christ was crucified, and I plan estates, not miracles. Besides, I already have my Maria."

"Have you changed my name, or is there something you've forgotten to tell me?" Dumping a startled Eennie on the floor, Lynne rose to help a smiling Elena who had entered with a tray of hors d'oeuvres and *yerba mate* tea.

Lynne spread the napkins and silverware on the coffee table, as Julio embraced his wife with real affection. "No, you're safe for the moment," he said. "We were just trying to pick out a video to watch this evening."

Elena wrinkled her elegant brow. "Just as long as it isn't one of your silent 'classics.' I always fall asleep."

Julio lifted a weary eyebrow at Rik. "So much for *Metropolis*. Actually, Rik suggested Terry Gilliam's *Brazil* and I wanted *The Magnificent Seven* with Steve McQueen. We're in love with one another's cultural myths. So we thought we'd leave it up to Lynne." Turning to her he gestured toward the cabinet under the TV. "If you don't see anything you like, the video shop we drove by today is just five minutes away down by the *futbol* stadium."

"Which one?" Rik asked.

"The old one, the *Independencia*. You know, where 'the Miracle on Grass' happened? Every American must know that story."

Rik shook his head. "Not if it has to do with soccer."

Julio frowned. "*Futbol*. It was where the World Cup was played in 1950, the United States vs. the United Kingdom."

"The United States *played* in that World Cup?"

"Yes, and not again for another forty years. The Americans were all amateurs, with only seven international matches over the previous fifteen years—which they'd lost by a combined score of 45-2. The British were the best team in Europe. The odds against them winning were 3-1; the odds against the Americans were 500-1!

"What happened?" asked Lynne, shaking off her indifference to sports.

"About what you'd expect." Julio smiled in satisfaction. "Twelve minutes into the game the Brits already had six shots on goal. At thirty-seven minutes the on-goal attempts were nine to one, and then an American player tried a kick from well up the field. The UK goalkeeper was in perfect position for an easy interception. Then another British defender dived in front of him and deflected the ball which found a corner of the net. It was the only goal of the game. I've watched the film many times."

Rik scowled. "Why have I never *heard* this story?"

"Provincialism," Julio answered airily. "That and the fact that there was only one American reporter here, and legend has it that he paid his own way."

"The Miracle on Grass." Lynne was somber. "Then you do believe in miracles."

"In *futbol*, yes," Julio laughed. "In social engineering, no."

"There are people in the *favelas* whose standard of living is worse than North Africa," she pressed him. "We all have an underworld we'll eventually have to face—if not in this millennium, then the next."

"Pay no attention to this naughty little boy," Elena chided them both. "My husband believes in the Miracle of Life," and she leaned over and tenderly kissed him.

"So sayeth the mother of my *yet* to be born sons," Julio growled indignantly.

For a moment Lynne studied them intently. Rik shook his head. "So, have you chosen a film, or is it off to the video store?"

Lynne returned to reality. "That won't be necessary. I see

what I want right here on the shelf—*The Third Man.*"

Rik smiled. "I might have guessed," he said, and sat next to Lynne, slipping his arm around her shoulders.

Elena, ever on the alert for a romantic moment, spoke up. "Am I right in sensing that there's a story here?"

"There is," Lynne admitted, "but it has almost nothing to do with the movie. Do you remember the plot of *The Third Man*?"

Julio snorted. "Of course! A naïve writer of American paperback westerns—white hats, black hats stuff—is invited by an old college friend to an occupied Post-War Vienna, which survives (barely) on deception and the Black Market."

Rik stood, picking up the narrative with enthusiasm. "When the American arrives, he's told that his friend is dead— killed by a hit and run driver in an accident witnessed by two Viennese friends of the victim. Another witness, however, saw a 'third man' help pick up the body off the street. The third man was the college friend himself, Harry Lime, played by Orson Welles, wanted by the police of every occupied zone for a host of crimes—the most despicable of which was the sale of contraband penicillin so watered down as to be deadly rather than life-saving."

Julio and Rik rose and crossed toward one another, circling melodramatically in the center of the room to the delight of Elena and the terror of Eennie, who scrambled for safety behind the bar.

"The two Americans meet at a Viennese amusement park, where in order to talk privately they ride the Ferris wheel."

"The *Wiener Riesenrad* in the Prater Park!"

"Harry opens the safety bar on their seat, showing Holly the people below, who are as tiny as dots. If it would make him incredibly rich, how many of those faceless dots would he sacrifice?"

"It's Satan tempting Jesus from the top of the mountain!"

"And then the greatest speech in cinema history!"

"You know what the fellow said." Rik's voice took on a world-weary blasé tone. "In Italy, for thirty years under the Borgias, they had warfare, terror, murder and bloodshed, but they produced Michelangelo, Leonardo da Vinci and the Renaissance. In Switzerland, they had brotherly love, they had five hundred years of democracy and peace—and what did that produce? The cuckoo clock."

Elena turned to Lynne in astonishment. "You don't mean to say that you know all these scenes too."

Lynne shrugged. "Of course. But the story comes from before I ever saw the movie."

Rik and Julio congratulated one another like tennis players after a five-set match.

"Welles wrote that speech, not Graham Greene. In the published script, it's a footnote."

Elena's curiosity was still focused on Lynne. "Then what is the connection?"

"The scene needed another beat for the sake of rhythm"— Julio and Rik continued to tell one another what they both already knew—"and Welles remembered something from a published lecture by the painter Whistler."

"The story goes back nearly forty years," Lynne explained. "To a young couple with little preparation and less money struggling to survive as graduate students."

"No truth in it, though. The cuckoo clock comes from the Black Forest in Germany."

"Were they people I know?" asked Elena. "Did they ever take a young Brazilian boy into their home?"

"And the Swiss army when the Borgias ruled was the most powerful in Europe."

"They may have. But that would have been twenty-five years later. Where they lived then there was barely room for the two of them."

At the bar Julio and Rik were freshening their drinks. "What are you talking about over there? We seem to have lost the thread of the conversation."

Elena shushed them. "Be quiet! I'm learning the truth behind *The Third Man*."

"I was just telling Elena about a couple of young graduate students from the early 1960s," Lynne explained.

"Anyone I know?" Rik brought the wine bottle from the bar and topped off her glass. She made room for him on the davenport, and Julio and Elena found places on the shining leather chairs that framed the coffee table.

"Looking at you, I doubt it. This couple could only afford two meals a day."

Julio laughed. "Score one for the better half! Don't worry, my friend. I will run those pounds off you on the tennis court." Elena cast a questioning glance at him. Having been English educated, her husband's American slang sometimes puzzled her.

Lynne continued. "And this couple would never have had such an erudite discussion about a film, because they hadn't been anywhere or seen anything."

Rik touched his glass against Lynne's. "Describe a night out for these hicks."

Her voice took on a "Once upon a Time" rhythm. "Every Friday night they went down to Griff's Drive-In and they each had a 12 cent hamburger. Then they went to the Massachusetts Street A&P for their groceries, and the last thing they bought was a pint of ice cream which they took home to their two-room apartment and immediately ate."

Rik looked grave. "It sounds like the freezer compartment in their refrigerator didn't work and that they had no air conditioning in 100 degree weather."

Elena looked astonished. "You had *no air conditioning*?"

Lynne fixed her with a pitying glance. "Of course, there was air conditioning! The apartment was one of six on the second floor and a cement walkway in front connected them all. When the sun went down and the wind came up out of the west, they poured water on the cement and the cooled air blew in the front door and window. "

"How ecologically sensitive they were! Were there other examples of their concern for the environment?" Rik asked.

"Every day they walked to the University. Gasoline was nearly 22 cents a gallon and not to be wasted on frivolities. Besides, their car wasn't insured. And almost every day they climbed the hill to the library behind the building where they took their classes."

"She must have awakened in the night with cramps in her legs," Rik said softly, "and he must have massaged them until she went back to sleep."

"He lost 25 pounds that first semester."

"Which he could probably afford to lose." Rik stroked Lynne's hair. "And she must have lost nearly ten—which she *couldn't* afford to lose."

Julio suddenly realized that Elena had moved to the arm of the chair beside him. He leaned forward. "What did this young couple do for entertainment?"

Lynne frowned. "Well, there was no going out to movies, of course. And no dancing!" She turned to Rik, who laughed at a joke lost on the younger couple. "No television. But there was music. She had a record player—not a hi-fi, mono. And records could be signed out of the city library. Broadway musicals, classical music."

Rik prompted, "Grieg's 'Wedding Day at Trollhaugen,' perhaps?"

"Perhaps, or Barber's 'Adagio for Strings,'"

"Or Ravel's "Le tombeau de Couperin."

"And the radio!" Lynne turned suddenly to Elena and Julio. "They spent $47 they didn't have for a radio. There was no public broadcasting then, but there was educational radio— news, lectures, sports (which she didn't care for, but he did), more classical music."

"He could have developed a phobia against Mozart's 'A

Little Night Music,'" Rik chortled, "because the university station played it every evening at nine, and all he could think about was the stack of books he still had to get through or fall even further behind the confident, better prepared students whom he imagined were either contemptuous of him or ignored him entirely."

"But that's when the entertainment came in, don't you see?" Lynne was smiling, but her eyes were shiny with moisture. "And the connection to *The Third Man* as well. At midnight, a Kansas City station would play an hour of old radio dramas. We'd stop work and have a slice of toast. Then we'd study for two hours more, and a different set of programs would come on at three a.m. Then we'd go to bed, and start all over again in the morning. The programs were our escape, our reward."

"What were the programs?" Elena asked, intrigued by the intensity the explanation seemed to arouse in Lynne.

"Some were American—*The Shadow*, *The Lux Radio Theatre*, *The United States Steel Hour*. Some were from the BBC—*Horatio Hornblower* with Michael Redgrave, *The Black Museum*, Marius Goring in *The Scarlet Pimpernel*."

"And your favorite? Rik asked, knowing the answer.

"*The Adventures of Harry Lime*, starring Orson Welles."

"*The Third Man*," Elena screamed with delight.

"Whatever for?" asked Julio.

"It was adventure, escape to exotic locales from a cramped apartment, a stressful present, and an uncertain future—we didn't know if we'd ever get our degrees, or if there would be any jobs when we got them. Then, the stories were well written, well-acted, with that wonderful zither music as a theme and to link the scenes."

Julio snorted. "It was just a radio rip-off of a great film." Elena, unfamiliar with the colloquialism but knowing it was derogatory, gave him a hard stare, but Lynne was not offended.

"No, there was something more—an idea that isn't in the film. Do you remember how Harry Lime died on the screen?"

"Shot by the police in a Vienna sewer, like the rat he was."

"That was how the radio program began! With the sound of running feet on a wet metallic surface and a shot, followed by Orson Welles speaking in a somber voice, 'Harry Lime died in a sewer beneath the streets of Vienna.' Then immediately he'd switch to a tone of amused detachment like the one he used in the movie (which I hadn't seen yet). 'But Harry Line had many lives. How do I know? I'm Harry Lime.' And the announcer would do the credits, underscored by the zither music, and we'd segue into the story."

"So?" Julio couldn't see the significance. "It was a prequel."

"That term didn't exist forty years ago," Lynne insisted. "Besides, to me it was something different. It was as if his life, or lives, existed simultaneously with his death. Seeing the film only reinforced the feeling. In the beginning you think he's dead; at the end he dies. But in the radio series Harry Lime was alive again—because the character had such a hold on our imaginations that we could visualize him in any number of situations. You say he was a rat, and he was! But he also saved the life of that actress—Anna—and she loved him. That was as real as his life as a con man or a black marketeer. Everyone saw Harry differently, and they were all right! Harry was—*is*—whatever we imagined him to be." Lynne leaned back, suddenly very tired. "As are we all. I used to think about that when we went to bed after listening to the program."

"Ho, ho, ho," Julio's eyebrows lifted. "What did you think about that, Rik?"

"I didn't care," Rik admitted. "I just held onto her as tight as possible. I figured that as long as she was there, I was there. If I hadn't been able to see myself in her eyes every morning, I would just have disappeared."

Elena's voice was soft. "Would you ever go back to those days if you could?"

Rik looked down at Lynne, who was nestled in the crook of his shoulder. "Go back to a time when I was always hungry, but didn't know for what? To a place where only one person knew me, and where I was afraid to be known?"

Lynne was beginning to sound sleepy. "To a country of many roads, but not a single map? Where the underworld was just a misstep away, and only one hand could be trusted?"

"In a heartbeat."

"In a heartbeat."

*****

Cabo Frio on New Year's Eve! Seven hours east of *Belo Horizonte* in the province of *Minas Gervais*, through mountains and coffee plantations, past termite mounds fifteen feet high and potholes almost as deep, is the coastal area of *Sao Paulo* province. Accessible from the Atlantic by the great cruise ships and from the air by charter flights from Uruguay, Argentine, and Chile, *Cabo Frio* has in June a population of about 150,000 people. Tonight, on its nine beaches, there will be three times as many.

The new millennium is twelve hours away, and two hundred feet above *Forte* beach, Rik—later to be followed by Julio—circles in an arc from the ocean to over the city and past the pre-Portugal fort that once guarded the entrance to the Bay. Their conveyance is a rowboat modified by an ultra-light sail, a prop engine, and guidance bars. Their link to earth is a thick rope attached to a power boat below. A transoceanic airliner is a prisoners' bus with numbing leg space and the occasional pacification of peanuts and orange juice. This is *flying*! It is a fantasy breeding appetite, not fulfillment. Next stop—hang gliding from the mountains above *Rio de Janeiro*!

Looking down, the hundreds of umbrellas on the beach looked like mushrooms growing out of the sand. Beneath one of them, dressed in matching Indian muumuus, leaning back in matching canvas chairs, sat Lynne and Elena.

As a young girl in a small town, Lynne had instinctively sought out older women with experiences that had complemented her own. As a new wife and mother, she was drawn to neighbors who had mastered domestic routine without losing their curiosity about the rest of the world—like the eldest sibling of a family of fifteen who had guided her through her own daughter's infancy, while simultaneously supplying her with the government flour she used to bake bread for anti-Vietnam War rallies. Now it was Lynne's turn to be mentor and sounding board.

It was a role she accepted gracefully, sensing that whatever concerns Elena had she could answer them herself simply by formulating them aloud.

Indeed, the life that Elena described seemed more like a fairytale than a seedbed of problems. Lynne found herself making fleeting comparisons to the fantasy existences of the Barbie dolls which Elena avidly collected. She had grown up beautiful, a beloved child in a well-to-do family. Her father was an engineer for a London-based aluminum company, and she was mostly educated at international schools in whatever part of the Empire to which her father's work took them— Canada, Russia, Australia, India ("like the children of the Raj," she joked). Her mother was a ceramics artist, effortlessly absorbing into her craft the cultures to which she was exposed. Elena studied business at the London School of Economics, and had just moved to *Belo Horizonte* from her mother's hometown of *Salvador, Bahia*, to begin a career in importing and exporting Brazil's exotic flowers when she was introduced to a young tax lawyer, educated in America and now a partner in his father's thriving business. What had followed—a whirlwind courtship, a huge wedding, successful careers, the apartment at the top of the city, and a second rooftop home owned by Julio's father here in *Cabo Frio*— hardly justified the occasional undercurrent of anxiety Lynne sensed in the younger woman's voice.

That voice paused and both women found themselves staring out at the incoming waves, which over the decades had thrown up low sand dunes on which they now crashed in frustration. Lynne had tried the surf and quickly wearied of its merciless pounding. Rik, on the other hand, had become addicted within a day, progressing from body surfing to kneeling on a board, confidently predicting a new life "hanging ten."

"What is it like here on New Year's Eve?" Lynne asked.

Elena answered with a wry giggle. "Just a quiet beach party with 400,000 of your most intimate friends. You should be glad you're not in Rio; there will be three million on the beaches there! At least a million of whom will be 'Tall and Tan *Ipanema* Girls' who have decided the only suitable dance partner for them is *your* man."

Lynne laughed. "I'm safe. Rik doesn't dance."

"He will tonight," Elena warned. "And so will you! The samba will be so loud that the tide will go out in self-defense, and the sand will be so hot you will dance or scorch your insteps. Above, the sky will have the mid-day Vesuvian brightness of simultaneous fireworks from the hillside, the hotel, and the fort at the entrance to the harbor. The only way to cool yourself will be with the spray of champagne, and when the new millennium comes in you will be very cool indeed!"

Despite herself, Lynne was awed. "You make it really sound like something to look forward to."

"To look forward to," Elena repeated somberly. "There is another thing we have to do before midnight—and as soon as Julio and Rik return from their little boy airplane thing, you and I must go back to town. We have to prepare our offering to *Yemaja*."

"Who or what is *Yemaja*?" Lynne asked, intrigued by her seriousness.

"Easier to answer what she isn't," Elena replied. "Where I come from in *Bahia*, she is a saint in the Church, 'Our Lady of Seafaring' and 'Our Lady of Conception.' You've met Hanisya?"

"Your maid, the woman who comes in to clean twice a week?"

"Yes, Hanisya is Yoruba. Her people came here as slaves. Slavery ended here only 110 years ago. To her, *Yemaja* was always there in the beginning and all life came from her. Her name means 'Mother whose children are like fish,' and everything living comes from the sea. In Haiti she is the Queen of Voodoo, *LaSiren*, who lured the god from the sky so that there might be life in the world."

"And you worship her on New Year's Eve?"

"Each of us buys a small wooden boat and makes a list of what is desired for the next year. These are *not* resolutions— nothing silly like that! They are *miracles* that only the goddess can grant. We place the list at the bottom of the boat, and over it and around it and every place possible, we pack and wrap and weave offerings to the goddess. That's my advantage, don't you see? I can give her flowers! You can too! My company has an outlet here in *Cabo Frio*. We're closed on the holiday, but I can get in and I have access to blooms from all over the world. She *has* to be pleased by that."

"Does *Yemaja* have a shrine here?"

"The greatest in the world—the sea!" Elena's voice became hushed. "About ten o'clock the tide goes out. (It's not true that the samba drives it away. The sea *loves* the samba.) We go to the high point of the beach and wade out as far as we can, to where the current begins, and set the boats afloat. They must be perfectly balanced or else they'll capsize. The boats drift out past the old Dutch fort at the entrance to the Bay, and if the goddess accepts the gift, they are never seen again, and your wish is granted."

"And if the gift is not accepted?"

"By morning, after the tide has come in, you will find the boat in the shallows or on the sand. *Yemaja* will not fulfill your desire."

Lynne persisted. "But you don't believe that, do you?"

"I have to!" Elena gripped Lynne's hand so hard that it hurt. "I need a baby. *Yemaja* is the mother of all living things. Julio needs a son to be complete. We've tried so hard! Everything ever born came from *Yemaja*. Oh Lynne, don't you want life?"

*****

At the bottom of the boat Lynne placed a slip of paper. Above it and around it she wove the wreath of flowers that was the tribute to the goddess. It began with the local Brazilian blooms—the golden Alstromerias, standing for friendship and devotion, and the sun colored Lisianthus, which means thoughtfulness. Then there were Azaleas, which urge one to "take care of yourself," Red Columbine, which signifies anxiety, Rosemary for remembrance, woven together with the Ivy that is the symbol of matrimonial love, and peeking through it the Clover which says, "I promise." On top was the green and yellow Herb of Grace that her English ancestors called Rue.

*****

On the beach, the *Conga* line snakes between the votive candles set into the depressions in the sand. It is the time of *Reveillon*, when the barrier between the *festa religiosa* and the *festa profana* melts away, when the holiness of the flesh is celebrated, when the sins of the old millennium are shed by the dancing feet of the new, exorcized by the throbbing beat of the drum. Beneath her toes, Lynne feels the shifting earth, as alive and as much a part of her as the blood which courses through her veins. Over her shoulder, she sees a line dressed in white stretching into a darkness beyond her perception, driven by a rhythm of which she is a part.

Then suddenly, as if the product of a cosmic rehearsal, the line rearranges itself from front to back to shoulder to shoulder. The *Samba* has replaced the *Conga*, and the movement of the feet of the dancers becomes barely perceptible, three steps per each 2/4 measure. Lynne yields to the muscle memory of a 35 years past chorus line. Step-ball-change. In a moment, she has adapted to the *Bahia* accent of the music and is tilting her legs toward the outside instead of keeping her knees together.

And then the old millennium passes and the fireworks rain down, seemingly dissolving into the spray of champagne above their heads. From out of the chaos a familiar hand finds hers, drawing her away from the exotic identity of the group into the intimacy of the duo.

*****

Encouraged by the growing quiet, the ocean is feeling its way back to the shore, as, hand in hand, Rik and Lynne walk barefoot through the shallows. Into her ear he pours the dreams of the new millennium.

"Three and a half years from now would be a good time for me to retire. Could you see yourself giving up your teaching position then? While we still have the energy to try something new? I'm not suggesting we give up the house or leave home entirely. But the stock portfolio has done very well in the last eight years! We could afford a condo here. Just spend the winter months? The kids have their own lives. They don't need us there anymore. And later, when there are grandchildren, imagine them coming down here—on the beach! Learning to surf, being exposed to new cultures and languages? Isn't that what we always wanted?"

Lynne presses close to his side, her eyes fixed on a hillock of sand in the distance. Something has been deposited there by the waves—flotsam of the sea or human detritus, she cannot tell. Rik's voice fades from her consciousness as they draw closer to a shipwreck in miniature, its soggy cargo of a wreath still topped by a yellow flower.

From her memory Lynne dredges a historic reminder: the Herb of Grace is also known as the Herb of Remorse.

Back in their room on the fifth floor they made love—spontaneously, almost desperately, their bodies still sweaty from the dancing on the beach, grains of fine sand barely perceptible on the wrinkled sheets below them. And when it was over, she lay beneath him, refusing to disengage, her head turned and her open eyes fixed on the waning moon cupped on the sill of the adobe window across the room.

And then she told him what the doctors had said the day before they left the States—that the cancer was back, why it had been so difficult to diagnose, how many months she might be expected to have. Details answering denials. And for a long time, she held him and soothed him while he cried.

*****

Lynne awoke slowly to the sound of her name being called from the garden. She sat up, leaning back against the metal frame of the Verona bed and looking through the open bedroom door. The outline of the dining room table was just visible in the dim light, and the doorframe of her parents' room on the opposite side was in deep shadow. The voice came again: "Lynnie, I could use some help out here." She slipped on her sandals and a summer dressing gown of her mother's and found her way to the back door. Moonlight flooded the garden and beyond it, the eastside housing development, which had gone up so many years ago, had morphed back into a September cornfield. Across the street from the front of the house, she knew without looking, would be the Tripp Lake Cemetery whose paths she had once memorized with her tricycle. In the garden a familiar figure steadily, unhurriedly, was turning over the dirt with a short-handled spade.

"Daddy, what are you doing?"

"I'm transplanting the perennials," came the answer, "and it's time you learned how to do it."

Without questioning, Lynne picked up the second shovel and began to dig. The soft loam offered almost no resistance and her body felt invigorated by its first sustained exercise in a long time. She glanced at her father's face, which as he labored appeared and disappeared under the bill of his work cap from the Old Creamery. It was focused and at peace, the way it always was when he worked in the garden.

Her shovel struck metal, and without being told, she joined her father in clearing the dirt from around a long rectangular box. Given its bulk it should have been impossible for them to move, yet they lifted it easily out of the ground, setting it beside the hole and moving on to a new patch of ground. One by one, boxes, differing in material and ornamentation but always similar in shape, were exhumed from the base of the garden and lined in rows around the two workers.

"Are these the perennials, Daddy?"

"Yes, they are, darling, and they all have to be brought to the surface now and then, and re-examined. Not for their sakes, they're content enough, but for ours."

"I thought that once people were buried, they stayed there forever."

Her father laughed gently. "You know that's not true. Do you remember that story from when you lived up on the Minnesota Iron Range? The one told by the woman who as a little girl watched from her upstairs window as they moved the cemetery to get to the ore underneath it?"

Lynne stood quietly, aware that she had been told that story more than ten years after her father died, but not wanting to say anything for fear that the truth would make him disappear. Somehow, however, he seemed to hear her thoughts.

"I know that story because you know it. The Iron Range and I are both alive in your memory, so it would be unusual if we didn't know one another—even as I know Rik and your children. After all, you measured him against me many times, just as you measured this garden against the Iron Range and the Wasatch Mountains. We're all perennials."

"Is everyone here in the garden a perennial, Daddy?"

"Yes, but they're *your* perennials, not mine. Yours are here because this garden is the first place you remember. *My* perennials are back on the farm in Old Johnstown."

"Then why are you here?"

"I'm here because you remember me here. I'll always be here as long as you remember me." Again, he anticipated her question. "Don't worry about me being forgotten. We're here for you, not for ourselves. Once this part of your life is over, you'll still be able to help others, but you'll be at peace. Would you like to speak with someone else?"

"Who else is here?"

The man walked further up the row between the boxes. "Well, there's your mother, of course. And the sister you never knew. You inherited her big doll and the teacup chest. Remember? You should meet her sometime. She's become a fine young lady."

"How could that be, Daddy? She died when she was a baby!"

"Well, that's a little difficult to explain. Maybe you should start with someone not quite so close. Over here is Sadie Wells, who was already living next door when we moved here and was your second-grade teacher over at Eastside School."

Lynne turned to see a thin, bespectacled woman in a shapeless print dress smiling at her. "My stars, Lynnie, I nearly didn't recognize you. You're almost as gray as I am."

Lynne stifled the urge to embrace Miss Sadie, who would have crisply rejected such a familiarity when she was a child. But like her father, her neighbor could read her unspoken thoughts. "You're not still worried about that time I kept you after because you wouldn't stop talking in school?"

"I cried, I know." Lynne was laughing and close to tears at the same time. "I tried to tell you that my mama would spank me if I got home late."

"I told you that if you ran all the way, you'd get home in time, and you did! When you were paying attention, you were always one of the best students I ever had. It was such a joy watching you grow up! I went to your high school graduation, your college graduation, and even your wedding. I didn't see you get your graduate degree, but I saw the pictures, and I saw the pictures of your children. I've been watching you for a long time, and it's such a joy to think that you can see me."

Her father interrupted from another part of the garden. "Here's someone else you haven't seen for a long time."

Lynne stared at the tall young man standing opposite her, struggling to turn a flicker of recognition into a name. "Billy Russell," she asked?

"None other and none less, Skinny Lynnie," he grinned back at her.

"Your first boyfriend," her father chipped in. "Although you got mad and he got embarrassed whenever we teased you about it."

"It didn't stop me from coming around though," Billy added.

"But how could that be?" Lynne was still staring. "You were only—"

"Twelve, when that cow kicked me in the stomach. No one realized that my intestines were blocked. I died of uremia four days later. You were eleven. We were about to start Junior High together."

"But now you're grown!"

"That's because of you," Billy answered patiently.

Her father took a step forward. "That's what I was trying to explain to you. What happened to your sister. The Christmas you were nineteen. You were so beautiful you made me wonder how *she* would have grown up. Then when I had my heart attack two months later, she was there waiting for me."

"I don't understand."

"The same thing happened with me," Billy explained. "When you were first dating Rik, you wondered if he was the one, but you had no one to compare him to. So you went away one weekend and thought about the future and the past. And one evening you tried to imagine what kind of a man I would have been if I'd grown up. Who I am now is what you imagined."

Lynne felt dizzy. "Then you're not real? You're just my imagination?"

Billy smiled. "I am real *because* of what you imagined. And I'm not the only one."

"Who else?"

"Rik. He became the man he is because *you* imagined who he could be. Remember the boy you first met—the farm boy with holes in his clothes from testing milk with acid in agriculture class, the careless student without a single educated family member or friend? Do you really think he could have become a distinguished university professor, a scholar, an artist, unless you imagined that he could?"

An early morning fog was drifting in from the cornfield beyond the fence. The corners of the lined-up boxes had become blurred, difficult to distinguish from the dirt that once covered them. Lynne struggled to focus on Billy's face. She was very tired.

"What will happen to Rik? How will he get along without me?"

Billy was gone, but she could still hear her father's

soothing, disembodied voice. "You haven't left Rik. You're his perennial. He'll miss you, but you'll still be with him. He'll go on. And every time he has a choice to make, he'll measure it by what you've imagined he can be. You never imagined him quitting."

*****

Slowly Lynne became aware of the grains of sand on the bunched sheet beneath her. The moon was down now. Behind, on the hard mattress bed, Rik clung to her, his arms wrapped around her as if he would never let her go.

Perhaps he would never have to.

*****

Over my head, I hear music in the air;
Over my head, I hear music in the air;
Over my head, I hear music in the air;
There must be a god somewhere.

TALE OF TEARS

In an album in my basement, there is a photo of my wife reading a story to three children. The setting is the living room couch of graduate school friends, the date (judging from the ages of the children and their clothing) is a winter holiday early in the 1970s, and the book is *Lyle, Lyle, Crocodile.* A red-haired boy of four snuggles up under Lynne's right arm, and to her left a delicate, younger girl stands so that she may better see the pictures. These children are the focus of the hopes and dreams of our friends. As an adult, the boy will go from the Marine Corps to Alcoholics Anonymous, to law school, and to success as a housing contractor and the husband of a lovely girl with his own baby daughter. The elfin beauty on the left has been missing for years, drown in a sea of drugs, the unthinking participant in a series of liaisons resulting in a brood of unfortunate offspring, all now removed from her by law. One child saved, one child lost.

Between Lynne and the smaller girl can be seen the blonde head and intent face of our daughter Annie. To her the story on the page is the most important thing in the universe. She will be so consumed by that world that at an early age she will be unwilling to wait for a narrator to admit her and will take the book from her mother's hands, never looking back to see the sense of loss there.

Until that day, however, there will be a number of photographs in the family albums of Lynne reading to Annie. Of Annie and me in the same configuration, there are not so many. Don't leap to conclusions; I was neither an absentee nor emotionally distant father. The same albums show Annie belching milk over my unshrinking shoulder, the two of us grinning at the camera—her with a cereal bowl balanced precariously on her head and me with a nursing bottle cocked in my right hand—or mesmerized by Fred Rogers on the television, or racing on a hillside above a cavernous iron ore pit.

It was only that as a reader of stories I was made inadequate by a propensity to weep. For example, I had only to pick up a book about a blonde little girl learning to cope with being the smallest and least coordinated person in her family.

Someone I know
can win first place
in a running race.
I can't.

Someone I know
can lose that race
with a smiley face.
I can.

And I was gone.

I should add that there was a time when it seemed that no one might ever read to Annie. Search through the album above and those of earlier years, and you will find dozens of pictures of our first child: Annie in pigtails, Annie in her bath, Annie in coveralls, Annie in a dirndl, etc. Once, at the park during another family's reunion photo, she left us and joined the group—reasoning inductively from her life experience that the presence of any camera required her. If *you* were to reason inductively from the albums, you might reasonably conclude that not a day passed without her being photographed.

You would be wrong. There is a stretch of weeks, perhaps months, from which there are no pictures of Annie—less than a page in the album, but a long time in our memories: a time during which our sunny and responsive daughter became progressively distant and tentative, a time when the children of our friends encountered and reveled in stages of development from which Annie seemed to be retreating rather than challenging. She commanded our attention with tantrums rather than laughter, and when she did communicate it was with a babble that refused to form itself into syllables.

Our doctor was of little comfort. "She's too fat. You're not feeding her right. Stop picking her up every time she cries. She has to learn not to expect you to solve all her problems." Lynne cried when she came home. A neighbor told her that the doctor had a retarded son, and when he examined a child whom he believed was feeble-minded, he became gruff and emotionally removed. Home once more, Lynne cried again.

It seemed an eon before we sought a second opinion, but it was only a matter of minutes before that doctor—a woman—made a suggestion: "Why don't we give her a hearing test?"

The diagnosis was a hearing loss of up to fifty percent in both ears. We were to receive quite an education on the subject over time, but the short explanation is this: The inner ear transmits sound through small, hair-like fibers. If there are fibers missing, or if they do not grow as the rest of the inner ear structure develops, a child's hearing ability deteriorates even as the sources of information around it increase. Thus, Annie, initially a verbally receptive child, became more and more lost as the weeks passed.

That she would ever find herself was by no means certain. We took her to the Medical Center at the University of

Missouri, Kansas City, which had one of the finest hearing departments in the country. During one of her examinations, I stood outside talking to an intern, trying to relate to a professional who was perhaps younger than I was. What I said I don't remember, but suddenly he raised his hand and smiled at me pityingly: "You realize, of course, that she'll never go to a regular school."

I never shared that assessment with Lynne, who was already making plans to enroll Annie at the Hearing Clinic at the University of Kansas.

Annie was three years old when she got her first hearing aid. I remember her systematically prowling the back lawn, delightedly identifying each new sound as she came upon it. The first trip to the Hearing Clinic was quite another matter.

There is a difference between voiced and unvoiced sounds. For example, the sounds represented by the letters "p" and "b" are formed the same way by the lips and the tongue, but "b" or "buh" involves the voice, and "p" or "puh" uses only air. This was Annie's first lesson, simple enough—if you are not crying. Her sobs began the moment she was separated from her mother, forced to watch from behind a one-sided mirror, and not a single "buh" or "puh" could be found among them. She did not cry alone.

That night as she gave Annie her bath, Lynne contemplated the future. Even if her daughter could not distinguish speech, she could still learn to read lips, to speak with her hands. Thomas Edison was a genius. Even Helen Keller learned to write. Deaf people married, had children, children who could hear, who had access to two worlds. A full and complete life was possible; it just had to be planned for.

In the bathtub, Annie played with her rubber ball. She held it out to her mother. "Buh," she said. In Lynne's mind twenty years of plans vanished like an erase-a-sketch. "Buh," Annie repeated, impatient with her mother for not taking the ball. Lynne wrapped the warm towel around her daughter and lifted her out of the tub. Annie wriggled one arm free and pointed to the toy dog on the dressing stand. "Puh," she said. "Puppy?" Lynne asked, and Annie beamed, puzzled as to why her mother was laughing and crying at the same time.

At the hearing clinic a few sessions later, we sat behind the one-way mirror and watched as the clinicians put Annie through her paces. A gaggle of speech and hearing students occupied most of the booth. In an animated stage whisper of a veteran watcher explained the procedures to her friends. "I always try to get here to watch this kid," she said. "She's just so *good*!" The glow on our faces could have lit up the room. Our daughter was a star! We had always known it.

It would be tempting to say that at that moment we knew that Annie's hearing loss would never hold her back, but the real proof came some months later. All parents should be warned that the passing of a great crisis in a child's life only serves to reveal a dozen smaller problems of everyday existence. For Lynne, one of those was Annie's penchant for leaving clothes and toys anywhere but their assigned place. Her most vehement lecture on the subject was inspired one Saturday by having kicked a Tommy-Tippy cup half-full of milk down the steps from the first landing to the doormat in front of the porch door. Annie watched her mother's red face as the torrent of reprimands reached new heights of pitch, pace, and profusion, and calmly reached up and turned her hearing aid off. Communicative *ju-jitsu*—turning a weakness into a strength.

But, I was talking about reading to Annie. We were very much alike, she and I, in our eagerness to escape from mundane everyday existence into the real world of stories, and in our ability to identify with them. Watty Piper never had a more fervent well-wisher than the enraptured Annie.

"I think I can," puffed the little locomotive, and put itself in front of the great heavy train. As it went on the little engine kept bravely pulling faster and faster, "I think I can, I think I can, I think I can."

It might have been the theme of her life. She strained with sympathetic magic as she listened, and no matter how often it happened, when the little engine reached the top of the grade, Annie's eyes shown with gratitude and triumph.

Still, I was older than Annie, a child of a different time, and only too aware of how close we came to leaving her behind in a world which we could not penetrate. I was able to distance myself enough aesthetically to get through *The Little Engine That Could*. *The Littlest Angel* was quite another matter.

Do you remember that story? Its creation was a small miracle in itself. Charles Tazewell wrote it in three days in 1939 as a backup radio script for a broadcast by Ronald Coleman, in case a planned piece wasn't available. It was, and it was another year before *The Littlest Angel* was broadcast, and it wasn't until after World War II that it was published as a book. When Tazewell died in 1972, it was in its 38th printing.

A small angel, perfectly well equipped to be a boy on earth, finds himself singularly unsuited to be in Heaven. He is homesick and lonely, forbidden to swing on the Golden Gate, always late for choir practice and unable to sing on key, always bumping into the other angels' wings and incapable of mastering his own, his halo falling over one eye or off his head entirely, and his robe grimy from his attempts to clean the halo with it. The littlest angel's conduct is improved when an understanding Angel of the Peace brings him the small box from under his bed at home, the box which contains all his little boy treasures. When the Christ Child is to be born and all of the angels plan to bring Him their finest gifts, all the littlest angel can think of to give is his box, and is immediately ashamed of its shabbiness in the midst of the other magnificent offerings. God, however, sees to the heart of the child, pronouncing the box as the perfect gift for the Son of Man, and transforms it into the Star of Bethlehem.

Tazewell and his wife had no children, but he once called

The Littlest Angel his "precocious son," equating the child and the book. Maybe that's why I could never read it aloud with any decorum. No book is complete without a reader, even as a tree falling alone in the forest makes no sound. As children we read adventure stories, imagining ourselves in them. As parents we read about lost children, imagining ourselves losing them. Years ago in Salt Lake City's now defunct Blue Mouse art theatre, we watched a documentary on the physicist Robert Oppenheimer. A Manhattan Project scientist who had gone to Hiroshima immediately after the Japanese surrender was explaining how he had determined that the bomb had exploded at the planned height by figuring the angle from a school room's window frame to its shadow burned into the blackboard across the room. Lynne turned to me, her face stricken. "Where were the children?" she asked.

Where indeed? On each occasion when I read *The Littlest Angel,* by the time I reached the bottom of page one, my nose had opened like the Canadian side of Niagara.

He was exactly four years, six months, five days, seven hours and forty-two minutes of age when he presented himself to the venerable Gate-Keeper and waited for admittance to the Glorious Kingdom of God.

I recognized, of course, the comforting moral of the story: that the loving honesty of a child was to be treasured more than the ritualized perfection of Heaven—even as I recognized similar triumphs of love over bureaucracy in incomparably better written stories, such as Oscar Wilde's "The Happy Prince." But nothing compensates for the loss of a child, even if one is so fortunate to experience it only through empathic imagination. I was with the lonely little boy looking up at the Towers of Unearthly Splendor so much higher than the olive tree that used to shade his mother's doorway, but I was also back in the doorway with the mother who knew every nuance of the "four years, six months, five days, seven hours and forty-two minute" measure of his life, and had imagined that she would continue to gaze upon it until the moment when her eyes closed forever. And so, as I continue to read, the lines become more and more blurred, and the gaps between their utterances longer and longer, until an impatient Annie takes the book from my hands and sets off in search of her more efficient mother.

*****

My inability to finish a children's story aloud and dry-eyed didn't end with Annie, but extended to her brother Karl. If it was less noticeable with him, perhaps it was because his favorite books, *The Rattle Rattle Dump Truck* and *Mike Mulligan and His Steam Shovel*, involved a sentimental connection with machines that always escaped me.

On one level, Annie's hearing condition was responsible for our having Karl. As Lynne neared thirty and my days as a graduate student wound down, we contemplated having another child. Two family members on my side were hard of hearing, so we could not ignore the possibility that Annie's problem was inherited. (Amazingly, in order to avoid lightning striking a second time in a known way, we contemplated adopting a child of whose genetic background we were absolutely ignorant!)

More to the point concerning the arrival of Karl was Malthusian theory. The publication of Paul Ehrlich's *The Population Bomb* in 1968 was followed by the "Zero Population Movement." In a finite material world with an infinitely expanding number of inhabitants, how could we justify the addition of even one more greedy mouth? Especially when so many of the existing tiny mouths were without protection and future?

Still, these were only theories, dry talking points we could utilize in argument, but which lacked galvanizing emotion. For emotion there was the War.

As a veteran educated almost entirely during the Cold War, I came later to anti-Vietnam activism than Lynne, but nobody came to it sooner than Annie. By the time she was two, weekend stroller rides at the front of marching, chanting friends of her mother were a regular feature of her life. In the corner of the kitchen, long-haired youths of both sexes made much of her while Lynne turned government-issue flour and cheese into bake goods for anti-war rallies, and she played with her dolls in the shade of the Sears store as red-faced Legionnaires shamed her mother for daring to hand out literature in the local mall. Another trip to the album shows Annie proudly holding up an orange and yellow autumn leaf to another photographer, whose federally mandated suit, narrow tie, and little hat defined his presence at the rally as less than benign.

And so we marched, hosted coffees, signed petitions, wrote letters, and the war went on. And we gradually drifted away from the Movement. Maybe it was not being trusted by students because I was over thirty (and not being trusted by the Establishment because I was bearded). Maybe it was the realization that Counter Culture clothing no longer came from the thrift shop, but off the rack at J.C. Penny's. Maybe it was a friend's announcement that he had given up being a Conscientious Objector because the draft was over and he just wanted to get stoned.

It could have been when a Weatherman-wannabee group blew up the Army Research Building at the University of Wisconsin, killing one man and wounding four others, or maybe it was when a SDS member suggested that since they would only grow up to continue Amerika's Racist Cultural Hegemony, all white children should be killed at birth. Only yesterday, it seemed, we'd heard them chanting "Hey, Hey, LBJ, how many kids did you kill today!" Now somebody wanted us to kill our own.

"You don't need a weatherman to know which way the

wind blows."

On June 9, 1972, our local newspaper carried a photo of a naked little Vietnamese girl running down the road, her back on fire. Her name was Kim Phuc, which in Vietnamese means "happiness." I left that morning to administer an exam at the Junior College where I taught. When I returned home in the afternoon, Lynne had a guest.

She was a Roman Catholic nun, and her name was Sister Rosemary Ilse Paulina, or "Elsie" when we'd all been students together a decade earlier. For the last three years, Elsie had been at the To Am orphanage in Vietnam, working for an organization called Friends For All Children. There were four such orphanages, with sixteen permanent workers from America, Australia, England, France, and Spain, complemented by a constantly swelling and ebbing flow of Catholic and Buddhist Vietnamese volunteers, plus American military and embassy personnel, airline pilots and stewardesses. To Am, Allambie, Newhaven, and Hy Vong: four nurseries and never less than hundreds of babies—newborn, abandoned, sick, malnourished, handicapped, and hopelessly incurable. Elsie had accompanied three of those babies to adoptive families in the city, and was on her way back. Lynne and Annie had run into her outside the Target Store.

I looked over at my wife, knowing from ten years of marriage that the decision had already been made, but made the obligatory arguments anyway.

"How would we know that the baby would be healthy, and wouldn't require years of medical care?"

Elsie looked around her, taking in the evidence of our comfortable, middle-class life. "You wouldn't," she said.

"We know nothing of Vietnamese culture. Would it be fair to take a child away from its origins and have it grow up totally separated from its roots?"

"Four out of the five children who never get out of these

orphanages die there—mostly because there is no one to hold them and give them a reason to live. If we could save one more child now, we could worry about the roots later."

One child saved, three children lost.

Three years later, on April 4, 1975, as America's plan for Vietnam limps toward the dustbin of history, Elsie and six other orphanage workers load 230 babies aboard a massive C5A Galaxy cargo plane headed for San Francisco. Fifteen minutes after take-off, as the huge transport neared cruising altitude, the rear cargo door blows out. Rudder control lost, the engines are throttled to turn the Mothra-like giant back to Saigon. The crew shares oxygen among the children in the upper level. Elsie is in the lower level, the level that is buried in a rice paddy just short of the Ton Son Nhut Airport runway.

One friend and seventy-eight children lost.

*****

He landed at Des Moines International Airport on a hot, muggy morning in June. A tornado had struck our town the night before, and as we crouched in the basement it occurred to me how ironic it would be for him to arrive and find us dead. From the time of our acceptance to the date of his arrival, we had waited 13 months (three months longer than he had been alive). We had a document signed by Henry Kissinger and Nguyen Van Thieu. We had a trip to Omaha to coax a bureaucrat to move that document off his desk. We had a nursery which had been converted out of my upstairs office. We were on time at the airport, and—insofar as it was possible—we were ready.

I sat with Annie, as she described the salient features of her new Raggedy Ann doll. It was black—one of those clumsy attempts at cultural conditioning socially concerned young parents were always trying in those days. (Like keeping her away from guns and urging her to be an engineer—which she did become, for the Department of Defense!) Lynne's eyes focused on the sky outside the terminal window, the same look of concentration on her face as the night of Annie's birth seven years earlier—a tractor-beam of will guiding her child down from the sky into her arms.

There are four pictures in the album of that morning in Des Moines. In the first, a tiny figure clutches at his mother's breast as she looks down at him with half-closed eyes. I tower above them, the only figure in the triad not obviously divine. In the second, Lynne sits with a crying baby in her lap, looking gratefully at someone just stage right of the frame. In the third, a little boy looks curiously off-screen as his mother coos in his ear. The fourth is like the first—mother and son forefront, but this time behind them stands Annie, for the first time displaced from the center of the photos of her family.

He is named Karl, the name that was taken away from his grandfather after *he* arrived in America. About 10 months old, Karl weighs only 12 pounds and is unable to sit up in his high chair without help. He has been dosed with aspirin so that his measles will not break out and keep him in Vietnam. His medical records—arriving six months later—list him as surviving whooping cough, scarlet fever, mumps, rotavirus, and haemophilus influenza. At the bottom of his impressive hospital rap sheet is an anonymous observation written in pencil, "Happy little boy." Despairing of his learning to stand, we try putting him in a walker, which he always tips over. One day in the yard he rises up from a crawl and breaks into a ragged trot. For years to see him not running is proof that he is asleep. He has scars on his heels, indicating that at his birth a Shinto priest made cuts there "to let out the devil." Our neighbor, an elderly German doctor, diagnoses from next door: "Obviously, they did not cut quite deep enough."

Karl is the center of play for Annie and all the little girls of the neighborhood. Does he know that he is different from them. Most assuredly, but what does that mean? His first babysitter, Grace Chin, is especially chosen. Karl cries because she does not look like his mother.

Yet, when he is three and we visit our *alma mater*, Karl stares delightedly out a window at an Asian professor and his own two small boys. "Look, Mama! Two Karls." Two years later in London's Victoria and Albert Museum, two Japanese children sit politely on a visitors' bench. Karl sails across the room and comes to a skidding halt beside them. "Hi, kids! I'm from Vietnam. Where are you from?"

Does he feel he belongs? He will have doubts, but they will come later. In the corner of the living room next to the hallway, the figures of a family have been carved out of one piece of African wood. Karl views the sculpture with satisfaction: "Mommy, Daddy, and Karl," he concludes, conveniently absenting his sister from the grouping. In that same living room, he and a friend pore over a platoon of GI Joe figures and the assorted hardware which has made this onetime War Orphan the 11th leading military power in the hemisphere. Lynne and Annie walk through the room. The visiting little boy stares at their matching English blondness, and then contemplates Karl.

"What's your real mother's name?" he asks.

Karl does not raise his eyes from the complicated tank maneuver he is executing. "Lynne Elizabeth Christine Chase Temple," he replies.

The friend seems satisfied.

*****

And yet I still cry sometimes when I read to Karl.

The most frequent precipitator of this precipitation is P.D. Eastman's *Are You My Mother?* It is the simplest of texts, with no page containing more than fifty words, and no word more than six letters. As for the drawings, the very best that can be said for them is that their assignment of human traits and emotions to animals is a challenge to the imagination of any reader.

It is a challenge I am capable of meeting.

A baby bird emerges from his egg while his mother is out hunting worms. In his search for her, he falls out of the nest. He cannot fly, but he is not helpless.

"He could not fly, but he could walk. 'Now I will go and find my mother,' he said."

The little bird encounters a kitten, a hen, a dog, a cow, an abandoned car, a boat, and an airplane, none of whom are his mother.

"'I did have a mother,' said the baby bird. 'I know I did. I have to find her. I will. I WILL!'"

Finally, the little bird meets a steam shovel, which deposits him back in his nest, just as his mother returns to it.

"'Do you know who I am' she said to her baby.

'Yes, I know who you are,' said the baby bird.

'You are not a kitten.'

'You are not a hen.'

'You are not a dog.'

'You are not a boat, or a plane, or a Snort!'

'You are a bird, and you are my mother.'"

My nose is draining on the suspender of Karl's coveralls. Annie sighs and gently removes the book from my hand. She takes her brother by the hand, and the two of them set off for the kitchen in search of their mother.

*****

A few days ago, I called Annie, who now lives on the other side of the country. She puts my six-month-old grandson on the telephone, and I sing to him a nonsense Cajun song that I used to sing to his mother.

Chikory Chick
Cha-La Cha-La
Checkela Roma-ka
In a Bannanna-ka
Polli-ka Wolla-ka
Can't you see?
Chikory Chick It's Me!

He gurgles and smiles at the sound whose source and meaning he can't place. It is just as well that he cannot see that I am crying.

CLOTHESLINE

"I should have known I'd find you out here."

Rik didn't have to turn to identify the voice. It was a crisp and bright late October Sunday—pleasant enough in the sun and out of the wind, but with a morning chill forecasting the death of Indian summer. At this time of year when he was a boy, the corn shocks would already be standing in the fields and the garden stripped down to a few huge pumpkins. He could smell the changing of the seasons as he hung the laundry on lines, which stretched from the grape arbor halfway past the garage.

"The sheets rippling in the breeze look like strolling nuns. You should take one of your famous photographs. Do you still have a camera?"

"No," Rik answered. "I stopped taking pictures when there were no people to be in them. I like the photos in my albums to be able to talk to one another." She would be standing in the driveway, where they had talked so many times before. Funny he hadn't heard the car. She would be dressed for autumn, with an orange sweater and a plaid skirt setting off her red hair. Her sense of style was impeccable. The only item that hadn't fit the ensemble was him.

"Poor you!" Her tone mocked him gently. "You still air the bedding every week? I'd imagined you'd given it up by now.

Or perhaps you still have the same reason?"

"The truth is I'm just a creature of habit. Once an idea gets in my head, I never let go of it." Rik studied the tattered edges of the bedspread he was hanging. It should be replaced. But then, no one but him ever saw it.

"I appreciated your thoughtfulness, you know. Because of my allergies." She went on when he didn't respond. "How is Boots?"

Boots had been Lynne's last cat. Emaciated and bedraggled, but purring, she had rubbed against Lynne one April as she planted beans in the garden on the other side of the clotheslines. The wavy rows maturing later that year were a sign of their courtship. In the house that afternoon, Lynne had confronted Rik with a question that was also a conclusion: "When a cat kisses you in a bean patch, you have to keep it. Right?"

When Lynne's head no longer occupied the pillow opposite him, Boots had taken her place. Now the cat was buried in the empty garden. Rik still made up the bed with two pillows. Another habit. "Long gone, I'm afraid, to a Better Place, with carpets of catnip and scratching posts that are legs to the throne of a god who never sniffles."

The laugh from the driveway was silvery. High strung and spontaneous, perfectly pitched to her dancer's body. "I appreciated that too. You always made me smile. I miss that."

"Humor equals pain, plus distance, the philosopher says. Someday I'll be far enough away to get the joke." Rik stepped over a broken sprinkler head. That would have to be fixed before the first freeze. A leak beneath the winter surface could be fatal to the whole system.

"Don't be bitter." Her voice was gently reproving. "You must have known it could never work out. We found one another too late."

Rik stooped to pick up a fallen clothespin and contemplated the gnarled fist that held it. When had his hands become his father's, he wondered? "If you will recall," he countered, "we were never free at the same time—though we might have been."

Her attention had shifted to the far end of the lawn. "What happened to the other pine tree?" They had been gifts from her own backyard—seedlings that had arrived in two huge cardboard pots.

"I had to cut one down. They were too close. Their root systems were twisted together. Allowed to grow, they would gradually have killed one another."

"You did the right thing. I would have hated to see them still standing there, both dead. This way I can look at the healthy tree and remember when they were young. What is the lighter green plant interlaced through the branches?"

Rik shivered. A harsh wind was blowing rain clouds in from the north. Perhaps this had been the wrong day to air laundry. "There's a grape vine on the fence which divides the lots. Early on it began using the tree as a trellis, and now they can't be separated."

She laughed again. "How Dionysian! Vine leaves in the hair of a tree that's always green! You must have to be pretty dedicated to fight all that prickliness for the grapes."

"That would be pointless. The vine expends all its energy in growth. It climbs and winds itself around the tree, but never produces grapes. It's barren."

"It's like the mistletoe we saw in the Polish *Bialowieza* Forest, engulfing the birch trees. Beautiful, symbolic, but ultimately parasitic." Her voice was sober now. "Which one is you, and which one is me?"

Rik fumbled with the clothespins. Was he always this clumsy? The baskets were nearly empty now, and he was determined to finish his task. "Why did you leave me?"

"Me?" The voice is part surprise, part mocking. "I never left you. Who do you think is talking to you now? I tried to leave you many times long ago, but every time I wanted to move on, you stood in my path. I was alone, but you would rather I were lonely than be free. You wanted me, but you would never tell me. Now you have your wish. I will always be with you."

On the lines on either side of Rik the past hung dark and stained. Had he forgotten to put detergent in the machine, or were some old things simply not washable? He couldn't understand why her reassuring promise of closeness seemed simultaneously menacing and further away. He stumbled down the row, searching for a gap through which he might answer. "You know why I could never speak."

"Yes. You called it 'fidelity.'" The laugh was harsher now. "But who were you being faithful to? Not to Lynne certainly. Not to me. You once accused me of being afraid of change, but it was you. Your idea of change was you having it both ways. You were faithful all right—to your own weaknesses!"

Rik grasped a line to steady himself as he struggled to find a metaphor. "That wasn't it. It was like... *Sergeant Pepper*. Paul McCartney wanted to continue making music; he just didn't want to be trapped into making 'Beatles music' forever. In order to keep loving, I had to find another way to love!"

"Then why, after Lynne was gone, did you make me move into her house?" The voice was shriller now, beating against his temples. "Did you think you could make other people replaceable parts of your life? Do you know what it was like, constantly surrounded by your relationship to her? Her furniture? Her friends? Her memories? You wanted me, but you wanted me to be her too. You were still the center of your own universe, and I was still to be your satellite—*but in her orbit*! I'm not a fool. You don't change. Once I became her, *who would have become me*?"

His head throbbing, Rik kicked a discarded basket into the garden. Around him a phalanx of sheets jerked in the breeze like a hangman's fantasy. An opening loomed ahead of him and he lurched toward it. He reached the end of the line, and in a final wrenching movement, turned himself to confront her. *"What do you want? Why can't you leave me alone?"*

The driveway was empty.

*****

All along the street the neighbors met in groups of two or three that week. It wasn't that anyone had reported the old man missing. He didn't mix with people much. Someone glancing into the backyard had noticed that, despite the weeks of rain, there was still laundry on the clothesline, and other pieces on the ground and blown up against the fence. Underneath a ragged quilt they found the body and called 911. Apparently he tripped over a sprinkler head and broke it. Face down in a spongy pool for god knows how long. It wasn't a pretty sight. Still, it could have been anything. When they're that age, it doesn't take much. It was funny to think how many kids in their witches and wizards costumes must have come to the closed front door on Halloween, not knowing the truly gruesome contents of the back yard.

And so the talk went that week, and occasionally the next, and was forgotten—to be reborn now and then, with the proper embellishments, beside Boy Scout campfires and in admonishments to children to stay in their own yards. The next summer a new couple moved in, with young children and a new Maytag washer-dryer. The clotheslines were taken down, and what had once probably been a garden was re-sodded. An expensive swing set took their place, and the yard rang with the laughter and shouts of those who had never heard the story of its previous owner.

Though nothing can bring back the hour
Of splendor in the grass, of glory in the flower;
We will grieve not, rather find
Strength in what remains behind;
In the primal sympathy
Which having been must ever be.

--William Wordsworth, *Intimations of Immortality*

ABOUT ATMOSPHERE PRESS

Atmosphere Press is an independent, full-service publisher for excellent books in all genres and for all audiences. Learn more about what we do at atmospherepress.com.

We encourage you to check out some of Atmosphere's latest releases, which are available at Amazon.com and via order from your local bookstore:

Saints and Martyrs: A Novel, by Aaron Roe

When I Am Ashes, a novel by Amber Rose

Melancholy Vision: A Revolution Series Novel, by L.C. Hamilton

The Recoleta Stories, by Bryon Esmond Butler

Voodoo Hideaway, a novel by Vance Cariaga

Hart Street and Main, a novel by Tabitha Sprunger

The Weed Lady, a novel by Shea R. Embry

A Book of Life, a novel by David Ellis

It Was Called a Home, a novel by Brian Nisun

Grace, a novel by Nancy Allen

Shifted, a novel by KristaLyn A. Vetovich

Because the Sky is a Thousand Soft Hurts, stories by Elizabeth Kirschner

ABOUT THE AUTHOR

Richard Scharine was born in the back room of a Wisconsin farmhouse, went to a one room grade school, and rode a school bus 52 miles to high school. He is currently a professor emeritus in the University of Utah theatre department, where his honors include University Professor, University Diversity Award, and College of Fine Arts Excellence Award. Dr. Scharine has published two scholarly books, five book chapters, and a score or more articles. A Fulbright Senior Lecturer at the University of Gdansk in Poland, he has directed a hundred plays and acted in seven foreign countries, including the title role in *Oedipus at Colonus* in Athens, Greece.

The smartest thing he did was to marry Marilyn Hunt Scharine.

CPSIA information can be obtained
at www.ICGtesting.com
Printed in the USA
LVHW041801210621
690774LV00005B/226

9 781637 528235